I0888955

RHETORIC AND WRITING STUDIES
IN THE NEW CENTURY

RHETORIC AND WRITING STUDIES IN THE NEW CENTURY

HISTORIOGRAPHY, PEDAGOGY, AND POLITICS

EDITED BY CHERYL GLENN AND ROXANNE MOUNTFORD

Southern Illinois University Press
Carbondale

Southern Illinois University Press
www.siupress.com

Printed in the United States of America

20 19 18 17 4 3 2 1

Publication has been partially supported by a grant from Penn State University.

Library of Congress Cataloging-in-Publication Data

Names: Glenn, Cheryl editor. | Mountford, Roxanne, [date] editor.
Title: Rhetoric and writing studies in the new century : historiography, pedagogy, and politics / edited by Cheryl Glenn and Roxanne Mountford; with an afterword by Adam J. Banks.
Description: Carbondale : Southern Illinois University Press, 2017. | Includes bibliographical references and index.
Identifiers: LCCN 2016049365 | ISBN 9780809335671 (pbk. : alk. paper) | ISBN 9780809335688 (e-book)
Subjects: LCSH: Rhetoric—Social aspects—History—21st century. | Rhetoric—Study and teaching. | Composition (Language arts)—Study and teaching.
Classification: LCC P301.5.S63 R484 2017 | DDC 808—dc23 LC record available at https://lccn.loc.gov/2016049365

Printed on recycled paper. ♻

To Andrea Abernethy Lunsford

CONTENTS

PREFACE

Andrea Lunsford is perhaps best known for her contributions to undergraduates: her influential textbooks, her work on basic writing and mediated writing, her founding of innovative undergraduate programs and research centers at Ohio State and Stanford, her national studies of error, her longitudinal studies of Stanford writers. But we would argue that in representing the field of rhetoric and composition to her graduate students over the years, she has had an equally profound impact on developing future leaders in the field. We are two of her students, and we owe our start in the field to Lunsford's generous mentoring and friendship.

Andrea Lunsford went to Ohio State at age thirty after learning of Edward P. J. Corbett's work connecting classical rhetoric with the teaching of writing. When she arrived, she quickly learned that there were no courses for her to take in rhetoric and composition; scholars like Corbett were still teaching literature. She took rhetoric courses in the Department of Communication and pedagogy courses in the College of Education. Corbett invited Lunsford to serve as his assistant editor for the journal *College Composition and Communication*, and it was through reading submissions that she became educated in the field. She was the first student at Ohio State to be examined in rhetoric and composition.

Lunsford moved from her first job at the University of British Columbia back to Ohio State in 1986, when we were just two years into our graduate program (Mountford at the MA level; Glenn at the PhD level). And while there, Lunsford brought her entrepreneurial spirit to the course offerings, and to the mentoring of graduate students, many of whom went on to establish themselves in the field. By 1986 the field of composition studies was developing its own research methods; Janice Lauer and William Ascher's

Composition Research was in manuscript form, and Lunsford asked Lauer to lend it for her first course on research methods in rhetoric and composition. In the years to come, Lunsford developed courses in the history and theory of literacy, of gender and rhetoric and composition, of postcolonial theory and composition, women's writing, performance and writing, and so forth. And for each of these courses, there was an edited collection, or a coauthored article, to which she invited her students to collaborate.

Thus, Lunsford's expansive knowledge of the field, coupled with her intellectual generosity, has long been invaluable to her students. We have grown to believe that graduate education is the process of linking the field's timeless and emerging research questions to the natural interests of new scholars. Or, as we tell our students, the best research projects connect what the field wants to know with what you want to know. A graduate program that creates such an environment for students creates foundations courses and cutting-edge seminars that bring students into dialogue with what is going on in the field. This seems a simple formula—obvious, perhaps—but we have been in far too many graduate programs in which faculty focused seminars so closely on their latest interest that it was impossible for students to do anything but reproduce that professor's work. Lunsford taught seminars in new areas, foundations courses with old and new research, and encouraged her students to link their passions with the research questions in the field.

One reason that Lunsford has been such a successful mentor to so many in the field is that her own research and scholarship stand at the forefront of rhetoric and composition studies. She has consistently helped define our major trends, leaving a legacy of titles that read like chapters in our discipline's history: "The Contents of Basic Writers' Essays"; "Aristotelian Rhetoric: Let's Get Back to the Classics"; "Audience Addressed / Audience Invoked: The Concept of Audience in the Composing Process"; "Intellectual Property, Concepts of Selfhood, and the Teaching of Writing"; *The Right to Literacy*; *Reclaiming Rhetorica: Women in the Rhetorical Tradition*; "Writing, Technologies, and the Fifth Canon."

This collection revisits four major areas in which Lunsford has been influential, asking its contributors to focus on where this trend is going, what work needs to be done, and / or to offer original research in this area. The goal of this collection is to offer new insights into rhetoric and writing studies in this new century, just as Lunsford has done throughout her career.

Cheryl Glenn and Roxanne Mountford

RHETORIC AND WRITING STUDIES
IN THE NEW CENTURY

INTRODUCTION
INTO THE NEW CENTURY

CHERYL GLENN AND ROXANNE MOUNTFORD

Well into the second decade of the twenty-first century, rhetoric and writing studies continues to thrive across our nation. Across the globe, programs in rhetoric, academic writing, and writing centers continue to take hold and grow—from China, Taiwan, and Qatar to South Africa, the Netherlands, Turkey, and Greece. Hundreds of these programs include attention to the digital, of course, but also to the visual, the oral, and the multimodal. Online composing, peer tutoring, writing in the disciplines, and writing across the curriculum are as commonplace as rhetoric programs, which encompass a full range of rhetorical inquiry, of history, pedagogy, theory, race, gender, the body, ability, activism, place, technology, community, medicine, politics, deliberation, vernacular, culture, translingualism, second-language acquisition, sexuality, and professional communication. Whether freestanding or under the aegis of an English department, rhetoric and writing studies appears to be one of the few growing fields in the humanities. Surely, it is among the most democratic of all the liberal arts, given its attention to diversity, representation, and inclusion—as this volume attests.

And just as rhetoric and writing studies has grown, so have the professional organizations and journals that help provide its infrastructure. The Council of Writing Program Administrators, the Conference on College Composition and Communication, Rhetoric Society of America, the Association of

Teachers of Technical Writing, Computers and Writing, the International Society for the History of Rhetoric, the Coalition of Feminist Scholars in the History of Rhetoric and Composition, and the International Writing Centers Association all provide venues for our ongoing professional development and collaboration, just as various (free access) online and print journals feature our scholarship and challenge our thinking and practices.[1] More and more presses publish books in rhetoric and writing. None of us can attend all the conferences, read all the journals and books, nor participate in all the scholarly conversations that are now so readily available. Rhetoric and writing studies is flourishing, indeed.

Only forty years ago, however, rhetoric and composition was just beginning to emerge as an academic discipline. For decades, freshman composition had been taught as a series of themes, genres, or static modes, with students reading literary essays and imaginative literature before delivering their own essays, which were to be modeled after the high literary quality of the assigned reading. In freshman composition, then, writing instructors taught literature, collected, corrected, and returned essays (or themes), and then moved on to the next writing assignment. Not until 1980, would fifteen or so graduate programs offer a concentration in rhetoric and composition, in comparison to the nearly ninety at this point in the twenty-first century. If MA programs are included, then the number is nearly two hundred.

Finally, after years of teaching writing in terms of grammatical correctness, 1970s freshman composition instructors began paying respect to the knowledge, practices, and language that students—all students—were bringing to the classroom. Following on the heels of the civil rights movement, open admissions took hold, promoting higher education for a new generation of college students, often including those who spoke and wrote in dialects of English other than the more prestigious standardized dialect. The "Students' Right to Their Own Language" document makes a compelling argument for recognizing the strengths and expertise of speakers of other dialects of English as well as of the power inherent in the ability to code-switch. The 1970s were pivotal in composition's history, with study of rhetoric, writing, and linguistics emerging within a renewed moment of democratic opportunity.

Numerous universities responded to open admissions and "Students' Right to Their Own Language" with support services for incoming students. Mina Shaughnessy was leading the way at City College of New York, where she administered SEEK (Search for Education, Elevation, and Knowledge), a prebaccalaureate program designed for students traditionally barred from entering college because of low grades or lack of money. The centerpiece of SEEK was the basic writing program, where Shaughnessy taught alongside such intellectual greats as Adrienne Rich, Barbara Christian, June Jordan, Toni Cade Bambara, and many others. This cohort worked closely with previously excluded students, employing a liberatory pedagogy that would transform the lives of many of their students, establish basic writing as a rich tool for engaging in scholarly inquiry, and profoundly influence colleges and universities across the nation.

Lunsford's response to the sea change in educational opportunities was her dissertation on basic writing. "A Historical, Descriptive, and Evaluative Study of Remedial English in the United States" prepared her to conceptualize and execute a basic writing program at Ohio State by the late 1970s. The task was so monumental—and political—that Shaughnessy flew to Columbus to assist Lunsford in analyzing her empirical data, honing her focus, and shaping the program. And they were not alone in this work. David Bartholomae, Suellynn Duffey, Theresa Enos, Sondra Perl, Mike Rose, Nancy Sommers, Lynn Quitman Troyka, and many other scholars were mining basic writing for the insights it could teach the field about how students learn to write, how they use their home language, and what a more inclusive, invitational, and supportive educational environment might generate.

Since 1977, Ohio State has become a leader in producing rhetoric and composition PhDs. The earliest programs were at Purdue University (led by Janice Lauer), the University of Southern California (led by Ross Winterowd), and the University of Texas (led by Maxine Hairston and James Kinneavy). All of these growing programs developed undergraduate and graduate courses in writing, professional writing, rhetorical history and theory, composition theory, and literacy studies. By the 1990s, many more programs had established themselves: the University of Arizona, Arizona State University, Florida State University, the University of Florida, Michigan Tech, the University of New Hampshire, Penn State University, Rensselaer Polytechnic Institute, the University of South Florida, Syracuse University, and the University of Wisconsin, Madison, to name just a few. Across the nation, the study of rhetoric and composition is well established as a scholarly discipline, worthy of the faculty who have piloted new concentrations that fuse questions of rhetoric and / or writing with various theoretical, methodological, and pedagogical concerns.

At the turn of the twenty-first century, rhetoric and composition programs are embracing their significance and influence. No longer does a program limit itself to first-year writing. The scholarly gaze as well as university-wide expectations have expanded to incorporate the digital, the multimodal, and the cross disciplinary in every way, whether the program is referred to as the Program in Writing and Rhetoric (PWR), the Department of Writing, Rhetoric, and Digital Studies (WRD), any constellation of Communication across the Curriculum, or some other nomenclature. Thus, the discipline of this new century pursues, shapes, and investigates rhetoric and writing practices that recognize the communicative competencies and potentials as well as the rhetorical displays of all human (and even nonhuman) animals.

Rhetoric and writing studies in the twenty-first century, then, speaks through and across various disciplinary discourses and collaborate across differences, while staying grounded in the needs of rhetors (whether student or professional). In *Writing Matters: Rhetoric in Public and Private Lives,* Lunsford assures her readers that she "is almost daily surprised about how writing and the teaching of writing have changed." "Every few years," she goes on to say, "a new body of literature needs to be learned, a new set of practices and a new kind of teaching mastered" (6). Such an assertion could be disheartening, even threatening.

Instead, *Writing Matters* strikes just the right tone of encouragement at just the right time. Lunsford reminds us of our legacy—we "teachers of writing and rhetoric have had to reinvent ourselves and our disciplines several times"—and projects that "more change is in sight" (6). Indeed, Lunsford herself is an exemplar of this process, having worked in literacy studies, rhetoric and feminism, postcolonialism, digital literacy, and other areas over the long arc of her career. The foundational truth is this: writing is one of the Western world's oldest technologies, and this rich, plastic art has consistently transformed itself in relation to new and emerging technologies (x). Thus, rhetoric's ability "to mold itself to new realities is the key to the new rhetoric, presenting special challenges and special opportunities for those who teach rhetoric and writing" (6).

The essays in *Rhetoric and Writing in the New Century* all attest to the challenges and opportunities within the field of rhetoric and writing studies—twenty-first century challenges of theory and praxis that prod us forward. To that end, these essays revisit four major areas of research, offering original insights and research into twenty-first-century disciplinary questions that continue to merit further consideration: (*a*) the nature of authors and authority, (*b*) the genres of student writing, (*c*) the politics of rhetoric, composition, and writing in the academy, and (*d*) the impermanence of a canon.

OVERVIEW OF THE COLLECTION

Part 1: The Nature of Authors and Authority

"Audience Invoked or Audience Addressed: The Concept of Audience in the Composing Process," written by Lunsford and her longtime collaborator Lisa Ede, won the 1985 Richard Braddock Award for best article published in *College Composition and Communication*. Their essay helped our discipline rethink the concept of audience. No longer was our audience simply our "reader," let alone a fiction of our intention. Rather, we asked ourselves, for whom are we writing and whom are we actually addressing—making a distinction between the two, sometimes overlapping, sometimes mutually exclusive audiences.

Twenty-first-century scholarship on the nature of the author and her authority continues to explore those same broad questions. For instance, in "Rhetorical Argumentation and the Nature of Audience: Toward an Understanding of Audience—Issues in Persuasion," Christopher W. Tindale reviews the scholarship on audience, from Aristotle to Perelman. Tindale's major concern is how, exactly, the identity of the audience affects the reception of any author's argument, any author's authority. Janice Fernheimer untangles the complications of multiple, sometimes conflicting identities in "Black Jewish Identity Conflict: A Divided Universal Audience and the Impact of Dissociative Disruption," heralding her concept of "dissociative disruption" as the means for making the rhetorical space necessary for reconsidering audience, identities, the author's authority, and the causes of conflict—thereby, prolonging the time necessary to reach justice. In "Rethinking Perelman's Universal Audience: Political Dimensions of a Controversial Concept," Antonio Raul de Velasco translates Perelman's audience from serving as the author's tool for "rhetorical invention" into, instead, the author's tool for "rhetorical criticism." Mike Duncan, in "Polemical Ambiguity and the Composite Audience," reconsiders Perelman's "composite audience," the one constituted of several heterogeneous audiences. Duncan argues that such an audience calls for purposeful polemical ambiguity, so that individual members might more easily interpret the author's message and authority as aligning with their own values. And in "The 'We' in 'Yes, We Can,'" Eric Dieter unpacks the rhetorical strategy of presidential candidate Barack Obama when he so successfully uses his authority to connect with his intended and addressed audiences, so much so that they become an endless circle of author and audience.

The essays in this opening section likewise focus on issues of author, authority, and, of course, audience, further interrogating the relationship between the author and audience as well as the authority of the writing itself to both author and audience. In "When *Not* to Write: Reflections on Words, Books, and Authors," MacArthur fellow Shirley Brice Heath opens with her thoughts about a different side of authorship: an author's conscious decision *not* to write. The prolific Heath reveals three pivotal moments during which she chose not to address an audience, not to give expression to her material. "Writing is about the writer," she asserts, and, sometimes, deciding to withhold expression requires all of the same questions of audience and kairos as writing. Woven among her stories are narrative accounts of her basic ethnographic research on sociolinguistics and literacy and the generative theoretical research that has shaped her career, influenced countless others, and reached audiences far broader than Heath could have ever imagined or addressed, let alone invoked.

Shirley Wilson Logan's "Troubling the Waters: Religious Persuasion and Social Activism" helps us rethink how nineteenth-century political women writers and speakers used their authority to effect change. While many of those women and their practices have already been documented (by Logan and Royster, for example), in this essay, Logan focuses on the ways that one previously overlooked woman rhetor distinguished herself by drawing on religious judgment and authority. Amanda Berry Smith claimed authority from God to challenge harmful appropriations of rhetoric. In this essay, Logan interrogates the reasons why Smith's success with nineteenth-century audiences has for so long been ignored.

Finally, in "Collaboration, Authorship, and the Resistance to Change," Lisa Ede charts the history of her many collaborations with Lunsford at the same time that she traces the academy's ongoing resistance to collaborative authorship, a resistance that has become even more entrenched through the decades. In the course of her essay, Ede also explains the ways collaborative writing has challenged the ideologically grounded concepts of "authorship," "'real' writing," and "intellectual property." Although our already networked students quickly take to collaborative writing projects (especially those composed and delivered online, as so much of their self-sponsored writing clearly represents), they rarely have the opportunity to leverage their expertise in the classroom. On a scholarly level, too few professors in the humanities write collaboratively, for they know that they will not be rewarded appropriately for collaborative publications or practices.

Part 2: The Genres of Student Writing

Always interested in the content and character of student writers' work, Lunsford has produced countless textbooks, built several major writing programs, led a longitudinal study of student writers, and produced numerous scholarly treatments of this important topic (e.g., "Crimes of Writing and Reading"; "Who Owns Language?"; and "Performing Writing, Performing Literacy"). The three essays in this section all speak to the genres of student writing while taking into consideration the context and material conditions in which students compose and deliver their writing.

At the point when writing scholars began taking student writing seriously (see Peter Elbow's *Vernacular Eloquence,* Geneva Smitherman's *Talkin' That Talk,* Keith Gilyard's *Voices of the Self,* Suresh Canagarajah's *Resisting Linguistic Imperialism in English Teaching,* and Vershawn Ashanti Young and Aja Martinez's edited volume *Code-Meshing as World English,* for instance), the field began to recognize how nonmainstream forms of English could transform student writing and student writers themselves. The genres of student writing moved beyond the singular memoir, proposal, evaluation, profile, or argument as students remixed, mashed up, and code-meshed, using their language or dialect to create alternative perspectives on the world.

Other researchers, such as those featured in *Crossing Customs,* edited by Andrew Garrod and Jay Davis, analyze student writing in terms of content, stance, and, of course, genre. The contributors in *Crossing Customs* find that much student writing remains anchored in a feeling of "difference" or even alienation, yet needing to resolve this dissonance by writing "American" about "American things," such as roommates, social life, classes. As these students try to fulfill the expectations of their genre-specific writing assignments, there's always leakage, for student writers feel the burden of what they left behind as well as the presence of their linguistic inexperience (wrong verb endings, weird synonyms, sentence constructions based on their home language). For too many of these students, their writing—regardless of genre—reveals more about their struggles with mainstream English language and culture than about what they know or who they are. After all, "Language is an especially well-guarded domain of the West" (Sharma 67).

Researchers of various authorial identities reveal the complexities for students whose identities shape their writing and concomitant genre, too often at cross-purposes with the expectations of their instructors. In "I Write It in a Way That People Can Read It," Amanda Kibler focuses on clarity as a genre in and of itself. Kibler studies adolescent L2 writers who struggle to negotiate the literacy tasks involved in writing "clearly," regardless of the genre, content area, or instructor. These writers steadfastly believe that their own concept of clarity markedly diverges from that of their instructors. When Gary Lemons challenges "whiteness in a black feminist classroom," he uses writing assignments to help his white students develop self-conscious, critical, antiracist, antisexist attitudes and practices, which unfold along with the genre (argument, investigative report, memoir, and so on) and content (linguistic and otherwise) of their own writing. Kathyn Rentz investigates the possible role professional writing could play in English departments, especially in terms of genre, since most English graduates go into business and industry (188). And, of course, in the Braddock Award-winning "Performing Writing, Performing Literacy," Jenn Fishman, Andrea Lunsford, Beth McGregor, and Mark Otuteye demonstrate all the ways that the genre and content of student writing regularly expand to embody explorations of "the realm of the possible" in order to bridge unfamiliar learning gaps "between theory and practice, abstract ideas and concrete examples" (233). For these three researchers, genres of student writing can be enacted, performed, even improvised.

Many of these contemporary studies have influenced the contributors to "The Genres of Student Writing." Longtime writing-program administrator Suellynn Duffey felt confident in approaches for teaching a graduate seminar in writing pedagogy—that is, until she arrived on an urban, MA-granting campus, where students with a wide range of professional and personal backgrounds came to study and write. Duffey thus uses her essay, "Teaching in Place: A Crucial Connection between the English Department and Its Community," to help readers understand the value of developing a site-specific graduate seminar, one leveraging the students' strengths at the same time that it is anchored and involved in the values and needs of the community in which the graduate students will continue to live and work. Duffey's "Sites of Writing" seminar urged students to investigate the "work" of writing within community settings, thereby sparking interest in a fresh genre. Students explored collaborative writing in engineering and scientific organizations, a women's writing group, the diary of a North Vietnamese physician, and African American sermons, thereby realizing that writing could serve as the foundation of community engagement and public scholarship.

Alyssa J. O'Brien takes readers into the realm of online teaching, focusing on an international collaboration that connects students and teachers across five continents, necessitating new approaches to traditional genres. In the

Cross-Cultural Rhetoric Project, which involves Stanford University, the American University in Cairo, Egypt, and Örebro University in Sweden, O'Brien and her colleagues focus on the production of visual (rather than verbal) rhetoric, which affected the genres students used. "Visual Rhetoric, Intercultural Writers: The University's Turn" demonstrates how students from the three campuses connected regularly via videoconference, allowing synchronous interactive teaching and learning, remixes, mashups, and other multimodal deliveries that helped build an international community. O'Brien argues that the purposeful inclusion of "visual texts promotes deep learning writing practices across cultures and enables students to develop as 'intercultural writers.'"

In "Pushing Generic Boundaries in Rhetoric and Composition: Three Sites, One Reader's Response," Melissa A. Goldthwaite responds to Lunsford's provocation that we "push against the boundaries of what is acceptable in traditional academic discourse, bringing in personal experience, colloquial language, other languages and dialects, and direct address" (*Writing Matters* 31). Goldthwaite works at the site of three scholarly exchanges in order to demonstrate the range of stylistic options and rhetorical genres that can be employed to convey information as well as to construct ethos. In her careful analysis of these exchanges—one heated (appearing in a professional journal), one pedagogical (based on her interviews with three leading writing specialists), and one scholarly (rooted in research studies), Goldthwaite asks us to reconsider the role of essay in academic writing. After all, we all study and teach a variety of genres, work to understand their effects, and yet continue to limit ourselves to the scholarly essay when we present our research to others.

Part 3: The Politics of Rhetoric, Composition, and Writing in the Academy

The contemporary view of the role of rhetoric in the curriculum is markedly different from that of the 1970s. Then, it was a question of allowing classical rhetoric to inform the teaching of writing. Studies of the history of rhetoric were often in service of this goal. The study of rhetoric is now more interdisciplinary and aims toward a broad range of goals. This rich landscape has offered new opportunities for scholars to enrich the curriculum. For instance, in "Teaching Rhetoric: Or Why Rhetoric Isn't Just Another Kind of Philosophy or Literacy Criticism," Gerard Hauser, reporting on behalf of the Alliance of Rhetoric Societies Pedagogy group, argues for the value of training in rhetoric for a broad civic education in order to recover rhetoric's "centrality to society's ongoing negotiation over how we shall act and interact" (41). His observations are underscored in "The Mt. Oread Manifesto on Rhetorical Education," in which William Keith, Roxanne Mountford, and their seminar participants argue for a revitalized and interdisciplinary study of rhetoric as the foundation of a civic education. LuMing Mao argues that comparative rhetorics should underpin our curriculum so that students and instructors alike can illuminate what he refers to as our "euroamerican-centrism," which too often blinds us to the incongruities among what is being said, meant, and enacted, between what we think we know and what we actually know, and what has to happen before we come to know and speak with / for others (211). Rhetoric's interdisciplinary partnerships—particularly between scholars in rhetoric and writing and rhetoric and communication—have raised questions about English as a home for the discipline. While some rhetoricians continue to argue for the place of rhetoric and writing in English (see especially Beth Boehm and Debra Journet), new departments of writing and rhetoric have emerged since the 1970s to take advantage of new partnerships.[2] Whatever the rhetorical approach or disciplinary partnership, rhetoric is firmly established as a part of the university curriculum and of the academy itself.

Lunsford has always built both her scholarship and teaching on a foundation resonant with Aristotle's definition of rhetoric: a way to "find something out" and "get it across." Most recently at Stanford, she and her colleagues devised a new writing course anchored in the following rhetorical principles:

- To identify, evaluate, and synthesize materials across a range of media and to explore how to present these materials effectively in support of the students' own argument;
- To analyze the rhetoric of oral, visual, and multimedia documents with attention to how purpose, audience, and context help shape decisions about format, structure, and persuasive appeals;
- To learn to design appropriate and effective oral and multimedia texts;
- To conduct research appropriate to the specific documents being created;
- To reflect systematically on oral, visual, and multimedia rhetoric and writing. (*Writing Matters* 11)

Given twenty-first-century enthusiasm for rhetoric as a part of any writing program, it may come as no surprise that three contributors to this volume would choose to explore the value of a rhetorical education for undergraduate and graduate students alike as well as for professors.

Gerard Hauser opens this section with his "Citizenship, Rhetoric, and Pedagogy," in which he renews his ongoing challenge that teachers of rhetoric help their undergraduate and graduate students develop a sense of engaged citizenship, one that will lead to a "new commonwealth of shared purposes and public goods." This concept of responsible and responsive citizenship will help ameliorate "the forces of radical individualism, unbridled special interests, and bitter division along economic and racial lines" that our nation currently endures. The main roadblock in the development of citizenship anchored in public works (rather than practical self-interest or high ideals) is that we rhetoric teachers do not agree on which model of rhetorical education we should "sustain and advance": the Athenian *paideia* or the Berlinian *Wissenschaft*. The first model, in which teachers exist for their students, focuses on the students' developing capacities to be responsible citizens. *Wissenschaft*, based in the German research-university model, expects students to help teachers achieve their research agendas. Hauser argues that we teachers must find a way to embed *Wissenschaft* within the values and philosophy of the *paideia*.

"Who, Then, Is This Rhetoric Major?" ask John Ruszkiewicz and Davida Charney in their contribution to this volume. Undergraduate programs (majors, minors, and emphases) in rhetoric, writing, and technology are popping up across the nation, with some seventy-two programs at last count. What courses? What sequences? What methods? Those have been the abiding questions in the development of such programs, when, according to Lunsford, a better critical question might be, "What do all these programs have in common?" In their essay, Ruszkiewicz and Charney investigate the center of gravity for all of these programs: the students. The authors argue that it is the students who give such programs relevance and permanence. Their research focused on students enrolled in the Department of Rhetoric and Writing at the University of Texas at Austin. According to their findings, undergraduate students enroll in these richly varied rhetoric and writing programs for three reasons: pragmatic (preparation for a career), personal (love of writing and arguing), and social (low student-teacher ratios).

The first two essays of this section focus the politic work of rhetoric and writing on the macro level; we conclude this section with "Networked Feminism: Mentoring in the New Economy," an essay that critically reflects on the micro-level work of mentoring. In their study of mentoring, Jenn Fishman and Andrea Lunsford have remarked on "how limited we are in our ability to talk about our experience of mentoring and being mentored" (28). Building on Fishman and Lunsford's research, we provide a taxonomy of approaches to feminist mentoring, which we label guru, generational, and networked.

We argue that a networked approach to mentoring draws on some of the best features of the other two models while providing a critical site where the circulation of knowledge challenges the hierarchal models upon which most mentoring is based.

Part 4: The Impermanence of a Canon

In 1416, Poggio Bracciolini discovered a complete manuscript of Quintilian in the basement of the monastery at St. Gall near Constance, Switzerland. After centuries of relying on mere passages of Quintilian's work, scholars finally were able to contextualize his rhetorical instruction, maxims, and examples. "A good man speaking well" became associated not only with Quintilian himself but also with the rhetor being formed. In the six hundred years since Poggio's discovery, scholars have continued to build the rhetorical canon, adding the work of non-Westerners and men and women of every color and class. Scholars representing all genders continue to spotlight society's disputed places, which have for too long been ignored. Fresh rhetorical histories and recovered or recognized rhetorical practitioners continue to shape our perceptions of rhetoric.

The rhetorical scholarship of critical race, feminist, and disability scholars has especially expanded our perceptions, setting new expectations and destinations for scholarship. The work of Smitherman has been crucial: her sociolinguistic investigations of the language and rhetorical power of African Americans continue to influence rhetorical research, practice, and canonicity itself. But hers is hardly the only scholarship to expand our vista. For instance, Ronald L. Jackson and Elaine B Richardson carried Smitherman's work a step further with *Understanding African American Rhetoric: Classical Origins to Contemporary Innovations,* taking her idea of "language" into the realm of rhetoric, diversifying the canon by tracing the roots of African American rhetoric to Africa (not to Greece or Rome) as well as by introducing such African terms as "nommo" and "kwaida." Their important contribution to the rhetorical canon makes it impossible to ignore African Americans' presence—and influence. When Keith Gilyard and Vorris Nunley edited *Rhetoric and Ethnicity,* they, too, linked the two concepts with essays on African Americans, American Indians, Mexican Americans, Italian Americans, and many other categories of Americans of dual heritage, each with a distinctive rhetorical practice and identity. Nunley's *Keepin' It Hushed: The Barbershop and African American Hush Harbor Rhetoric* unveils the rhetorical practices of blacks, some of which include camouflaging their ideas as well as speaking frankly in front of white people, of "speaking truth to power," as Nunley writes. In other words, as Muhammad Ali once said, "Get used to me" (qtd. in Nunley 5). And editor Damián Baca introduces our field to *Rhetorics of the Americas, 3114* B.C.E. *to 2012* C.E., refocusing our view in order to appreciate indigenous rhetorics that arose within uniquely pre-Columbian American cultures. The contributors to Baca's collection present the rhetorical power and personages of the Taínos, Incas, Nahua, Moche, Hawai'ians, among others, indelibly changing the rhetorical canon.

Feminist rhetorical scholars, too, continue to diversify the canon, as the explosion of recent books on the subject attests. Perhaps no venue for this work is more prominent than Studies in Rhetorics and Feminisms, a Southern Illinois University Press series edited by Cheryl Glenn and Shirley Wilson Logan. In the past fifteen years alone, they have produced twenty-four monographs. Both Glenn and Logan have published at this intersection as well, though not with the series, with Glenn offering the first longitudinal history of rhetoric inclusive of women, and Logan supplying long-unpublished texts by nineteenth-century African American rhetors. And they are not alone in this work: Jessica Enoch, Gesa Kirsch, Roxanne Mountford, Krista Ratcliffe, Elaine Richardson, Jacqueline Jones Royster, and many, many others are constantly diversifying the rhetorical canon. Lunsford, too, has helped mitigate the aristocratic male's traditional dominance of the field with her edited collection *Reclaiming Rhetorica,* which helped introduce our discipline to such rhetorical powerhouses as Diotima, Margery Kempe, Christine de Pisan, Sojourner Truth, Margaret Fuller, and Julia Kristeva. And, of course, disability scholars such as Brenda Brueggemann, Cynthia Lewiecki-Wilson and James C. Wilson, Paul Heilker, and many others have already expanded our understanding of the rhetorical concepts, practices, and displays of those who embody a range of physical, emotional, and intellectual abilities.

The contributors to this section reflect some of the most powerful contemporary efforts to broaden the canon—by supplying new research methods, theoretical methodologies, and academic practices or by recovering and recuperating new rhetors. Susan C. Jarratt opens this section by arguing for new and different methods of reading ancient rhetorical texts, particularly in light of the recently discovered and as-yet undiscovered female figures who have been intentionally marginalized, if not (nearly) erased. In "The Empress and the Sophist: Power and Artistry in Third-Century Greek Rhetoric," Jarratt explains that emerging interest in new canonical figures and less commonly studied periods and geographic sites requires new ways of reading and specific rhetorical strategies for reading, rereading, and interpreting. Jarratt suggests turning to rhetorical tactics characteristic of the age in which a historical figure lived, including shifting the *topoi* under which female figures are placed in order to read ancient texts. She demonstrates the reading process with multiple readings of the sophist Philostratus's intellectual biography in order to draw conclusions about the representation of the empress Julia Domna.

In "Rhetorical Education at Catholic Colleges for Women in Ohio: 1925–1940," Nan Johnson considers Lunsford's scholarly values and practices by using "small stories" attuned to the local. Johnson argues that too often the local story disappears in the wake of a grand narrative, so she rescues and preserves a small story about the women in Catholic colleges in the early part of the twentieth century. For Johnson, small stories offer rich starting places for dialogue, engage readers (or listeners) in speculative thinking, and, therefore, reflect the collaborative spirit that has informed so very much of Lunsford's own scholarly life.

In "Feminist Perspectives on Postcolonial Rhetorical Practices: Cosmopolitan Erudition and Surveilled Silence," Elizabeth Flynn complicates the category of "postcolonial woman" by contrasting the lives of two influential writers, the relatively privileged Gayatri Spivak, originally from India, and former slave Mende Nazer, originally from the Sudan, who needed the assistance of a coauthor. Within the comparison, Flynn explores the ways Spivak writes theoretically to other cosmopolitan scholars, rather than to the subaltern, whom she frequently references. Nazer, on the other hand, is a subaltern writing to the subaltern, providing an excruciatingly detailed account of her subaltern status. Flynn advises those of us who engage in transnational and postcolonial rhetorics to focus on women from diverse backgrounds (rather than only on the canonical female figures) in order to demonstrate the range of transnational and postcolonial feminist rhetorics and strategies.

In many ways, Bo Wang's contribution to this collection, "Translating Nora: Chinese Feminism and Global Rhetoric," echoes parts of Mao's argument for the value of comparative, cross-cultural, and transrhetorical practices. Wang writes that such practices stimulate our critical abilities to produce and transmit "knowledge across cultural and geopolitical boundaries and discern the shaping of discursive and cultural relationships." Wang's consideration of the Chinese productions of Ibsen's *A Doll's House* (and interpretations of the character of Nora) offers a case in point, a way for readers to understand the scholarly necessity of integrating global and transnational studies of rhetoric into academic offerings. The inclusion of a global perspective will challenge "existing theoretical assumptions" and "parameters of analysis" that have long underpinned traditional studies of rhetoric, including traditional feminist, comparative, and critical race studies of rhetoric.

Afterword

In "Ain't No Walls behind the Sky, Baby! Funk, Flight, Freedom," Adam Banks weaves together many of the themes of this volume: our authority as a discipline, our investments in some genres (the scholarly paper, the academic essay) over others (especially multimodal), the politics surrounding our work, and the future. At a moment in which higher education continues to feel the aftershocks of the economic downturn of 2008, Banks challenges the field of rhetoric and composition to remember the struggles of the past: "Even the respectability of bigger budgets will not save us. As real as our struggles are, we act like being broke is new. We always been underfunded. . . . We took care of our students anyhow. We transformed one discipline and created our own anyhow." Banks challenges the field to move away from comfortable genres and to *innovate* with the affordances of the digital, to take flight even when there seems to be no freedom on the ground, to engage in jubilee acts of justice at a moment in which there is so much injustice within and without. By embracing "boldness, complexity and even a little irreverence and messiness . . . ," Banks writes, "we will be able to take flight into intellectual, pedagogical and programmatic places that we might partially see, but cannot yet fully know."

Like Banks, the authors of this volume consider both our legacy as a discipline and our possible futures. One legacy is our investment in the student experience and student writing. Lunsford studied basic writers, errors in student writing, the kinds of writing students do after the explosion of social media. Her instinct has long been to treat student writing and the teaching of writing as inherently interesting and worthy foci of study. These instincts drive several of our contributors to seek meaningful curricular change that will benefit students and their experience. Johnson, Hauser, and Ruszkiewicz and Charney consider the ways that curricula might aid students' ability to participate in society. Ede, Duffey, O'Brien, and Goldthwaite challenge long-standing biases in the humanities toward single-author essays, training graduate students to serve national rather than local constituencies, print over multimodal assignments, and narrowly conceived genres of academic writing. These contributors and others challenge us to keep the discipline "funky," to use Banks's words, by destabilizing or flipping such hierarchies as national over local, print over digital, academic over nonacademic.

Banks also challenges members of the field to attend to issues of social justice—particularly racial inequality. This theme is addressed in several essays, including those of Logan, Flynn, and Wang, whose chapters in this volume address problems of race, class, and gender. Flynn and Wang also participate with Logan, Jarratt, Johnson, and us in bringing a feminist perspective to the field, a project long dear to Lunsford. Finally, the field's increasingly global reach emerges in the essays of O'Brien, Flynn, and Wang, who illustrate the fruitfulness of considering broader contexts for our teaching and research.

Throughout her career, Andrea Lunsford has fought for the idea that no writer works alone. Our thoughts are nested in community. Lunsford claims she always wrote in the company of others, even when she was alone at her keyboard. The inverse is also true: Lunsford's contributions (alone and with others) enrich and make possible innovations in the fields of rhetoric and writing studies and in this volume. The essays in *Rhetoric and Writing Studies in the New Century* reaffirm the long-standing, richly generative interanimation between studies of rhetoric and studies of writing at the same time they transport us into the twenty-first-century politics, pedagogies, and practices that now shape and propel our discipline.

Notes

1. Such journals now include *Across the Disciplines*; *Assessing Writing*, *Basic Writing e-journal*; *College Composition and Communication*; *College English*; *Community Literacy Journal*; *Composition Forum*; *Composition Studies*; *Computers and Composition: An International Journal*; *Computers and Composition Online*; *Currents in Electronic Literacy*; *Enculturation: A Journal of Rhetoric, Writing, and Culture*; *://English Matters*; *Harlot: A Revealing Look at the Arts of Persuasion*; *Inventio*, *J.A.C.: A Journal of Composition Theory*; *Journal of Basic Writing*; *Journal of Second Language Writing*; *Journal of Teaching Writing*; *Kairos: A Journal of Rhetoric, Technology, and Pedagogy*; *KB Journal*; *Philosophy and Rhetoric*; *Present Tense: A Journal of Rhetoric in Society*; *PreText*; *Journal of the Council for Programs in Technical and Scientific Communication*; *Readerly/Writerly Texts: Essays on Literature, Literary/Textual Criticism, and Pedagogy*; *Reflections*; *RhetNet*; *Rhetoric Review*; *Rhetorica*; *Rhetoric Society Quarterly*; *Teaching English in the Two-Year College*; *Technical Communication Quarterly*; *Writing Center Journal*; *Writing Lab Newsletter*; *WPA: Writing Program Administration*; and *Written Communication*.

2. The University of Texas at Austin and Syracuse University were among the first to establish independent departments. Since then, interdisciplinary graduate programs have been established at Clemson University and North Carolina State University, among others.

Works Cited

Baca, Damián, and Victor Villanueva, eds. *Rhetorics of the Americas, 3114 B.C.E. to 2012 C.E.* Palgrave, 2010.

Boehm, Beth, and Debra Journet. "Across the Curriculum: Rhetoric and Composition." *Teaching Narrative Theory*, edited by David Herman, Brian McHale, and James Phelan, Modern Language Association, 2010, pp. 61–69.

Brent, Doug. "Reinventing WAC (Again): The First-Year Seminar and Academic Literacy." *College Composition and Communication*, vol. 57, no. 2 2005, pp. 253–76.

Britton, James, Tony Burgess, Nancy Martin, Alex McLeod, and Harold Rosen. *The Development of Writing Abilities (11–18).* Macmillan, 1979.

Brueggemann, Brenda Jo. *Lend Me Your Ear: Rhetorical Constructions of Deafness.* Gallaudet UP, 1999.

Canagarajah, A. Suresh. *Resisting Linguistic Imperialism in English Teaching.* Oxford UP, 1999.

Corbett, Edward P. J. *Classical Rhetoric for the Modern Student.* Oxford UP, 1965.

Dieter, Eric. "The 'We' in 'Yes, We Can': Obama's Audience, the Audience's Obama, and Consubstantiality." *The Rhetoric of Heroic Expectations: Establishing the Obama Presidency*, edited by Justin S. Vaughn and Jennifer R. Mercieca, Texas A&M UP, 2014, pp. 50–66.

Duncan, Mike. "Polemical Ambiguity and the Composite Audience: Bush's 20 September 2001 Speech to Congress and the Epistle of 1 John." *Rhetoric Society Quarterly*, vol. 41, no. 5, 2011, pp. 455–71.

Ede, Lisa, and Andrea Lunsford. "Audience Addressed / Audience Invoked: The Role of Audience in Composition Theory and Pedagogy." *College Composition and Communication*, vol. 35, no. 2, 1984, pp. 155–71.

Elbow, Peter. *Vernacular Eloquence: What Speech Can Bring to Writing.* Oxford UP, 2012.

———. *Writing without Teachers.* 2nd ed., Oxford UP, 1998.

Emig, Janet. *The Composing Process of Twelfth Graders.* National Council of Teachers of English, 1971.

Enoch, Jessica. *Refiguring Rhetorical Education: Women Teaching African American, Native American, and Chicano/a Students, 1865–1911.* Southern Illinois UP, 2008.

Fernheimer, Janice W. "Black Jewish Identity Conflict: A Divided Universal Audience and the Impact of Dissociative Disruption." *Rhetoric Society Quarterly,* vol. 39, no. 1, 2009, pp. 46–72.

Fishman, Jenn and Andrea Lunsford. "Educating Jane." *Stories of Mentoring: Theory and Praxis,* edited by Michelle F. Eble and Lynee Lewis Gaillet, Parlor, 2008, pp. 18–51.

Fishman, Jenn, Andrea Lunsford, Beth McGregor, and Mark Otuteye. "Performing Writing, Performing Literacy." *College Composition and Communication,* vol. 57, no. 2, 2005, pp. 224–52.

Garrod, Andrea, and Jay Davis, eds. *Crossing Customs: International Students Write on U.S. College Life and Culture.* Falmer, 1999.

Gilyard, Keith. *Voices of the Self: A Study of Language Competence.* Wayne State UP, 1991.

Gilyard, Keith, and Vorris Nunley, eds. *Rhetoric and Ethnicity.* Boynton, 2004.

Glenn, Cheryl. *Rhetoric Retold: Regendering the Tradition from Antiquity through the Renaissance.* Southern Illinois UP, 1997.

———. *Unspoken: A Rhetoric of Silence.* Southern Illinois UP, 2005.

Glenn, Cheryl, and Andrea A. Lunsford, eds. *Landmark Essays in Rhetoric and Feminism, 1973–2000.* Routledge, 2014.

Glenn, Cheryl, and Krista Ratcliffe, eds. *Silence and Listening as Rhetorical Arts.* Southern Illinois UP, 2011.

Hauser, Gerard. "Teaching Rhetoric: Or Why Rhetoric Isn't Just Another Kind of Philosophy or Literary Criticism." *Rhetoric Society Quarterly,* vol. 34, no. 3, 2004, pp. 39–53.

Heilker, Paul, and Melanie Yergeau. "Autism and Rhetoric." *College English,* vol. 75, no. 3, 2011, pp. 485–97.

Jackson, Ronald L., and Elaine B. Richardson, eds. *Understanding African American Rhetoric: Classical Origins to Contemporary Innovations.* Routledge, 2003.

Kibler, Amanda. "'I Write It in a Way That People Can Read It': How Teachers and Adolescent L2 Writers Describe Content Area Writing." *Journal of Second Language Writing,* vol. 20, 2011, pp. 211–26.

Kirsch, Gesa. *Women Writing the Academy: Audience, Authority, Transformation.* National Council of Teachers of English, 1993.

Lemons, Gary. "When White Students Write about Being White: Challenging Whiteness in a Black Feminist Classroom." *Counterpoints*, vol. 473, 2004, pp. 213–33.

Logan, Shirley Wilson. *We Are Coming: The Persuasive Discourse of Nineteenth-Century Black Women*. Southern Illinois UP, 1999.

———, ed. *With Pen and Voice: A Critical Anthology of Nineteenth-Century African American Women*. Southern Illinois UP, 1995.

Lunsford, Andrea Abernethy. "An Historical, Descriptive, and Evaluative Study of Remedial English in the United States." Diss. Ohio State U, 1977.

———, ed. *Reclaiming Rhetorica: Women in the Rhetorical Tradition*. U of Pittsburgh P, 1995.

———. *Writing Matters: Rhetoric in Public and Private Lives*. U of Georgia P, 2007.

Mao, LuMing. "Beyond Bias, Binary, and Border: Mapping Out the Future of Comparative Rhetoric." *Rhetoric Society Quarterly*, vol. 43, no. 3, 2013, pp. 209–25.

Mountford, Roxanne. *The Gendered Pulpit: Preaching in American Protestant Spaces*. Carbondale: Southern Illinois UP, 2003.

Murray, Donald. *A Writer Teaches Writing*. Houghton, 1985.

Nunley, Vorris L. *Keepin' It Hushed: The Barbershop and African American Hush Harbor Rhetoric*. Wayne State UP, 2011.

Ratcliffe, Krista. *Anglo-American Feminist Challenges to the Rhetorical Traditions: Virginia Woolf, Mary Daly, and Adrienne Rich*. Southern Illinois UP, 1996.

———. *Rhetorical Listening: Identification, Gender, and Whiteness*. Carbondale: Southern Illinois UP, 2006.

Rentz, Kathryn. "A Flare from the Margins: The Place of Professional Writing in English Departments." *Pedagogy*, vol. 1, 2001, pp. 185–90.

Richardson, Elaine. *PHD to PhD: How Education Saved My Life*. Parlor, 2012.

Richardson, Elaine, and Ronald Jackson, eds. *African American Rhetorics: Interdisciplinary Perspectives*. Southern Illinois UP, 2007.

Royster, Jacqueline Jones. *Profiles of Ohio Women, 1803–2003*. Ohio UP, 2003.

———, ed. *Southern Horrors and Other Writing: The Anti-Lynching Campaign of Ida B. Wells, 1892–1900*. Bedford, 1996.

Royster, Jacqueline Jones, and Gesa Kirsch. *Feminist Rhetorical Practices: New Horizons for Rhetoric, Composition, and Literacy Studies*. Southern Illinois UP, 2012.

Shaughnessy, Mina. *Errors and Expectations: A Guide for the Teacher of Basic Writing.* Oxford UP, 1979.

Sharma, Devyani. "Living by Leaving Behind." Garrod and Davis. 53–71.

Smitherman, Geneva, and H. Sami Alim. *Articulate While Black: Barack Obama, Language, Race in the United States.* Oxford UP, 2012.

Smitherman, Geneva. *Talkin and Testifyin: The Language of Black America.* Wayne State UP, 1977.

———. *Talkin' That Talk: Language, Culture, and Education in African America.* Routledge, 1999.

———. *Word from the Mother: Language and African Americans.* Routledge, 2016.

"Students' Right to Their Own Language." *College Composition and Communication*, vol. 25, 1974.

Tindale, Christopher W. "Rhetorical Argumentation and the Nature of Audience: Toward an Understanding of Audience—Issues in Argumentation." *Philosophy and Rhetoric*, vol. 46, no. 4, 2013, pp. 508–32.

Valasco, Antonio Raul de. "Rethinking Perelman's Universal Audience: Political Dimensions of a Controversial Concept." *Rhetoric Society Quarterly*, vol. 35, no. 2, 2005, pp. 47–64.

Wilson, James C., and Cynthia Lewiecki-Wilson, eds. *Embodied Rhetorics: Disability in Language and Culture.* Southern Illinois UP, 2001.

Young, Vershawn Ashanti, and Aja Y. Martinez, eds. *Code-Meshing as World English: Pedagogy, Policy, Performance.* National Council of Teachers of English, 2011.

PART 1
THE NATURE OF AUTHORS AND AUTHORITY

WHEN *NOT* TO WRITE
REFLECTIONS ON WORDS, BOOKS, AND AUTHORS

SHIRLEY BRICE HEATH

Every piece of writing is ultimately about the writer.

Teachers of composition and rhetoric emphasize this truism again and again. They tell students to take ownership of their writing. They urge them to choose with care their topic, purpose, and audience, for when they write, they write themselves.

As writers move through life, some choose as carefully what they will *not* write as what they will write. This chapter describes what *not writing* has meant for me as an author.

Over the course of my life in the academy, I have, no doubt, written too much. Though I remember what every piece I've written is about, I have forgotten what many of these pieces say. What I have *not* forgotten, however, is what the pieces I chose *not* to write were about and what they could have said. I have also not forgotten that only I could have written those pieces that never came into existence.

Yet I chose not to write those pieces. Make no mistake about my use of the word *chose.* Deciding not to write takes as much, and sometimes more, mental work than writing does. Some pieces a writer may think desirable for print never get written, because the writer determines that neither energy and will nor time and resources are sufficient. The pieces I talk about here were not the victim of such circumstances.

In this chapter, I tell the stories behind three unwritten pieces that remain with me. I then offer my conjectures on what is happening within the readership of extended texts such as books, and how shifts in readership preferences may well increase the importance of choosing when and what to write.

UNCONTESTABLE "ORIGINALITY"

I once chose not to write when I knew that doing so would bring charges from people I cared about that I had stolen what was original with them. These people were literary artists—famous American poets and novelists I first met in the 1980s.

As a linguistic anthropologist, I maintain a desire to know how carefully crafted writing is created and how the language of the ultimate product is received by devoted readers. Throughout the 1980s, I spent hundreds of hours hanging out in independent bookstores in twenty-seven cities and midsized towns across the United States. My haunt in these bookstores was the American literature section, where I watched others while I looked through books and lingered. When I saw a patron select a book by either a current prize-winning American writer or a classic writer from earlier decades, I followed them to the checkout counter carrying a randomly chosen book in my hand. In line for the cashier, I started a conversation in which I got around to asking the patron I had followed: "Do you mind if I ask how you came to select the book you've chosen?" I kept track of these answers, but I also continued the conversation by briefly explaining who I was and asking if these individuals would allow me to phone them in six weeks to have a chat about the book. Most agreed.

When I phoned them, I reintroduced myself and initiated talk about the book. I asked questions that revealed to me: a) whether or not they indeed had read the book, b) what they had read since, c) the impressions they had of the language within the book I had seen them choose, and d) whether or not they had talked about the book with anyone else and what they had said in those conversations. I ended my talks with these readers by asking if I might phone again about six weeks later to learn what else they had read of American literary works and how they had made their choices.

During most summers of the decade of the 1980s, I also attended writers' conferences, often playing a minor role on the faculty, and once again pursuing the same questions of participants there. These visits also enabled me to get to know the writers who taught at these conferences. During that decade, a majority of the best-known American poets and novelists did not hold regular faculty positions throughout the academic year. Instead they taught in several writing conferences each year, enabling them to supplement incomes from their royalties that at that time sufficiently rewarded these best-known American creative writers (e.g., novelists such as Raymond Carver and John Irving and poets such as Marvin Bell and Mark Strand). At various times throughout each academic year, I visited these writers in their own homes to learn (*a*) who and what they had read, (*b*) how they had made their selections, (*c*) how they would describe the language of those writers who most influenced them, and (*d*) what they most wanted their readers to think and do with the language they had created in their own works.

I have never published this research. The fact that I did the work became known only because, in the early 1990s, Jonathan Franzen, a promising young American writer whom I had met in the course of my research, was asked to write an essay for the *New York Times Magazine*. The topic the editors wanted Jonathan to address was "the great American novel." He phoned to tell me of this opportunity and asked what I had ever done with the study he remembered my working on some years ago. I reported that I had never written about the work, and if he wanted to use ideas from the study, I was happy to send him a summary, have conversations about the work, and see what he would do with it. He agreed, though I cautioned him: "Every major writer in America will hate you, claim what you say came from them, and maintain that your ideas are either wrong or stolen."

Franzen said: "I know." He was very familiar with the fact that his fellow writers held the view that any original idea related to "great American writing" came from them. The piece for the *New York Times* never happened, but in April of 1996, Jonathan published in *Harper's Magazine* an article entitled "Perchance to Dream: In the Age of Images, A Reason to Write Novels." In this piece and in an essay he later republished in his collection *How to Be Alone: Essays,* he drew heavily from what I had told him about my research. His piece argued that creative writers feel compelled to be estranged from the world around them and find their comfort in inhabiting their imagined world. Don DeLillo, American novelist, had conveyed this idea to me just as he did when he wrote a letter responding to Jonathan's piece. DeLillo maintained: "The writer leads, he doesn't follow." This claim sounds heathen to academics schooled in M. M. Bakhtin's writings that assert that all language echoes "common language"—words that others have spoken but that authors purposively rework.

Just as Jonathan and I had predicted, swift and harsh responses to his piece came from major American literary writers. Readers of this literature, however, wrote supporting testimonies to confirm the ties between loneliness and social isolation in their lives and their retreat into reading the words of others. Many maintained that without reading, they would feel completely adrift in the world, for they found their closest friends within the words that literary writers gave them in novels and poetry.

So why did I not write the book about my research on the power of language for writers and readers of American literature? Perhaps because writers and readers feel socially isolated, many had welcomed me into their lives. They relished my company, for they trusted my genuine interest in their work. Highly private people, they feared the general public, and often found encounters with readers at bookstores and book fairs invasive and threatening. My approach to writers and readers did not threaten them, for they found that talking to me as a linguistic anthropologist about styles, influences, and lasting words gave them new insights into their own views. Moreover, we shared a love of literary language.

However, as DeLillo and others who responded to Jonathan's piece asserted, each writer has to believe that the words he or she puts on the page originate with the author. Jonathan, as one of them, lived within that same world, knowing that writers consistently feel that they betray and steal from one another. Thus his piece may have been viewed by other writers as expected or "normal."

For me to write about them and their words, however, could never have such normality for the writers that had become my close friends. With understandable extension, these authors believed that anything I said about how they created and felt about their words came from them. If used by me, these ideas would be "stolen." These writers had trusted me with what they viewed as their very own private and exclusive secrets about literary language. My revelations as a social scientist would be incomprehensible to them as anything but theft and an irreparable breach in our friendship, a betrayal of their trust.

Since every piece of writing is ultimately about the writer, I chose *not* to write. Doing so would transform me into a traitor who revealed secrets others had entrusted to me.

NOTES TO FRAGMENTED MINDS

"Happy families are all alike; every unhappy family is unhappy in its own way." This opening line of Leo Tolstoy's novel *Anna Karenina* has become so familiar as to be at times laughable. But some of us can never laugh at this line.

Unhappiness came to my own happy family with the simultaneous double blow of my husband's stroke and our daughter's accident in August of 1984. Both were left with fragmented minds that remained the rest of their lives. My husband, the well-known linguist Charles Ferguson, had a stroke and entered intensive care. Two days after Charles's stroke, our eighteen-year-old daughter, Shannon, suffered severe head injuries in a fall while mountain climbing in Colorado.

Their fractured minds robbed them of their personalities and many of their linguistic and cognitive abilities.

A truism that often surfaces in composition courses claims that "writing about pain" can bring relief and release. I never found this to be the case. Over the years after Charles's stroke, as he grew more distant from the intellectual and loving companion who had made me so happy in our marriage, I did try writing to him, but only once.

I distinctly remember sitting on a bench one spring in a park in Cambridge, England, and missing him so deeply, I broke into a loud wail with a flood of tears. Looking around at the startled strollers in the park, I pulled out my notebook and began to write a letter to Charles asking him all the questions I had stored away since his stroke. "Do you ever remember . . . ?" "Do you miss . . . ?" Of course, I never mailed the letter, but instead I tucked it away in the back of my address book. Years later, after he died, I pulled it out and read it to a grief counselor who was urging me to shed my anger. I had lived for fourteen years with a man whose fractured mind had created someone whose personality I could no longer recognize or respect. My letter opened to my counselor the depth of loss that comes to a family that includes a stranger caught in "living death."

And what of my daughter, Shannon, in the years between Charles's stroke and her accident and his death? She too transformed into someone barely recognizable as the daughter who, during her teenage years, had become my closest friend. While Charles was gone after fourteen years, released from his "living death," she remains in hers. And I have never written to her and will not, for some lessons of life, one does not have to learn twice. That letter to Charles written in such anguish on a park bench brought no relief from knowing that he and I had to go on living with his fractured mind. I did not have to write to Shannon to feel the sharpness of that reality for her and to know that her years of "living death" were likely to go on and on, even beyond my own death.

Written words do not heal; they reveal. And some revelations simply have to be endured.

KEEPING ETHNOGRAPHY OUT OF THE ADVICE BUSINESS

Some reasons for *not* writing are personal. Others spring from one's sense of professional identity. Ultimately, all reasons derive from self-identity and the need to keep that intact.

I am a linguistic anthropologist whose academic career has centered on understanding the uses and structures of symbol systems ranging from language (oral and written) to visual representations (such as gestural systems, choreography, and music). To this central interest in structured symbol systems, I have, since the late 1990s, added an intense interest in neuroscience and what it can tell us about the ways that learning across symbol systems may be affected by cultural and social conditions during childhood and adolescence.

The genre of my books has been ethnography narrating the lives of working-poor and working-class families, black and white, over one or more decades. The primary lens of these books has been the socialization of children and teenagers in various learning environments, such as families, classrooms, and communities. In particular, the role of work and play interactions between the young and adults stands out in my studies of socialization.

Responses to the longitudinal range of my ethnographies invariably ask whether or not changes that have taken place in child and adolescent socialization over decades brought about losses. On some occasions, responses raise the matter of what is gained over time that makes socialization more successful, effective, and rich than was the case in past decades.

Since the earliest years of ethnographies, anthropologists have heard the warning: "Beware the fallacy of the ethnographic present." What is written of the here and now in ethnographies never remains as it is described; people, places, and policies change. Moreover, ethnographers who attempt to do their work with as little disruption as possible to those they study refrain from making judgments concerning who or what may be good or bad, successful or ill-fated.

Two of my ethnographies have raised particular challenges for readers who have a strong urge for such judgments. In the first (*Ways*), I described the lives of three hundred families in the Piedmont Carolinas during the 1970s, the decade following the landmark legislative and legal achievements of the civil rights era. In the second (*Words*), I described the ongoing lives of these same families during the tumultuous economic ups and downs of the next three decades (from 1980 to 2010). The roller-coaster economy of this period brought geographic relocation and shifts in valuations and patterns of traditional family structures. Work and family life alterations resulting from technological changes changed parental influence on children's socialization. My ethnography describes not only how language structures and uses changed over these decades, but also how times and places of projects of play and work shifted.

Readers of the first ethnography who met many of the characters whose lives are narrated in the second have a nostalgic view of what life was like in the 1970s. Consequently, as they read the changes that three decades of economic and technological swings and innovations brought about, they make judgments that they ask me to confirm. "Isn't it the case that teenagers today have lost a sense of responsibility and morality?" "Don't you see a huge drop-off of interest in reading by today's young, compared to what you found in your first book?" "Isn't it true that what has been lost (in language, play, and work patterns and habits) is more than compensated for by what we have gained through having the Internet and its associated technologies?"

The only answer that I can make as an ethnographer to these questions is "yes, but . . ." The equivocal answer from me indicates that it is certainly the case that adolescents of the families I followed did indeed change their oral language habits and with increasing speed from the middle of the 1990s forward. In everyday discourse among their peers, their extended conversations (more than four minutes on the same topic) showed sharp changes in verb usage. Simple present and past tenses dominated, while their marking of events to come relied in large part on forms such as "is going (plus infinitive)," with "going to" generally uttered as "gonna." The perfect tense was rarely used in everyday speech, and subjunctive forms were seldom spoken. Only through threats or warnings ("If you don't come, I'll be really upset") did they use "if-then" constructions. They rarely uttered hypotheticals that contained multiple variables on either side of the "if" or "then." Their narrations often centered on retelling shared experiences (including television programs, films, and Internet viewings of YouTube or Vimeo), with exaggeration of content and dramatic sound effects (such as yells, loud noises, and laughter). They marked the degree of their responses to these retold events with modifiers such as "awesome," "totally," and "actually." Their imperatives to friends generally came in frozen forms, such as "check it out."

What is missing in their conversations in comparison with those of their counterparts of the 1970s, 1980s, and early 1990s? Any list of earlier language patterns that occur today with much less frequency than in earlier years would be interdependent with altered contexts for conversations between children and adults. Projects of work and play occur relatively rarely compared to such occurrences in earlier years. Because project talk involves planning and projecting, hypotheticals and "what if?" and "what about?" questions occur in such talk. Without project talk between the young and adults during events such as playing board games, planning construction of a dog house, or projecting ways to redecorate a child's bedroom, the young do not hear perfect tenses that juxtapose the time of action of one event with another. They also are far less likely to hear comparatives. They are far less likely to read extended texts that do not relate to their special interests. Thus they are far less practiced than their counterparts in prior generations in remembering what extended texts say or mean. None of the linguistic forms or habits noted here is modeled in project-centered contexts with sufficient frequency for young speakers today to reach a level of fluency and inclination that would bring these forms into their everyday behaviors.

Yes, we must conclude that today, in comparison with earlier decades, teenagers hear and use less frequently certain forms of language. But much that relates to language has been added to the repertoire of what teenagers today know and use. For example, today's young have a broader lexicon of "rare words" than their counterparts in earlier years. As the young have increasingly learned to explore the Internet and to develop communities of interest, they have gained vocabulary. In comparison with their counterparts in the 1980s and early 1990s, today's teenagers have a wider range of acronyms and abbreviations through their use of the Internet. As diversity has increased in schools and other peer interactional contexts such as sports teams, today's young have a wider range of genres and styles of speaking (and writing) than their peers of earlier decades. Moreover, today's young have more strategies of research through which they can gain information and skills related to their special interest. They know much more about routes of access to information, and they read and write more often in more genres, for a wider array of purposes and audiences, and in a greater number of styles than their earlier-age peers.

However, it seems easy for individuals who entered adulthood during the 1980s or 1990s to see today's youth as lacking the language structures and usage they recall from their childhood and teenage years. This tendency to note what is absent rather than what is present has several causes. Foremost is the fact that today's young, especially older children and teenagers, more often than not talk, write, and read outside the presence of adults. Hence, adults lack information about what is actually happening in the oral and written language of the young. A second reason is that academic assessments rarely tap into any of these "new" ways of talking, reading, and writing among today's teenagers. What is demanded in these assessments comes from assumptions regarding the dominance of information presented in extended texts, interactive deliberative discourse, and means of expression tied to academic subjects and ways of reasoning, comparing, and analyzing.

The central question of this chapter is when should we choose *not* to write? I did write these two ethnographies. What is it that I decided *not* to write?

Audiences of readers and listeners to my public lectures repeatedly express both their guilt and their regret at "not knowing" what my 2012 ethnography says about modes of parenting and language development in today's young. Therefore, they point to my social science studies and conclude that I "should" write a guide to tell parents what they see as the perils of not playing and working on family projects with their children. They believe that I am "obligated" to tell parents what is happening to the language uses and knowledge bases of their children as a result of "spending too much time on the Internet and socializing with their friends." The list of warnings they wish they could hear from me goes on and on.

I tell those who offer such recommendations to me only that I have chosen not to transform my social science research into guides to parenting. I do so for several reasons. Foremost is my belief in what was termed in the 1980s and 1990s "basic research." Such research explores what is happening under certain conditions and derives theories of explanation that rely on the response of specific phenomena under these circumstances. Theories thus generate explanations of changes in behavior in relation to co-occurring conditions. Judgments of what is right or wrong in either these behaviors or co-occurring conditions have no place in "basic research."

On the other hand, since the late 1990s, the drive for "applied research" has intensified from clinical fields such as education, medicine, and social work, as well as areas such as transportation, agriculture, climate change, and housing. After 2010, journalists and academics saw the value in drawing from both basic and applied research to create summaries based in interdisciplinary research. Such journalists include David Brooks, Malcolm Gladwell, Adam Gopnik, Tracy Kidder, and Fared Zakaria. Such academics include Dan Ariely, Noam Chomsky, Jared Diamond, Howard Gardner, George Lakoff, Jonah Lerer, and Deborah Tannen. Not included in these brief lists are the increasing numbers of academics from the fields of biography, finance, history, psychology, and politics who have contributed works that bring together basic research and practical recommendations. These works have done a major service to both the academy and the reading public who engage with such texts.

However, I am not such a writer. I have chosen to create the genre of ethnography as a narrative form that presents basic research in ways that I trust will lead readers to enter their own lives into the theories of explanation I offer. Because of the time span and number of individual lives covered in these ethnographies, the ethnographies I write cannot be transformed into guides for others. Theories are by their very nature generative. Thus each reader can respond to the weaving of theories into narrative through relating what is given to a chosen context the reader knows. It may be that which belongs to the reader as an individual. It may be that which the reader believes applies to one or more groups who share specific aspects of life stories with the characters in the ethnography. Some readers may come away from longitudinal ethnography without a need to apply theories in the work to any individual or group. They will remember only the characters. Either outcome is fine.

I do not want those who read my ethnographies to sense that I judge either my readers or the characters about which I write. Life as it moves along cannot be reduced to more then, less now. Most of us do what we must and move on as best we can. That is the stuff I try to tell in the ethnographies I write.

THE CHANGING LIFE OF EXTENDED TEXTS AND WHY *NOT* WRITING COULD BECOME MORE POPULAR

In the opening decades of the twenty-first century, scenes of readers engaged with extended texts have little in common with such scenes throughout most of the twentieth century. Asking readers about their memories of extended texts they read in past years brings about few details surrounding these texts, and often the texts themselves are nowhere to be found in the readers' households.

With technologies linking the Internet to every space and point of time as the twenty-first century moves forward, individuals read in short spurts, often while multitasking. Readers remember little of what they have read. Focus on the language of the texts before them calls on different skills and intentions, takes more time, and links to self-identity. Advances in the technologies that enable neuroscientists to observe what happens in the human brain during specific activities reveal how the brain works during rapid-fire scanning of texts and within multitasking. Long-term memory storage calls on the brain in ways that differ significantly from short-term-memory engagements called for during scans of texts. Readers who do not undertake the brainwork necessary to read and retain extended text information and language features reason that there is no need to do so: they can always quickly re-access these texts.

With each decade of the twenty-first century, writers who struggle to craft their language in memorable ways for their extended texts have fewer and fewer readers. They have their fans—their ready readers, and they write for them. Review outlets that in years past filled their pages with language-rich fiction and poetry have replaced these works with popular works on current topics such as politics.

Extended texts are increasingly likely to reach primarily three types of readers. These include: those with curiosity, those with highly specialized interests, and members of personality cults. The curious tend to be those who keep up with what is going on in the world. They scan reviews, sometimes browse bookshops, and check the Internet for publications related to the latest focus of their curiosity. Their travels often generate points of curiosity that lead them to read extended texts. Those with highly specialized interests read widely and purposefully about their particular hobby, need, or passion. If their pediatrician identifies their toddler as being on the autism spectrum, they seek out help groups, read any source that comes their way, and find books they believe speak most helpfully to them and their needs. Those who follow politics, finance, or environmental issues closely seek out and read extended texts on these topics. Finally, members of personality cults want to keep up with their favorite film or music star, author, or historic figure. They watch for biographies and autobiographies and works of different types of history, ranging from military history to narrative and social histories. They may read these as either e-books or as printed texts between book covers. All three types of readers see little reason to remember or to attend to the nature of the language, though they are likely to have general impressions about how specific authors or books came across to them through particular styles of writing.

In short, with each decade, extended text production shrivels. Chief among the many causes of this shrinkage has been the acceleration of access to information combined with the shrinkage of time available for contemplative reading that extended texts have called for in past eras. In the Western world, from the eighteenth century until recent years, members of the leisure class have been educated to immerse themselves in extended texts and to learn through them. They have been asked to recall specific features of these texts, including ways in which individual writers created the language of these texts. But such is the case no more.

Now and into the foreseeable future, extended texts will not serve these purposes. Such texts will primarily serve functions specific to governmental, legal, and financial institutions. These institutions demand written records. Their public functions require them to preserve and store documents as public records that can be retrieved when legal decisions and property dispositions must be made. Most of such documents find few readers. To be sure, journalists review governmental budget documents as well as legislative rulings and appropriations bills. Legal scholars and journalists read legal decisions when they relate to publicized rulings or alterations of legal precedent. Journalists also read the writings of other journalists. Attorneys, officers of financial institutions, and government officials at state and local levels often collect documents, though they read them for detail or in full only when legal outcomes depend on textual detail. Simply knowing specific documents exist and having the gist of what they "say" often counts as "reading."

Competition for attentive reading has always been fierce, in part because reading has always insisted on exclusive attention. No one can vacuum, dig in the garden, or ride a bicycle while reading a book. Today, audiobooks allow readers to take in their content while doing something else. The age-old dedication to sitting down with a book, newspaper, or magazine to read from cover to cover has come close to vanishing in modern economies. The act of reading has been taken over by skimming, reviewing, glancing, and "checking it out." Reading a review often substitutes for reading the book; reading the abstract, first paragraphs, and looking over graphs, figures, and illustrations amounts to "knowing" what has been written. No one feels these realities more than young people attending academic institutions. Assignments from instructors across the span of formal schooling have decreased the amount of reading and writing required. Survey after survey taken by publishers indicates this shrinkage and the move of instructors toward acceptance of Internet sources as legitimate references needed to fulfill assignments. Open courses increase annually in numbers and types of content as well as age of targeted audiences.

My reasons for not writing have been personal and professional. Others may recognize and even share some of these reasons. Yet such reasons will, by no means, be the major determinant into the future of continuing disinclination by writers of all types to write extended texts. As Franzen's 1996 article noted, some writers will find "in the age of images, a reason to write." They will have to do so, however, while recognizing the value of images as complement and supplement to their written words. The huge growth in audiences for graphic novels attests to this point, as does increased use of images on the Internet. As "swiping" replaces keyboarding, the components of language will increasingly decline as the way into informational access.

In 1992, Daniel Pennac, French novelist and thriller writer as well as creative writing teacher, wrote *The Rights of the Reader.* The book, a collection of 144 short chapters, has been translated into more than thirty languages. Reading the book today suggests to me that this author could see coming in 1992 what would rapidly characterize readers and writers in the twenty-first century. He describes responses from his creative writing class to questions he puts to them. One day, he asks them to describe a book. Their response may well be the best possible foreshadowing of what is to come that may well convince more and more writers *not* to write.

> When I ask them to describe a book for me, a UFO lands in the classroom: a mysterious object that almost defies description. Deceptively simple to look at but with multiple functions. A foreign body with all sorts of powers and dangers. A sacred object, infinitely cherished and respected, placed with priest-like solemnity on the shelves of a spotless library and worshipped by an adoring sect with enigmatic expressions.
>
> The Holy Grail.
>
> Right. (140)

Works Cited

Bakhtin, Mikhail Mikhailovich. *The Dialogic Imagination: Four Essays.* Translated by Caryl Emerson and Michael Holquist. U of Texas P, 1981.

Franzen, Jonathan. *How to Be Alone: Essays.* Picador, 2003.

———. "Perchance to Dream: In the Age of Images a Reason to Write Novels." *Harper's Magazine,* April 1996, pp. 15–17, 38–54.

Heath, Shirley Brice. *Ways with Words: Language, Life and Work in Communities and Classrooms.* Cambridge UP, 1983.

———. *Words at Work and Play: Three Decades in Family and Community Life.* Cambridge UP, 2012.

Pennac, Daniel. *The Rights of the Reader.* Translated by Sarah Adams. Walker Books, 2006.

TROUBLING THE WATERS
RELIGIOUS PERSUASION AND SOCIAL ACTIVISM

SHIRLEY WILSON LOGAN

> For an angel went down at a certain season into the pool, and troubled the water: whosoever then first after the troubling of the water stepped in was made whole of whatsoever disease he had.
>
> —John 5:4, King James Version

> In considering the authors I have chosen to focus upon, our understanding of the rich, complicated, and understudied relationships among literature, piety, and nationalism that were in play as the United States struggled to assume its place among the world's powers will be enriched.
>
> —Joycelyn Moody, *Sentimental Confessions*, 2001

Many will recognize the expression "troubling the water," especially as found in the King James translation of the Christian Bible. It is also a line from the Negro spiritual "Wade in the Water," with various implied interpretations. Twentieth-century jazz pianist Ramsey Lewis recorded a well-known version of "Wade in the Water" as did singer Eva Cassidy. In 2008, in the aftermath of Hurricane Katrina, a documentary titled "Trouble the Water" was issued as a call to action and change. I use it in the title of this chapter to allude to the strong ties between the social activism in which black women were involved across the nineteenth century and the religious warrants they employed to support it. These women "troubled" social and political waters to make changes in people and circumstances. They understood their faith not only as a source of comfort during troubling times, of which there were many, but also as a powerful source of motivation for action.

> From the moment I experienced the change, I felt a strong desire, with the help and assistance of God, to devote the remainder of my days to piety and virtue, and now possess that spirit of independence, that, were I called upon, I would willingly sacrifice my life for the cause of God and my brethren. (Stewart 29)

This is Maria Stewart (1803–79) describing a conversion experience in her 1831 essay "Religion and the Pure Principles of Morality, the Sure Foundation on Which We Must Build." In this passage, although she writes of a commitment to "piety and virtue," she avows a twin commitment to the cause of her oppressed and enslaved "brethren," all in a spirit of independence. Scholar Marilyn Richardson observed that black women like Stewart—Julia Foote (1823–1901), Jarena Lee (1783–18??), and Zilpha Elaw (1790–18??), who explicitly invoked religious warrants, "were neither isolated nor atypical, but were inheritors of a black female tradition of activism founded on a commitment to religious faith, human rights, and women's struggles," a syncretic blend she refers to as "religious social activism" (viii).

A careful consideration of nineteenth-century African American women's social-activist rhetoric might fruitfully include an analysis of the extent to which this activism finds support in the belief that it is sanctioned by some moral authority, nearly always their Christian God. Reminding an audience of this shared belief then becomes for the rhetor one of the chief means of persuasion. Many of the women who used this strategy operated outside of traditional organized churches, primarily because they were prevented from assuming roles usually performed by the males within those institutions.

These women—often referred to as "Sisters of the Spirit," "Daughters of the Church," "Holy Sisters," "Righteous Women," or negatively as "Ungodly Women" (for speaking publicly)—who asserted their claims solidly in the context of their religious beliefs and under the authority of some sacred text or deity, are frequently not viewed as social activists. As a result, the texts produced by women so labeled often do not receive the same level of rhetorical attention that texts framed politically receive, although their texts were not necessarily apolitical or otherworldly in focus. When we do study these women as social activists, we give limited attention to the influence of their beliefs. Further, African American women's spiritual autobiographies are rarely included in literary anthologies, even in specialized collections of African American literature.[1] Katherine Bassard notes that the form taken by these sanctified women for relating their life stories is rarely considered in taxonomies of Afro-American *literary* discourse (121).

Both Sojourner Truth and Frances Harper, fully versed in the Christian Bible, applied their rhetorical skills in support of women's rights, suffrage, and abolition. Nonetheless, their arguments against slavery and discrimination are bolstered throughout with religious references. Harper closes her 1891 speech to the National Council of Women of the United States with a call for American Christianity "not to show us more creeds, but more of Christ; not more rites and ceremonies but more religion glowing with love and replete with life" (42). Cooper's arguments in a speech to a group of black Episcopalian clergy for the promotion and protection of southern black women naturally employ religious appeals. In addition, the final chapter of her collection of essays, *A Voice from the South* (1892), is powerful witness to her belief in the benefits of faith and the importance of acting on one's beliefs.

> To me, faith means *treating the truth as true.* Jesus *believed* in the infinite possibilities of an individual soul. His faith was a triumphant realization of the eternal development of *the best* in man—an optimistic vision of the human aptitude for endless expansion and perfectibility. . . . And religion (ought to be if it isn't) a great deal more than mere gratification of the instinct for worship linked with the straight-teaching of irreproachable credos. Religion must be *life made true.* (298–99).

Such statements from scholars like Cooper demonstrate the extent to which religious persuasion can lay the foundation for public activism; for believers, it is "life made true." Even Ida B. Wells (1862–1931), in her attacks on the perpetrators of mob violence and lynching, points to the hypocrisy of such actions by citizens of a "Christian nation" (94). Wells's approach to religious persuasion seems to have been to call out those who claimed to be religious rather than to attest to her own faith. In her address to the members of the Society for Christian Endeavor, Victoria Matthews (1861–1907) appealed to a common, shared Christianity and linked it to the nation, to womanhood, homes, work, virtues, law, and even to the government. Her appeals to Christian womanhood call for specific action against such practices as separate train cars for blacks, discrimination against blacks in the penal system, and prohibitions against interracial marriage. Thus, the activism of these women was rooted in the same commitment to religious principles, both theirs and those of others.

In this essay, I consider how this blend of faith and activism took shape in the writing of Amanda Berry Smith (1837–1915), an evangelist missionary who traveled throughout the United States and to India and West Africa from 1878 to 1890. These travels were partially supported by the Methodist Episcopal Church, a primarily white denomination, although she maintained her membership in the African Methodist Episcopal Church. Shortly after she returned to the States, she documented her experiences in her 1893 work, *An Autobiography: The Story of the Lord's Dealings with Mrs. Amanda Smith, the Colored Evangelist: Containing an Account of Her Life Work of Faith, and Her Travels in America, England, Ireland, Scotland, India, and Africa as an Independent Missionary.* As the descriptive title of her autobiography indicates, Smith was greatly influenced by the evangelical movement of the Second Great Awakening. In addition to supporting a general belief in a divine being, Protestant evangelicalism attracted large numbers of African Americans, free and enslaved, with its emphasis on individual freedom and direct communication with God, particularly during the mid-nineteenth century. It was during this period that camp meetings were held with enthusiastic preaching and large audience participation. Traveling preachers during the Second Great Awakening converted many with their plain-styled message and manner of worship, incorporating African beliefs and traditions of spirit possession, call and response singing, shouting, and dancing. Amanda Smith was a well-known participant in this tradition. Known by such epithets as "God's image carved in Ebony," the "Colored Evangelist," and the "Singing Pilgrim," she often blended singing and preaching, even at women's gatherings like the 1895 convention of the British Woman's Temperance Association.[2] Smith styled a religious rhetoric of social activism. Missionary and evangelist Rev. Marshall W. Taylor, himself a Methodist minister, ranked her higher in achievement than any of her black female predecessors: "Without the genius of Mrs. Wheatley, the daring of Sojourner Truth, the logic of Mrs. Harper, Mrs. Smith has a greatness born not of self nor of mind, but of *soul culture* by contact with God. Herein is she great, the equal of either and greater than any" (58). Now Taylor's 1886 comparison of Smith to Phillis Wheatley ("*brilliant genius*"), Sojourner Truth ("*indomitable revolutionist*") and Frances Harper ("*scholarly agitator*") ranks her above them in rhetorical prowess because of what he implies is her special ability to communicate with God (emphasis in original; 57–58). In Taylor's view, this is what distinguishes Smith more than a difference in message or purpose.

Smith was born into slavery in 1837 in Long Green, Maryland, near Baltimore. After her father purchased himself and subsequently his family, they moved to Pennsylvania. With considerable difficulty, Smith received the equivalent of only about three months' formal schooling and acquired most of her literacy skills from her parents, who were both readers. In the context of the Second Great Awakening, Smith was converted at a revival meeting when she was thirteen. Over the next sixty years she became an evangelist who preached in the United States, England, India, and West Africa. Three years after she returned to the United States in 1890, she settled in Chicago. In 1899, Smith opened the Amanda Smith Orphan Home and Industrial School, raising money to build and support it by preaching at events around the country.

On September 27, 1897, the Denver *Daily News* reported on such an event in an article titled "Homely Originality: Secret of Amanda Smith, the Colored Evangelist's Success." This event was an address to a packed audience at Denver's Trinity Methodist Church where she drew on her evangelist ethos to solicit funds for the orphanage, observing: "The Holy Spirit came into my heart and asked me what I had done to help my people; what I had done definitely to assist my own race. I tried to edge out of it, but failed. 'Why not start an industrial orphans' home for colored children?' came to me. It was the very thing, and I am wedded to the idea." Smith also used this occasion to call for action against the September 10, 1897, killing of twenty-two, mostly immigrant, striking miners by a sheriff and his deputies near Lattimer, Pennsylvania. Referring to the incident, Smith speculates, "If those officers had gotten down on their knees and had a season of prayer, that catastrophe would have been avoided." She goes on to describe the "horrible poverty" she found in the mining districts where saloons were open on every corner, although the mines were shut down, asking, "Where were your Wesleyans and Salvationists? Why didn't they get out and help matters a little?" This speech is emblematic of her "homely originality," and her ability to blend the evangelical, the political, and the entrepreneurial.

Margaret McFadden notes the irony that women used their assigned roles in the church as a training ground for activism; they developed female networks in women's prayer groups, camp meetings, and Bible study such that they modeled a form of rebellion. In the tradition of evangelist Phoebe Palmer (1807–1874), once you receive the second blessing of sanctification, you make a choice to live a new life. Central to this second blessing or "altar transaction" is the principle that "a woman could lay all the details of house and children on the altar and thus be freed from worldly attachments and responsibilities." It did not mean that women should neglect or abandon their prescribed roles as homemakers, but that those roles "should cease to be absorbing" (McFadden 70). Smith's own sanctification allowed her the freedom to address matters of concern beyond the domestic sphere and outside of traditional Methodism. Denied the pulpit, black and white women were more apt to engage in their own biblical interpretations based on their own experiences. Their marginality gave them a type of freedom, and their sanctification gave them the personal authority and the "spiritual self-reliance" to branch out on their own. William Andrews explains that "what the experience of sanctification confers on the believer is the sense of being in total harmony with the will of God, of being perfectly pure in intention and action insofar as his or her acts are determined by individual attention" (14–15).

Smith was greatly influenced by Palmer and attended the Tuesday Meetings, a female prayer group held at Palmer's home in New York. In 1868, following one of these meetings, Smith experienced "entire sanctification" and began her ministry in earnest, empowered with the belief in her sanctification (McFadden 71). Jualynne Dodson, in her introduction to the 1988 edition of Smith's autobiography, comments on Smith's ability to establish a "relationship with missionaries of the white Methodist Episcopal Church." In 1878, leaving her daughter Mazie, who was in her early twenties, Smith "traveled to London for the beginning international phase of her preaching ministry, a phase that no other black woman had experienced" (xxxiv).

Still, references in her autobiography and her speeches suggest that Smith's religious and social activism in various evangelical settings was not free of awareness of racial and gender differences, especially in her own country. None of her experiences among the holiness reformers or the Methodist church provided a haven from racism. At camp meetings, while running revivals, and during her travels, Smith faced racial prejudice, from the general public and from fellow Christian reformers. Smith's narrative of her early years of enslavement and subsequent freedom was filled with the kinds of injustices born of the peculiar institution. Commenting on the intersection of race and salvation in one passage, Smith writes, "I think some people would understand the quintessence of sanctifying grace if they could be black about twenty-four hours" (Smith, *Autobiography* 116–17). Leading up to this statement, Smith had been responding to off-handed queries from whites about what it was like to be black. As Carole Stewart points out, "Smith interprets the issue of American racism within the context of religious experience" (354). The world of her religious experiences provides the lens through which she observes and engages with racial tension in that world. During the years following her conversion, when white and black worshippers seeking sanctification were invited to come forward during camp meetings, the white worshippers did so hesitantly at first, but gradually white and black came forward together. It should be noted that these meetings were not all integrated, and even at most "integrated" meetings, blacks and whites sat in separate sections. In an 1873 sermon Smith delivered at the Sing Sing (New York) Methodist Episcopal integrated camp meeting, Smith makes the following observation: "White people used to be afraid to kneel down among us; they've got over that. I saw a white lady right down among a lot of colored people, and she got converted, glory to God! And I guess she was just as well satisfied there as if there had been white people around her" (*Christian Recorder*).

She also writes of the need to hold some meetings "with my own people," given that much of her U.S. preaching ministry took place among white congregants, and she wanted to and did return to her African Methodist Episcopal roots. She describes a surprisingly uneventful and, in fact, welcoming visit to a white church after having been warned by her aunt that "we never go to the white people's church here. I would laugh if they put you out" (Smith 248). Smith discusses a long debate with herself and with other members of the evangelical movement as to whether she should attend a convention in Knoxville, Tennessee, because of its location in the South near the "KuKlux." She eventually decided to go, with the financial support of the members (Smith 205–14). Smith incorporates these ongoing but unsurprising racial concerns into her autobiography and sermons, not as separate anecdotes but as natural consequences, part and parcel, of her encounters.

She also writes of gender limitations, in many evangelical settings, resulting from being a woman speaking in public. In 1879, when she spoke in Scotland, she was told that only women would be allowed at the meeting, so when a few men slipped in, Smith ignored them. The local women, unaccustomed to mixed meetings, however, lost courage in the presence of men. Smith recalled how she had to coax one woman into praying after the men arrived (Smith 278–79).[3] She comments on the prejudice against women preachers, exhibited by an elderly clergyman in a town near Monrovia, Liberia (354). On the treatment of women in this same region of Africa, she observed that a boy would not bring his own mother water, because toting water was "woman's work" and describes the terms of the arranged marriages whereby girls are claimed for marriage soon after they are born. Upon witnessing the abusive treatment of Frances, a Bassa girl who had run away from a cruel husband, Smith was able to acquire her in order to protect her, advocating that other missionaries make the same effort, and explaining, "If a girl has been bought by a missionary, she is free as long as she lives; no one will ever claim her: but if otherwise, she can be claimed years after, by anyone of her people who chooses to make trouble" (391–92).[4] Now I don't mean to suggest that her autobiography is filled with commentary on the treatment of blacks and women in the United States and abroad, but it is there and unfolds in interesting ways.

Still another result of Smith's evangelical perspective is her understanding of the uses and abuses of literacy. It was during her early postconversion period that she was sensitized to the persuasive force of what was commonly known in the nineteenth century as "pernicious reading," an activity that many believed had the potential to poison the minds of readers, causing them to stray from their moral principles. As a result, she began to question the existence of God and engaged her aunt in an argument on the subject. Smith recalled in her autobiography her initial response to a persuasive piece that led to her doubt.

> I remember reading a book. I forget the title of it, but it was an argument between an infidel and a Christian minister. As I went on reading I became very much interested. "Oh," I thought to myself, "I know the Christian minister will win." It starts with the infidel asking a question. The minister's answer took two pages, while the question asked only took one page and a half. As they went on the minister gained three pages with his answer; and the infidel seemed to lose. And then it went on, and by and by the minister began to lose, and the infidel gained. So it went on till the infidel seemed to gain all the ground. His questions and argument were so pretty and put in such a way that before I knew it I was captured; and by the time I had got through the book I had the whole of the infidel's article stamped on my memory and spirit, and the Christian's argument was lost. (29)

Smith describes the shame she felt at being persuaded by the infidel and thanks her aunt for restoring her faith. She closes the chapter with the admonition to "beware how you read books tainted with error. There are enough of the orthodox kind that will help you if you will be content with them and the Book of books" (29–30). While many men and women who were developing literacy found it empowering, for Smith and other women evangelicals, "the misuse of language is a sin" (Bassard 126). This view represented a different relationship to literacy. Because female African American spiritual autobiographers were placed in the further marginalized category of evangelicalism (in addition to race and gender marginalization), they were careful to avoid the slipperiness of human communication even though they relied on it to share their message. Bassard argues convincingly that "the radically different social position of black women preachers like Jarena Lee, Zilpha Elaw, Julia Foote, and Amanda Berry Smith caused them to see their relationship to language and literacy quite differently from even Harriet Jacobs or Harriet E. Wilson." She draws a distinction between black women who wrote slave narratives and those who wrote spiritual autobiographies (119). The spiritual autobiographies were published outside of any political movement, though they addressed important issues of their time. They were not driven by pressures from a sponsor or publisher to authenticate their words, although they were keenly aware, as indicated in Smith's observations above, of the need to monitor their "pernicious" reading and writing. The authors felt that they had received their sanction to write from God and often invoked godly intervention to insure that the words were properly written and properly interpreted.

Amanda Smith's belief in the doctrine of sanctification separated her from the African Methodist Episcopal Church, which itself represented a departure from the Methodist Episcopal Church. "Though it is tempting," Bassard writes, "to dismiss spiritual autobiographers as apolitical, their politics, much more so than that of the slave narrators, involve a kind of [liberating] *politics of language itself*"(122). These writers, already marginalized, functioned more as free agents who could publish and write outside of any political movement, claiming authority from God. Their sanctification implies that the writers are in total harmony with God and free to do God's will. They emphasized the defectiveness of language as well as its power. Bassard adds that the "silencing of these texts by critics of black literature has resulted in a missed opportunity to study the ways in which religion (especially Holiness Methodism) relates to social position and thus to ideological formation and resistance within Afro-American letters" (122).

For these Christians, then, persuading is a religious act, if we understand "religious" as believing in some power or entity outside yourself who has moral authority over your behavior. The difference, it seems, between the women who wrote spiritual narratives and gave sermons and those who wrote slave narratives and gave speeches with minimal references to their faith or beliefs is more of a difference in degree than kind. Was Maria Stewart's writing more "religious" than Sojourner Truth's? Maria Stewart wrote more about the extent to which her beliefs—or to use Anna Cooper's term, her truths—guided and informed her actions and arguments than did Sojourner Truth. It turns out that intellectuals like Harper (whom Marshall Taylor refers to as a "scholarly agitator") or Anna Cooper (who is always described as a scholar or intellect) had strong religious beliefs, as the last chapter in *A Voice from the South* reveals, and those beliefs undergirded the ideas advanced in her book. Perhaps it was the extent to which the women became a part of secular, mainstream discourse that determined whether they were accepted and their words were eventually anthologized.

I end this discussion with a statement Adrienne Israel makes at the close of her biography of Amanda Berry Smith.

> Smith fused personal faith with social reform: in her early life as a champion of the temperance cause and education for African women and in her latter life as founder of an orphan home and industrial school meant to save black children from destitution and forced labor. Rather than being a panacea that discourages social involvement and diverts attention from reality to a distant heavenly reward, Christian faith for Smith was a source of motivation that sustained her efforts to reform both individuals and society in the face of formidable opposition. (157)

Amanda Smith and her contemporaries were all indeed troubling social, religious, and political waters.

Notes

1. The most widely used anthology of African American literature, the *Norton Anthology*, includes Maria Stewart's 1832 Franklin Hall address and the introduction to her essay "Religion and the Pure Principles of Morality, the Sure Foundation on Which We Must Build" (1831).

2. The *New York Times* carried this description of Smith preaching at the 27 August 1905 Ocean Grove, New Jersey, camp meeting: "Amanda Smith, the venerable negro evangelist, was present. In a high-pitched key she sang 'I'm So Glad.' As she sang she danced up and down the aisle. Those about her were infected by the quaint refrain, and for five minutes there were salvos of 'Amens' and 'Hallelujahs.'"

3. The incident brings to mind the often-repeated legend that as a result of Sojourner Truth's 1851 speech at the Akron, Ohio, Woman's Rights Convention,

she handled a hostile white crowd, stopped a malicious male attack on women and "saved a mass of cowering white women." However, Nell Painter argues persuasively that none of this is true. (See *Sojourner Truth: A Life, a Symbol*, 129.)

4. Smith also adopted a Gredebo boy, Bob, and placed both Bob and Frances in school in England, with the idea that they would return to their own country as missionaries.

Works Cited

Andrews, William L. Introduction. *Sisters of the Spirit: Three Black Women's Autobiographies of the Nineteenth Century*. Indiana UP, 1986, pp. 1–22.

Bassard, Katherine Clay. "Gender and Genre: Black Women's Autobiography and the Ideology of Literacy" *African American Review*, vol. 26, no. 1, 1992, pp. 119–29.

Cooper, Anna Julia. *A Voice from the South*. 1892. Oxford, 1988.

Dodson, Jualynne E. Introduction. Smith, *Autobiography*, pp. xviii–xlii.

Harper, Frances. "Duty to Dependent Races." 1891. Logan, pp. 36–42.

"Homely Originality: Secret of Amanda Smith, the Colored Evangelist's Success." *Rocky Mountain News*, vol. 27, 1897, pp. 1–2.

Logan, Shirley Wilson, ed. *With Pen and Voice: A Critical Anthology of Nineteenth-Century African-American Women*. Southern Illinois UP, 1995.

Matthews, Victoria. "The Awakening of the Afro-American Women." 1897. Logan, pp. 149–55.

McFadden, Margaret. "The Ironies of Pentecost: Phoebe Palmer, World Evangelism, and Female Networks." *Methodist History*, vol. 31, no. 2, 1993, pp. 63–75.

Moody, Joycelyn. Preface. *Sentimental Confessions: Spiritual Narratives of Nineteenth-Century African American Women*. U of Georgia P, 2001, pp. ix–xiv.

Painter, Nell Irvin. *Sojourner Truth: A Life, a Symbol*. Norton, 1996.

Richardson, Marilyn. Foreword. *Sisters of the Spirit: Three Black Women's Autobiographies of the Nineteenth Century*, edited by William Andrews, Indiana UP, 1986, pp. viii–ix.

Smith, Amanda. *An Autobiography: The Story of the Lord's Dealings with Mrs. Amanda Smith the Colored Evangelist*. 1893. Oxford UP, 1988.

———."We Don't Wonder at Christ Instituting a Living Ministry." *Christian Recorder* 21 August 1873. Accessible Archives, accessed 18 May 2015.

Stewart, Carole Lynn. "The Quintessence of Sanctifying Grace: Amanda Smith's Religious Experience, Freedom, and a Temperate Cosmopolitanism." *Journal of Africana Religions*, vol. 1, no. 3, 2013, pp. 348–75.

Stewart, Maria W. "Religion and the Pure Principles of Morality, the Sure Foundation on Which We Must Build." *Maria W. Stewart, America's First Black Woman Political Writer: Essays and Speeches*, edited by Marilyn Richardson, Indiana UP, 1987, pp. 28–42.

Taylor, Marshall W. *The Life, Travels, Labors, and Helpers of Mrs. Amanda Smith the Famous Negro Missionary Evangelist*. 1886. Google Books, accessed 18 May 2015.

Wells, Ida B. "Lynch Law in all Its Phases." 1893. Logan, pp. 80–99.

COLLABORATION, AUTHORSHIP, AND THE RESISTANCE TO CHANGE

LISA EDE

When Andrea Lunsford and I were PhD students in the department of English at Ohio State University (OSU), it wasn't possible to declare rhetoric and writing as a major area of study. It was not a stated area of emphasis in the PhD program at that time at OSU, or at most other universities. Nevertheless, Andrea came to OSU to study rhetoric and writing with Edward P. J. Corbett. And Andrea did in fact succeed in cobbling together the first program in this area in the department and completing her dissertation, a study of the basic writing program that she created as a graduate teaching assistant. In the decades since, the field of rhetoric and writing has become fully professionalized, with a wide-ranging complement of PhD programs, journals, monograph series, scholarly awards, and the like. As a result, the role of rhetoric and writing in the university curriculum has been radically revised at the level of graduate study. But what about the situation in terms of the undergraduate curriculum? What impact, for instance, has Andrea's and my research on collaborative writing had on the typical first-year writing class? Just as importantly, what impact has this research had on understandings and enactments of authorship as they circulate in the academy?

These are questions that Andrea and I have asked ourselves in recent years as we have attempted to assess the significance and impact of our three decades of work on collaboration and on collaborative writing. In 2001, for instance, we published an essay in *PMLA* on "Collaboration and Concepts of Authorship" where we asked if scholars in English and foreign languages are "prepared not only to critique conventional understandings of subjectivity and authorship but also to act on the implications of that critique" (180). We raised this question again in 2011 when we wrote "Collaboration and Collaborative Writing: The View from Here," an essay that is included in *Writing Together: Collaboration in Theory and Practice,* a collection of previously published and new work that appeared in that same year. While we discuss many issues in these and other reflections, one observation stands out with particular clarity. This is our recognition that at the level of pedagogical and scholarly practice resistance to significant change surrounding issues of collaboration and of authorship is much more powerful, and much more entrenched, than we ever could have imagined when we began our work thirty years ago.

EARLY CONTEXTS AND QUESTIONS

Andrea and I first began to study—and advocate for—collaborative writing in the early 1980s. This research was stimulated by our own experience as coauthors. Our first coauthored essay happened almost by accident. With our friend Bob Connors, we were coediting a collection of essays in honor of Edward P. J. Corbett, and one day Andrea and I decided that rather than contributing two separate chapters, we would write one together. (In that predigital era, our physical proximity—Andrea lived in Vancouver, British Columbia, and I had just moved to Corvallis, Oregon—was essential to our collaboration.) We were sure that Ed would be pleased at our collaboration. We went on to write "On Distinctions between Classical and Modern Rhetoric" together, but Ed was anything but pleased that we had done so collaboratively. Don't get me wrong: Ed liked the essay. What he didn't like—or at least didn't understand—was why and how Andrea and I had written it together.

So the story of our long collaboration begins with an irony. Andrea and I coauthored our first essay to honor our friend and mentor Ed Corbett, but the collaborative process we undertook to write it shocked and worried him. Indeed, when Ed saw that Andrea and I were not going to take his advice to give up coauthoring, he made us promise to alternate our names as first authors, rather than present them in alphabetical order, as we'd been planning to do.

Ed Corbett was, it turned out, right to be concerned about responses by colleagues in the humanities to our collaboration. Despite the fact that Andrea and I each had numerous single-authored publications, our penchant for coauthorship was clearly a problem for our colleagues. Andrea was awarded early tenure and promotion at the University of British Columbia, but her colleagues were careful to inform Andrea that "of course" they had to discount all of her coauthored work when they reviewed her. My chair was more willing to credit our coauthored research but, anticipating that others might have reservations, he "informally" asked Andrea to write a "formal" letter describing our collaboration and assuring readers that we were equal partners in our various publications. This letter became part of my dossier and made its way up the chain of review, where at one point the college promotion and tenure committee asked Andrea and me to go through all of our publications and use magic markers to highlight just who had written which words, sentences, and paragraphs. Fortunately, when we explained that given our writing process this magic marker trick was literally impossible, the committee accepted our claim to equal authorship. So we both were tenured and promoted, though in my case my dean felt compelled to warn me that "you will never be promoted to professor if you insist on continuing to coauthor" when he met with me to inform me of my promotion. I am grateful to have proven him wrong.

Given these responses, perhaps there *was* a hint of defensiveness in Andrea's and my decision in the early 1980s to challenge the academy's (and our culture's) basic assumptions in regard to authorship, particularly the commonsense understanding that "real" (i.e., valued) writing must be single authored. (I'll return to the issue of "real" writing later in this essay.) In hindsight, our original goals for the research project that we initiated in 1984 were pretty naïve. To put it most simply, we wanted to demonstrate that much of the writing that goes on in the workplace is collaborative. Then we could say "told you so!" to our colleagues in English and the humanities.

Thanks to a Shaughnessy Scholars grant from the Fund for the Improvement of Postsecondary Education (FIPSE), we were able to develop an ambitious research agenda, one that involved three stages: an initial questionnaire sent to fourteen hundred randomly selected members of seven professional associations: the American Institute of Chemists, the American Consulting Engineers Council, the International City Management Association, the Modern Language Association, the American Psychological Association, the Professional Services Management Association, and the Society for Technical Communication. Our goal was to understand their collaborative writing processes as fully as possible and, especially, to learn what conditions and factors made for productive, satisfying, efficient, and effective collaboration. We followed this first survey with a second questionnaire sent to twelve members of each association, members we chose because of the thoughtfulness of their responses to the first survey. Finally, we held on-site interviews (some lasting several days) with a small number of survey respondents from each association.

The results of this study appeared in our 1990 *Singular Texts / Plural Authors: Perspectives on Collaborative Writing*. These results confirmed our hypothesis that much of the writing that goes on in these professions is done collaboratively. (Predictably, members of the Modern Language Association reported the least amount of collaborative work.) But our study also demonstrated the limitations of a data-oriented approach to collaboration, as we quickly recognized that it is impossible to separate any effort to study the material practices of collaborative writing from larger, and deeply ideologically embedded, assumptions about authorship and intellectual property, particularly as they inform conventional notions of what constitutes "real" forms of writing in the humanities.

We gained an insight into the power of these assumptions early in our study. As I have noted, our research project included several surveys. Andrea and I knew that we needed to field test our surveys, so at one point I asked several of my colleagues to respond to an early version of the first survey. One of these colleagues was at the time the coauthor of the second best-selling technical writing textbook in the country. He and I had worked together for years and had coauthored many committee reports. So imagine my surprise when my colleague returned his survey to me—a survey that indicated that he had never written a single document collaboratively. When I questioned my colleague about his response he said, "Oh, I thought you meant *real* writing." "Real writing." This comment forcefully demonstrated to us that while the data gathered in our surveys would be important, Andrea and I needed to better understand and convey the ideologically grounded history of such constructs as authorship and intellectual property. Doing so added several years to our research project, but it also significantly enriched our analysis. This exploration has remained central to our engagement with collaborative writing, authorship, and intellectual property—issues that we have continued to explore over the years.

From one perspective, our early research on collaborative writing was wonderfully timed, as it coincided with a broad and deep interrogation of notions of authorship, writing, and intellectual property in both literary and rhetorical theory, an interrogation that resulted in the social "turn" in composition theory as expressed in such important studies as Anne Gere's

1987 *Writing Groups: History, Theory, and Implications* and Karen LeFevre's 1989 *Invention as a Social Act.* As readers are undoubtedly aware, despite this revolution in theory, in practice assignments in first-year writing classes continue to view single-authorship as the norm. While first-year writing textbooks may devote a chapter to "Working Together as a Team" or "Writing Together," most assume that students will complete major writing assignments independently. Indeed, when Andrea and coauthor Karen Lunsford conducted a national study of first-year writing, not a single collaborative assignment emerged. For an analysis of their results, see: "'Mistakes Are a Fact of Life': A National Comparative Study."

COLLABORATIVE WRITING: CHALLENGES AND OPPORTUNITIES, THEN AND NOW

As we note in *Singular Texts/Plural Authors,* when Andrea and I began our FIPSE-funded research on collaboration, we anticipated that we would develop "detailed, specific guidelines for teachers—guidelines that would address such issues as the characteristics of effective collaborative writing assignments and the most efficient ways to organize and evaluate group efforts" (121–22). We hoped that such advice would encourage teachers to integrate significant collaborative writing assignments into their curriculum, particularly in required first-year writing courses. Our chapter titled "The Pedagogy of Collaboration" does address issues such as these, but it also acknowledges that our effort to reflect on this topic raised more questions than answers thanks to "the capacity of collaborative writing to 'open out' or problematize both theory and practice" (122). Our research on collaborative writing also made us acutely aware of the extent to which academic assumptions, practices, and structures work against collaboration. Most obvious, perhaps, are the individual grades that students receive at the end of the term and the power and authority that teachers hold in the classroom as the grantors of those grades. In addition, as we note in *Singular Texts/Plural Authors:*

> The hierarchical bases of power in our classrooms reflect the larger structure of our educational institutions. Most university calendars, divided neatly into semesters or quarters, reflect a positivistic approach to learning: knowledge is "packaged" into discrete segments and dispensed to passive recipients, fast-food style, through four years. Such a system posits students as isolated units, all of whom learn in similar ways and at

> similar speeds. The time necessary for group cohesion to occur, for examination of group dynamics involving consensus and dissensus to take place, much less for a consideration of the issues at stake in a seemingly simple question such as "Who is the author of this essay?" is not easily found in such a system. (120)

Though these words were published in 1990, they still, alas, ring true. Indeed, a shift toward a corporatized, client-based university and an increased emphasis on distance education has created new challenges for those who wish to engage their students in significant collaborative writing projects.

Andrea and I now recognize additional challenges—and also opportunities—that were not apparent to us in the 1980s and early 1990s: these challenges and opportunities grow out of students' self-sponsored online writing, much of which is collaborative. The digital world that we and our students inhabit today represents an even starker contrast between many first-year writing classrooms and the world of students' self-sponsored writing. For most of our students, email now seems both old fashioned and formal, as they rely increasingly upon instant messaging and social networking sites, such as Facebook, YouTube, and Twitter. Add to these venues the staggering array of writing sites involved with fanzines, blogs, and wikis—and the ready accessibility of almost infinite amounts of information to be sampled, shared, and used in the design of "new" or "patchwork" texts—and the opportunities for self-expression and collaboration increase exponentially.

In such a setting, it is hardly surprising that students are more and more used to thinking of themselves as part of a network of people engaged in various discursive practices rather than as individual authors—at least when they are at work on self-sponsored activities. Think of how various cause-oriented status updates circulate on Facebook, or of the pleasure that Facebook friends take in sharing and commenting on YouTube videos, quiz results, or other apps. Our students consult Wikipedia regularly; some also contribute to it. But students also engage in other kinds of online collaborative projects, often simultaneously as author and audience. In *Convergence Culture,* for instance, Henry Jenkins notes that more than 60 percent of the content for the video game *The Sims* has been generated by its fans (166). In his study, Jenkins provides numerous additional examples of online collaboration in action, such as a group called the Cloudmakers that banded together to play "The Beast," a videogame created to promote Steven Spielberg's 2001 film *Artificial Intelligence: A.I. (123).*

Clearly, much of the collaborative online writing that students undertake is writing that can be characterized as communicating for entertainment. But not always. Consider, for instance, Heather Lawver, a home-schooled teenager who, at the age of fourteen, launched *The Daily Prophet,* a Web-based school newspaper for Harry Potter's fictional Hogwarts. By 2006, the newspaper had a staff of 102 children from around the world (Jenkins 171). More importantly, when sites devoted to the Potter series began to be threatened by Warner Brothers, Lawver formed the association Defense against the Dark Arts and worked with fans throughout the world to protect their freedom to publish fan fiction online. Pressing health issues (Lawver was diagnosed with Dercum's disease) led to the closure of *The Daily Prophet,* though Lawver continues to collaborate on a site she developed devoted to education about this disease and support for those living with it.

These examples emphasize the gap that currently exists between the highly collaborative, self-sponsored online writing that many students do and the writing they are asked to do when they enter many of our classrooms. From one perspective, of course, this gap is hardly new. A gap has always existed between the values, expectations, and interests that students bring to the academy and the values, expectations, interests, and experiences of their teachers. Yet as these examples emphasize, the gap seems especially wide and deep: students out of class are composing across a range of multimodal genres, most often in concert with other writers; yet in their first-year writing classes they are most often still the "singular authors" that Andrea and I described decades ago.

Students' immersion in online self-sponsored writing clearly represents an opportunity to call attention to the everydayness and power of collaboration. But it also represents a challenge, for there is considerable evidence that in spite of all the extracurricular writing students are engaging in today, they may not think of it as "real" writing—a term and concept whose staying power is clearly evident. Nor would they necessarily characterize the highly participatory forms of such writing as "collaboration." The Pew Internet and American Life Project's 2008 report, "Writing, Technology, and Teens," for example, found that while as many as 93 percent of teens say "they write for their own pleasure" and "most teenagers spend a considerable amount of their life composing texts . . . they do not think that a lot of the material they create electronically is real writing" (2). This report goes on to say that students view "real" writing, which they associate with school writing and other high-stakes discourse such as resumes or letters of application, as very important, but they fail to include the informal writing they do online in that category. In a similar vein, researchers involved with the Stanford Study of Writing asked student participants every year of the five-year study to describe their collaborations. Most students reported that they did virtually no collaborative writing. In response to different questions, students regaled researchers with accounts of writing that they did with others, primarily in extracurricular online settings.

ON AUTHORSHIP AND THE RESISTANCE TO CHANGE

This tendency for contemporary students not to view the online writing they engage in every day as "real" writing is one demonstration of the power that deeply entrenched notions of authorship continue to hold. Not surprisingly, what is true of our students is even more true for those engaged in scholarly research and publication in the humanities. In a world where, for tenure-line faculty at least, the maxim of "publish or perish" still holds supreme force, the question of what it means to be an author whose work is credited as having value remains a central issue. As Andrea and I noted in our 2001 *PMLA* essay, "Collaboration and Concepts of Authorship," at the level of theory this question has been interrogated from just about every imaginable angle, as the status of the author has been problematized, deconstructed, and challenged to such an extent that even in 2001 discussions of the author problem seemed decidedly old hat. Scholars have, Andrea and I have argued, nevertheless found it much more difficult to *enact* contemporary critiques of the author and of the autonomous individual in their own scholarly and academic practices. Andrea and I are hardly alone in our concerns over disjunctures or contradictions between theory and practice in the academy. Literary scholars such as Jonathan Arac, James Sosnoski, Evan Watkins, Maria-Regina Kecht, and Paul Bové have commented on the extent to which contemporary academic practices in the academy constitute, as Sosnoski puts it, "modern skeletons in postmodern closets." In his *In the Wake of Theory,* Bové explores the relation of theory and practice in English studies, noting that too often scholars have assumed "that 'theory-work' somehow would or could stand outside the given realities of our times and place" (5).

Similarly, in *Work Time: English Departments and the Circulation of Cultural Value*, Watkins calls attention to the importance of acknowledging that "actual practices of resistance depend on specific working conditions" and to the danger of "the dream of transubstantiation"—the dream that work done in one location (the writing of an article or book, for instance) will effect political change in another location" (28–29). In his study, Watkins is concerned with (among other things) the ways in which "ideologies of 'the new' circulate as a privileged form of value" in English studies (15).

Perhaps we should not be surprised, then, that the more things change (at the level of theory) the more they remain the same (at the level of practice). For at the material level of practice, clearly the individual author remains supreme. Tenure-line assistant professors in the humanities don't need to be told that what finally counts when they come up for promotion and tenure is the work that they publish as individual authors. They know this at the level of disciplinary common sense, where ideology works most powerfully.

This disciplinary common sense is exposed quite clearly in the MLA's 2007 "Report on Evaluating Scholarship for Tenure and Promotion." From one perspective, this report is positive in that it recommends that "the profession as a whole should develop a more capacious conception of scholarship by rethinking the dominance of the monograph, promoting the scholarly essay, establishing multiple pathways to tenure, and using scholarly portfolios" (12). As the report makes clear, however, on the ground the reality is significantly bleaker. Research undertaken by the task force conclusively demonstrates that in recent decades adherence to the single-authored monograph in English and foreign language departments has strengthened, not weakened—and that this has occurred "despite a worsening climate for book publication" (10). Indeed, the authors of the report note that "the status of the monograph as a gold standard is confirmed by the expectation in almost one-third of all departments surveyed (32.9%) of progress toward completion of a second book for tenure. This expectation is even higher in doctorate-granting institutions, where 49.8% of departments now demand progress toward a second book" (10). As the MLA report suggests, in recent years profoundly conservative assumptions about authorship appear to have become even more deeply entrenched, at least at major research universities.

Andrea and I are not the only scholars who have attempted to challenge conventional scholarly norms and practices of authorship in the humanities. Others have made similar efforts. In 1995 David Damrosch's *We Scholars* made the case for replacing the academic culture of agonism and alienation with one of genuine collaborative community. Two years later, in "Shop Window or Laboratory: Collection, Collaboration, and the Humanities," Jonathan Arac asked why a model of exclusively individual ownership is, as he puts it, "the fundamental way that we seem to value our intellectual activity" (123). In answering this question, Arac notes the degree to which humanities scholarship has focused "on the figure of the creator, treated as a distinctive, single, isolated individual" (118), and he goes on to explore knowledge produced by such isolated individuals (the shop window model) and to offer an alternative arena in which knowledge is produced collaboratively (the laboratory model). Arac's thoughtful essay sums up the obvious disjunction between the work that theory has done to critique "expressive totalities," such as the originary author, and the extent to which that work is carried out in "ways wholly compatible with a thoroughly discredited individualism" (12). In her 1999 "What If Scholars in the Humanities Worked Together, in a Lab?" Cathy Davidson returns to Arac's question from a slightly different perspective. In productive labs, she says, "collaborative thinking" should be the outcome of work even if collaborative writing does not always, or even often, occur: "In a lab—or at least the platonic ideal of a lab—discovery of one sort or another is the shared overt goal. . . . Labs are built around the process of discovery [and require] collaboration across fields and disciplinary subfields, as well as across generations" (B5). Kathleen Fitzpatrick continues this conversation in her 2011 *Planned Obsolescence: Publishing, Technology, and the Future of the Academy.*

There are, I'm happy to say, exceptions to the traditional and conservative privileging of the single author. One example I would point to is HASTAC. This acronym stands for Humanities, Arts, Sciences, and Technology Advanced Collaboratory. (Cathy Davidson, formerly at Duke and now at CUNY, played, by the way, an important role in conceptualizing this project.) Here's how HASTAC describes itself on its "about" pages.

> HASTAC ("haystack") is a network of individuals and institutions inspired by the possibilities that new technologies offer us for shaping how we learn, teach, communicate, create, and organize our local and global communities. We are motivated by the conviction that the digital era provides rich opportunities for informal and formal learning and for collaborative, networked research that extends across traditional disciplines, across the boundaries of academe and community, across the "two cultures" of humanism and technology, across the divide of thinking versus making, and across social strata and national borders.

Anyone is free to join HASTAC and to participate in its many sponsored projects, some of which are digital and others of which involve face-to-face collaboration.

Projects like this are exciting, and they serve the important purpose, among other things, of bringing together faculty and students who are genuinely interested in working—and even at times writing—together. The first Distinguished Scholar in Residence at HASTAC, for instance, was Dr. Allison Clark. Her research interests "involve the creation and examination of culturally specific approaches and tools as intervention strategies for the creation of digital literacy and equity. As codirector of the Seedbed Initiative for Transdomain Creativity, she explores the feasibility of using technology to create self-sustained interdisciplinary communities of collaboration involving artists, humanists, social scientists, technologists from around the world" (HASTAC).

Dr. Clark's work (and that of other scholars connected with HASTAC) suggests that long-held assumptions about individual authorship will continue to be challenged. But it is also important to recognize that change comes very, very slowly when it comes at all. And, frankly, change also involves risk for those who wish to challenge the status quo, as Andrea's and my tenure and promotion stories show. Universities are beginning to respond, particularly when they recognize that the norms of singular authorship that play such a primary role in the humanities work against the kind of interdisciplinary and transdisciplinary collaborations that many university presidents and provosts now wish to emphasize. A recent article in *Inside Higher Education* titled "Tenure Across Borders," for instance, calls attention to efforts at the University of Southern California (USC) to encourage interdisciplinary collaborations by rewriting promotion and tenure guidelines, by holding workshops on collaboration and creativity on campus, and by creating a fund to support interdisciplinary and collaborative projects.

Efforts such as those taking place at HASTAC and USC are certainly laudable, but it is important to remember that they are occurring in a context where, as the 2007 MLA "Report on Evaluating Scholarship for Tenure and Promotion" indicates, the most highly valued form of writing in most English departments is the individually authored monograph. These efforts are also occurring, as I noted earlier, in a context where there is a stark contrast between the collaborative writing that students engage in throughout their busy days—online writing that is intensely collaborative but that students do not view as "real" writing—and the writing that they do in schools and colleges.

As Andrea and I note at the conclusion of "Collaboration and Collaborative Writing: The View from Here," those who wish to advocate for collaboration and to challenge conventional norms of authorship and of intellectual property confront a "devilishly complex and difficult terrain" (204). The resistance to change is real—both in the academy and in the culture at large. Finally, however, Andrea and I remain optimistic: today "the stakes are higher, the difficulties are greater, but the possibilities are more exciting for us as learners, educators, and as citizens than we could have imagined some thirty years ago" (204). The field of rhetoric and writing has played an important role in calling attention to issues involving collaboration, authorship, and intellectual property. May it continue to advocate for progressive, pluralistic practices.

Works Cited

Arac, Jonathan. "Shop Window or Laboratory: Collection, Collaboration, and the Humanities." *The Politics of Research,* edited by E. Ann Kaplan and George Levine, Rutgers UP, 1997, pp. 116–26.

Barrett, Dan. "Tenure Across Borders." *Inside Higher Ed.,* 22 July 2011. Accessed 24 July 2011.

Bové, Paul. *In the Wake of Theory.* UP of New England, 1992.

Damrosch, David. *We Scholars: Changing the Culture of the University.* Harvard UP, 1995.

Davidson, Cathy. "What If Scholars in the Humanities Worked Together, in a Lab?" *Chronicle of Higher Education,* 28 May 1999, pp. B4–B5.

Ede, Lisa and Andrea A. Lunsford. "Collaboration and Collaborative Writing: The View from Here." *Writing Together: Collaboration in Theory and Practice,* edited by Andrea A. Lunsford and Lisa Ede, Bedford/St. Martin's, 2011, pp. 186–206.

———. "Collaboration and Concepts of Audience." *PMLA,* vol. 116, no. 2, 2001, pp. 354–69.

———. *Singular Texts / Plural Authors: Perspectives on Collaborative Writing.* Carbondale: Southern Illinois UP, 1990.

Fitzpatrick, Kathleen. *Planned Obsolescence: Publishing, Technology, and the Future of the Academy.* New York UP, 2011.

Gere, Anne Ruggles. *Writing Groups: History, Theory, and Implications.* Southern Illinois UP, 1987.

HASTAC. Humanities, Arts, Science, and Technology Advanced Collaboratory. http://hastac.org. Accessed 6 August 2011.

Jenkins, Henry. *Convergence Culture: Where Old and New Media Collide.* New York UP, 2006.

Kecht, Maria-Regina, ed. *Pedagogy Is Politics: Literary Theory and Critical Teaching.* U of Illinois P, 1992.

LeFevre, Karen Burke. *Invention as a Social Act.* Southern Illinois UP, 1999.

Lenhart, Amanda, Sousa Arafeh, Aaron Smith, and Alexandra Rankin Macgill. "Writing, Technology and Teens." *Pew Internet.* Pew Research Center and American Life Project and the National Commission of Writing. 24 April 2008. Accessed 6 August 2011.

Lunsford, Andrea A., and Karen J. Lunsford. "'Mistakes Are a Fact of Life': A National Comparative Study." *College Composition and Communication*, vol. 59, 2008, pp. 781–806.

Lunsford, Andrea A. and Lisa Ede. "On Distinctions between Classical and Modern Rhetoric." *Essays on Classical Rhetoric and Modern Discourse*, edited by Robert J. Connors, Lisa S. Ede, and Andrea A. Lunsford. Southern Illinois UP, 1984, pp. 37–49.

———. *Writing Together: Collaboration in Theory and Practice.* Bedford/St. Martins, 2011.

"Report of the MLA Task Force on Evaluating Scholarship for Tenure and Promotion." *Profession 2007.* Modern Language Association, pp. 9–71.

Sosnoski, James J. *Modern Skeletons in Postmodern Closets: A Cultural Studies Alternative.* UP of Virginia, 1995.

Stanford Study of Writing. http://ssw.stanford.edu. Accessed 6 August 2011.

Watkins, Evan. *Work Time: English Departments and the Circulation of Cultural Value.* Stanford UP, 1989.

PART 2

THE GENRES OF STUDENT WRITING

TEACHING IN PLACE
A CRUCIAL CONNECTION BETWEEN THE ENGLISH DEPARTMENT AND ITS COMMUNITY

SUELLYNN DUFFEY

> Humanities disciplines are being rejustified in epistemological and civic terms, and older questions of culture and identity are being resituated. A complete retransformation has not occurred, but . . . the New Academy [is] . . . a broad-based movement that has grown up around the edges and increasingly within the departments of the "old academy." It is composed of new ways of thinking, reconfigurations of disciplines, new modes of teaching and assessment, and new forms of scholarship.
>
> —Julie Klein, *Humanities, Culture, and Interdisciplinarity*

In this volume that asks us to project into the future by building on the legacy of the past, I ask us to build our conception of the *discipline,* the hybrid that is composition / rhetoric / writing studies, with a necessary and nuanced sense of the *local* in which it is embedded. I ask us to engage a local disciplinary thinking particularly as we shape graduate courses, my focus in this essay, but also as we conceive of the overall shape and nature of our discipline. Such a move is compatible with but different from moves in the last third of the twentieth century to expand the literary canon. This expansion, in its simplest version, entailed including minority and women's voices and texts. Weaving the material conditions of the local into a sense of the discipline is, however, a more complex and fluid move along the lines that

Julie Klein's words above suggest, more complex moves than the addition of texts to a canon.

I have not always held a flexible view of disciplinarity. Decades ago, when composition / rhetoric was new as an area of study in English departments and when I was relatively early in my career, certain material conditions sent me longing for a canon of texts so that conversations I directed at Conference on College Composition and Communication workshops and Special Interest Groups meetings, for example, would be easier and more productive. I believed that if all of us in the room had read the same dozen or so texts, disagreements about pedagogy would not have been so heated. Then, on the WPA listserv or in some similar forum, I saw posted the wide range of texts my national colleagues considered essential to a canon. Some of the posted versions of a canon had no overlap with others, but I could usually see the logic in each version. Thus began my journey to reconstruct my sense of our discipline, one that has led me to my current sense of the importance of the local in it.[1]

My adjustment to local conditions, often but not always because of institutional structures, has repeatedly taken my thinking in new directions and parallels a move Lunsford made very early in her professional career. Planning to write a dissertation on Scottish rhetoric, she was persuaded instead to do a dissertation on basic writing (BW), in conjunction with starting up a BW program for the department in which she was completing her doctoral studies. The institutional need and desire for a BW program, instantiated by the department faculty and administrators, shaped the direction of Lunsford's scholarship in the late 1970s.

Local conditions shape a discipline—in many ways. Thus, I hope you will read the particular instances I include here as more than anecdotes. As Robert Stake helped educationists see—long before Clifford Geertz introduced such concepts as thick description to us and Nedra Reynolds and others taught us to look at geographies and material locations—particularity leads to a kind of knowledge that generalization does not. The "full and thorough knowledge of the particular" becomes "useful understanding, especially as one recognize[es the particular] in new and foreign contexts," Stake says (6).

Following what Stake tells us about the power of the particular to shape our thinking beyond the simple enjoyment of an anecdote, my contribution to this book is grounded in my lived experience teaching graduate courses in an urban university that offers only the MA in English, not the PhD. The MA-only nature of our graduate program and the demographics of our student population have urged me to reshape my graduate teaching practices, the texts I use in classes, the goals of my courses, and, ultimately, my sense of the shape of our discipline—which had been shaped by Research 1 institutions, primarily Ohio State. I came to learn that the students in my graduate classes at the University of Missouri-St. Louis (UMSL) would not respond to canonical texts and thus the discipline in quite the same ways as had my OSU doctoral students. At UMSL, my first assignment was Teaching College Writing (TCW), a course similar to one I had cotaught at OSU and similar to one most universities offer to incoming graduate students. This course started my adjustment, but additional ones, particularly one I'll speak about at length below, illustrate the distance to which my adjustments to the *local* have traveled.

As I prepared to teach at UMSL, the first sign of something besides business as usual was that only a small number of students in Teaching College Writing were actually teaching assistants, maybe only three out of twelve. My experience at Ohio State left me surprised and somewhat unprepared to face a class without a homogeneous set of circumstances its students were facing—teaching writing for the first time at the college level. Clearly, if I conceived of the course as strictly a practicum for TAs, I would fail to address the needs and experiences of a majority of the students who in that year included high school teachers, a former nurse, a few students seeking a master's degree with literature emphasis who were in the course for unknown reasons, a person who'd taught developmental writing previously with only a bachelor's degree (which I didn't even know was possible), a computer programmer and experienced fiction writer who hoped to teach college writing in his second career.

In subsequent years, the course has enrolled editors with local publishing and non-profit organizations, Walmart managers who worked night shifts, a Lowe's customer service rep, an airplane engineer at Boeing, a former Monsanto account manager with biotech credentials who was a poet at heart, a creative writer who brought a strict Mormon religious background to her sense of writing, and an immigrant whose parents were political exiles from Poland. Many, many of my students are the first generation in their families to attend graduate school. All but the smallest percentage have spent most, if not all, of their lives in our city and region, and many are place-bound. All come with the desire to move into new circles of literacy (usually literary) study and their sense of graduate education and current concepts of literacy are usually vague. These aspects of their lives heavily influence their entrance into graduate study.

I knew from having taught basic writing for years that creating student access points into a course of study is necessary, so I began to pay close attention to where my students "were," that catchphrase we use to invoke Lev Vygotsky's "zone of proximal development" and other concepts through which good teachers learn to know their students. I pushed myself to explore how they were "inventing the university"—David Bartholomae's concept that has helped us understand what students new to academic settings do. I began to look for the logic of student error, the logic behind their conceptions of what I was trying to teach, as Mina Shaughnessy, Mike Rose, and others have taught us to do. These concepts had guided my teaching at the undergraduate level, but now, I had to employ them at the graduate level as well, something that caused me to adjust my techniques of educating our graduate students, of course, and ultimately has made me think that the discipline, as I've shaped it for my master's students, should play a significant role in how we conceive of the whole discipline. Most of my students will never seek a doctoral degree, and while it's easy to think that what they want or need is a master's level degree in "applied" rhetoric / composition, that conception truncates the range of their needs and desires to learn.

Over several years and several different graduate courses, my students have brought the richness of their diversity to me, and I've learned (*a*) to teach theory through narrative (so we often read less canonical texts), (*b*) to teach history of the discipline only or primarily by grounding it in pedagogical issues the students would be familiar with through their own experiences as learners and teachers, (*c*) to include students' literacy experiences as analytic not merely anecdotal parts of the class content (via class discussion and writing topics), and (*d*) to require and grade weekly, short, guided reading responses so that it's harder for my students, many of whom hold full-time jobs or several part-time ones, to let the busyness of their nonacademic lives lead them to skip this week's readings, and next week's, and . . . I have found ways to engage students deeply in disciplinary concepts and issues, but I don't introduce students "to the discipline" as one would if she led them through a history of scholarship or a collection of canonical works in composition studies

This chapter, now, goes on to discuss a graduate class that shows an additional inflection the local can bring to bear on disciplinary thinking. I move from how the local required me to reshape graduate education to how I asked students to engage in local communities of writing. Then I suggest ways in which these emphases on local disciplinary thinking might nudge my department toward change.

COMMUNITY ENGAGEMENT IN ENGLISH STUDIES

Traditionally, literature and creative writing faculty have had limited interactions with communities, and when they do so, it is in indirect and somewhat narrow ways, such as when their scholarship sometimes focuses on authors of local interest.[2] At my university, this kind of community interaction is usually left to tenured faculty who are comfortable moving away from scholarship that departments and institutions traditionally recognize and reward. A more direct means of engagement occurs when scholarship is sometimes disseminated to the community through lay publications and public lectures and when creative writers give readings in the community at public libraries and such. These means of interaction, however, embody few of the principles of community engagement and public scholarship now circulating through the academy because, in them, faculty *deliver* and a community audience *receives* that which is delivered. Drawing on Thomas Deans's work, Julie Ellison and Timothy K. Eatman offer instead this broad and inclusive definition: "Publicly engaged academic work is scholarly or creative activity . . . [that] encompasses different forms of *making knowledge about, for, and with diverse publics and communities.* Through a coherent, purposeful sequence of activities, it contributes to the public good and yields artifacts of public and intellectual value" (iv, emphasis mine). As concepts of community engagement have evolved, they have thus moved far beyond the unidirectional model most common in literary and creative studies.

In contrast is our discipline. Composition courses across the country send students into the community through various service-learning routes, especially ones through which undergraduate students tutor in local schools and at other community locations or use their business writing skills to design fund-raisers for campus projects. Both kinds of projects, tutoring and fund-raising, are embedded in a few of the advanced writing courses in my department; they are valuable, and many undergraduates and community members have been involved. But this community involvement is in many ways peripheral to the English department even though it is brought to the fore whenever a campus office wants to account for the university's outreach efforts. It escapes the notice of most tenure-line English faculty and English majors and has no effect on the undergraduate major and none on the graduate program, both mainstays in disciplinary identity. Our compositionists, some of whom teach the community outreach courses, are isolated from undergraduate English majors, as well, because we teach almost none of the English courses they take.

As you can see, mine is a department that has not embraced community-engaged scholarship as a central feature of its disciplinary and institutional identity. But the small way in which I have enacted community engagement in a graduate seminar is located centrally within the department. It involved me, a tenured faculty member, and graduate students in English, instead of nontenure-line faculty and undergraduates across the disciplines. Both of these facts create a greater likelihood that tenure-line faculty will hear, informally, about the course and potentially give it some thought, mechanisms that in the long run help facilitate change. As Julie Thompson Klein writes, "Change . . . results more often from a slow and even unidentifiable shift of viewpoint, not a single argument or sudden epiphany" (218). Arguments built to directly espouse community engagement and public scholarship can't be counted on to change my department's graduate or undergraduate curriculum or to move it toward community engagement, but informal and indirect means may.

LITERACY AND INQUIRY IN "SITES OF WRITING"

One of my main disciplinary reasons for designing this course, entitled Sites of Writing, was to urge students to envision the world of writing as much larger and multipurposed than they usually think of it, given their undergraduate and graduate emphases on literary writing, an emphasis the vast majority of our students come with.[3] Compositionists, rhetoricians, linguists, and some literary scholars understand ordinary writing and language to be worthy of scholarly inquiry and recognize that language serves many purposes besides ones of cultural and aesthetic preservation. I wanted our students to learn that those other worlds are worthy of study—one of my ways of introducing them to the discipline. As Richard E. Miller writes, "Within composition studies, we tend to be more receptive than most to the idea that valuable academic work can occur in a variety of contexts" (223). Miller goes on to say that "revitalizing the project of higher education begins with the revision of where one understands valuable academic work to occur and committing oneself to working in those places" (223). The readings I chose and the tasks I set not only required students to move far outside what they already knew to be the arena of English studies but also involved them in work that the New Academy sanctions.

Instead of works that would be considered literary, we looked at writing in community settings in which the community was at least as important as or more important than the text. (For a complete reading list and a research assignment, see Appendix A.) We looked at collaborative writing in engineering and scientific organizations, a women's writing group in the Tenderloin district in San Francisco, the diary of a North Vietnamese physician written during the Vietnam War, African American sermons with pastors and congregation both contributing to the emergence of the sermonic event, and other locations. In this last instance, we encountered evidence that the sermon does not actually exist prior to or without the congregation's interaction during its delivery, a concept new to my students, and so postmodern literary theories about what constitutes a text were literally grounded in an ethnographic study of the formation of a sermonic text. We also read about how the academy (in English studies particularly) embraces the natural but only insofar as it is an abstraction, rarely as a geographical or material location where scholars and teachers live and work. The materiality in many of the readings grounded our inquiry outside of academic abstractions and inside of communities. For example, one of the chapters in *Placing* is entitled "What I Learned from the Campus Plumber," and another, by a philosopher in the Pacific Northwest, "Six Kinds of Rain: Searching for a Place in the Academy." As is apparent, the writers we read and read about are not part of any English literary canon nor was their primary value aesthetic (although some books were beautifully written). Although many of them were written by compositionists, the collection of them does not comprise a canon, I would argue. Yet my department's graduate director allowed students to "count" the course for *either* a composition *or* literature credit.

Located in distinct communities, these books and our class discussions focused on what each showed us about the "work" writing did, the multiple layers of work it did, and the range of audiences for whom it did its work. This kind of focus is closely tied to public scholarship as it is being performed in the New Academy. For example, the North Vietnamese physician wrote her diary during the Vietnam War to record her work in South Vietnam tending injured soldiers and questioning her own communist identity. She wrote it primarily for herself and secondarily as a contribution to her family's long tradition of journal writing. It was only by the efforts of an American soldier and his Vietnamese translator during the war that the diary became part of that tradition when it was returned to the writer's family thirty years after it was found at the site where the writer had been killed by American soldiers.

But it also did much more work than originally intended. By the combined efforts of the former soldier, his brother and other relatives, a host of Vietnamese citizens, and a Quaker organization, the diary built bridges between nations formerly at war and between families on what were then opposing sides. The processes of bridge building were multiple and involved many communities: the American locating the doctor's family, his family and the diary-writer's traveling across continents, the writer's family's donating the diary to the Vietnam Center and Archive at Texas Tech University, and the Americans creating a website and a documentary film devoted to the book and the processes of reunification.

We did not try to fit the readings into any classification system used in literary studies nor did we use much of the theoretical frameworks often applied to literature and creative writing that my students were familiar with. We did, however, undertake scholarly analysis at the same level of complexity that graduate English courses involve, but the subject of the analysis and its purposes were different. Theories about the "work" writing does called for an expansive analysis of writing and a significant engagement with diverse communities, activities much closer to public and engaged, local community scholarship.

Because we focused so much on ordinary writing and ordinary people, we redefined the subject matter of the course away from individual, great authors. Women writers in the Tenderloin in San Francisco were community members. Collaborative writers in engineering and industry were workers serving industry needs. Pastors in African American churches wrote for their jobs. When we scanned history, we did not try to create a narrative of the historical development of writing; instead, we took samples of it from various real-world communities, like the nineteenth-century rhetorical education of African Americans that occurred primarily outside of educational institutions. When we studied the Vietnamese physician's diary, as I suggested above, we focused on the writer and the text but equally on the American soldier who preserved the diary after the war, the communities intertwined when it was written, and their interrelationships when it was eventually published in English in 2007.

When we read *A Murder in Virginia: Southern Justice on Trial,* a book written by a historian not an English scholar nor a compositionist, we focused on illiteracy and literacy in multiple communities and how the community literacies and politics intersected with the trial outcomes of four illiterate African Americans accused of murdering a white woman in 1895 Virginia. In this book, students found a dramatic but entirely factual narrative that reached back to a brief period between the Civil War and the dominance of Jim Crow laws. Through this narrative, students learned the power of the

African American press and African American women's clubs. And they saw cooperation between blacks and whites to right racial wrongs in the justice system. The students learned American history unknown to them; they learned about literacy, politics, culture, and more, all through a tale of mystery. The power of narrative, especially when it is well written, has the potential for lasting impressions on readers in ways that purely abstract, analytical, factual, historical, or theoretical texts do not.

We also read *Beyond the Archives: Research as Lived Process,* a collection of narratives about where research originates and how it proceeds. This book astonished many members of the class and, perhaps, more than any other, foregrounded inquiry methods completely unfamiliar to most, if not all, of them—serendipitous processes grounded in the ordinary. Students had never known, they proclaimed, that a grandfather's trunk or a graveyard could yield the beginnings of legitimate research. Nor had they known the recursive processes scholars undergo as they first get hooked on a hunch or an idea and let that lead them into scholarly endeavors. Schooled to conduct research that synthesizes what other scholars have said, that argues for one or another critical reading of a text, that is thesis-driven and tightly argued, they were astonished to learn that there were other possibilities—that published scholarship could involve the personal and include narrative and that subjects besides high art and culture were worthy of study. That knowledge, that awareness alone, changed the students, but the changes went deeper. One student, who had suffered from writer's block throughout her graduate career, caught glimpses of why she was blocked via alternative inquiry the course presented, inquiry that Candace Spigelman would call "personal academic argument." She began on a path that, a semester later, left her unblocked and reveling in her writing.

Some of the students' comments, in fact, are probably the impetus for this article I write now. When we read and discussed *Beyond the Archives,* one and then another and another of the experienced graduate students asserted and then defended their assertion that the class should replace or be taught concurrently with or in addition to the department's required course on "bibliography, research methods, and literary criticism," a course the department treats as introductory to graduate study (http://www.umsl.edu/~umslenglish/graduateprograms/masters.html). If this course were to become part of the required introduction, it would "introduce" students to composition studies as well as lay the foundations of community engagement and public scholarship the New Academy seeks to explore. Excited when I began the course about the inquiry it offered, I had no certainty that students would be equally excited to do work they were largely unfamiliar with. Nor could I have foreseen the particular inquiry the students would pursue nor the exact influences it would have on their lives and, potentially, on our graduate program. But I had learned much about how to teach our students, and so I forged ahead—as I have seen Lunsford do time and again. I turn now to the students' final projects.

FROM TEXTUAL INQUIRY TO COMMUNITY ENGAGEMENT

Prepared by this extensive study of divergent communities and how writing and other literacies functioned in them and prepared by several weeks' study that disrupted their traditional notions of knowledge and inquiry, the students were ready for the final course project, one that took them into communities for their research. (See Appendix B.) Most of the communities students entered were local and all had local ties. Most involved living writers and literacy learners whom the graduate students interviewed, adding a living component to the textual study they had always engaged in.[4]

A sampling of the projects will help readers further imagine the community interactions these graduate students undertook. One student studied the writing center at a local community college because he knew little about writing centers but knew a worker at this one. Through observational research, he saw writing center theory in action in ways that he proclaims will influence his high school teaching and his future doctoral studies. Another student studied her sister's journal. The initial impetus was the student's conviction that her sister was an excellent writer even though the sister herself did not believe so. Through close reading of the text and interviews with her sister, my student unearthed definitions of "writer" that had shaped her sister's belief about what constituted real and true writing. While her journal writing felt real and true, her school writing did not, she said, and yet school writing is the measure by which the writer judged herself.

The process of this research, not surprisingly, touched on the nature of the sisters' identities and their relationship, a very intimate community. The inquiry process created moments of tension between them and caused the journal writer to stop writing for a while. The tension abated and the writing quickly resumed, and what the student in my class learned, first, is the real power of community inquiry, emotional as well as intellectual. Additionally, learning how her sister defined "writer" gives my student an awareness that urges her to cross the boundaries between school writing and "real" writing, lessons I expect her to carry with her, long-term, into a sustained teaching career.

Another student, following accepted scholarship in psychology and other fields, studied how three local women had used journal writing as a mechanism of healing. She herself was personally connected to such uses of writing, and it's clear that her study helped her solidify a philosophy of teaching that honors students' diverse needs, a crucial perspective for one who teaches in an urban, low-income school as she does.

Another student studied a local language-learning institute for nonnative speakers of English. A volunteer there, she learned, through observational research and interviews, the depths of community ties among the students and between them and the institute's leader. The student has also, most probably, found the focus for her continuing graduate studies. Other students studied electronic communities that mattered to them and a magazine that grew out of a local arts community in the mid-twentieth century.

"THE 1926 LISTS"

One of the most interesting projects, and one I'd like to present, in some detail,[5] was a student's study of her grandfather's writing, its content and significance to her as a family member and as a reflection of the century of his life. She interpreted his writing in the context of current literacy research that shows literacy's intersection with technological, economic, and other changes (Brandt, 2001). With her permission, I include an extended excerpt from her essay, which won the department's award for the best essay written in a graduate composition studies class. It's called "The 1926 Lists" and the writer is Mirra Anson. She begins with a narrative, a pattern she had seen in our course readings, and she interweaves it into a scholarly analysis of literacy in community domains.

> One of the most vivid and earliest memories I have of my grandfather is the way he washed his hands. The bathroom in my grandparents' house was right off the kitchen, and my grandfather would ceremoniously wash his hands in the bathroom sink after working on the farm all day in preparation for the dinner prepared by my grandmother. I remember one day specifically when I was about six years old, I was in the kitchen with my grandmother "helping" to put dinner on the table. My grandfather came inside and said to me, "Come on, and let's wash up for dinner." He

turned on the water, lathered up, and took my hands inside his. I remember thinking how small my hands looked next to his; how pale, and how untarnished mine were in comparison, even under the guise of suds and running water. It was amazing how he got his hands clean everyday for supper—he removed every speck of dirt from under his nails, scrubbed clean the ashes that settled there after burning the trash, and washed away all evidence of outside work to reveal squeaky clean hands.

It was as if this hand washing ritual represented an important transition from his day identity as an Iowan farmer during the 20th century to his other role as husband, father, and grandfather. Those working hands became hands that would not only eat dinner with the family, but engage in newspaper fights, games of checkers, and draw silly looking cartoons characters on blank sheets of butcher paper—all at the amusement of the grandchildren. Those hands would sometimes wave throughout the air as he told stories of his youthful shenanigans, or those of people he grew up with that had long ago passed away. But what I didn't realize until his death was that he also used those hands to write—and write a lot and write everywhere [including on the barn walls, according to Anson. She goes on.].

My grandfather was a serious journal writer in that he kept a journal for about every year of his life [nearly one hundred]; even during his stay in the health care facility. One of those journals was from 1926 when he was twenty years old. Inside the front cover was a list titled, "Top Things of Importance in Life in 1926." On the back cover was another list, "Events of 1926."

Below is an image of his 1926 lists.

The following image may be difficult to read; therefore a typed version is below:

Things of importance in life in 1926

1. Graduated from Olds High school.
2. In an Operetta and play.
3. Visited the Colorado Mts.
4. Visited Chicago, Denver, and Omaha.
5. Went up in an airplane.
6. Purchased a Doge Sedan.
7. Purchased a Fordson Tractor.
8. Entered the Swedesburg Orchestra playing clarinet.

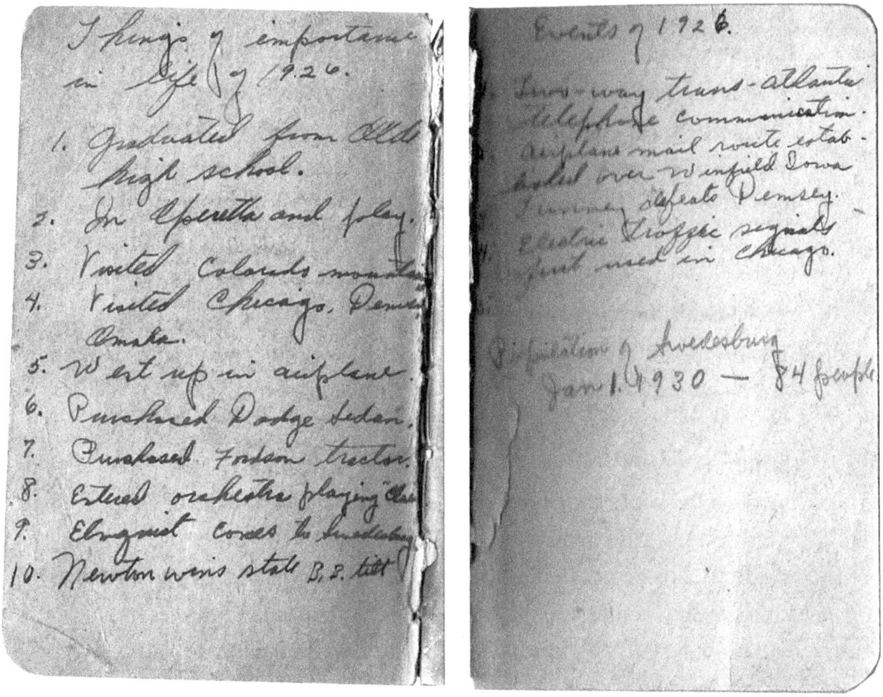
Things of importance in life of 1926.
1. Graduated from high school.
2. In Operetta and play.
3. Visited Colorado mountains
4. Visited Chicago, Omaha.
5. Went up in airplane
6. Purchased Dodge sedan.
7. Purchased Fordson tractor.
8. Entered orchestra
9. comes to Swedesburg
10. Newton wins state B.B. title

Events of 1926.
Two-way trans-atlantic telephone communication.
Airplane mail route established over Winfield Iowa
Tunney defeats Dempsey.
Electric traffic signals first used in Chicago.
Population of Swedesburg Jan 1. 1930 — 84 people

Left: "Things of importance in life in 1926"; *right*: On the back cover, another list: "Events of 1926."

9. Elingwist (?) comes to Swedesburg
10. Newton wins the State BB title

Events of 1926

1. Two way trans-Atlantic telephone communication
2. Airplane mail route established
3. Tunney defeats Dempsey
4. Electric traffic signals first used in Chicago

. . . These lists were certainly not ordinary to my grandfather, but yet they are in the sense that they articulate the accumulation of his observations from just one year. They are made extraordinary by the fact that for years, he kept the diary in which these lists were embedded (he kept all his journals / diaries), and his daughter (my mom) discovered them, and passed them along to me. The mere idea that someone has preserved and analyzed his lists, makes them do extraordinary work. Further, the lists communicate themes or elements of how he lived his life; they convey the

> forces that were shaping his literacy, and ultimately represent the forces that have shaped our own.
>
> . . . In *Literacy in American Lives,* Deborah Brandt explores how literacy changed the lives of Americans over a fundamental 100 years, from 1895 to 1985. Literacy, according to Brandt, is a concept that can be viewed as a "staple of life," alongside with any other manmade convention or material system. Literacy, she argues, is a double edged sword in a sense. On one hand literacy has been instrumental in expanding our democratic ideals and providing for individual upward mobility. Yet, it also has sorted and bracketed us economically and socially. Literacy, in other words, is complicated.

Although Anson is pursuing a doctoral degree in education and is thus familiar with multiple inquiry methods, discovering the personal and ordinary as subjects of study was new to her. Because of the background of all the other students, the course asked them to study in completely new areas with unfamiliar research methods and to write and organize material in formats they'd never before used.[6] With few exceptions, the students conducted their inquiry and their writing tasks exceptionally well, particularly given how far they were from their comfort zones. Many of the students were, unusually, in their first semester of graduate study, so I feared that the unfamiliarity of the course might exacerbate any lack of confidence they felt as beginners. But it seemed not to. In addition, their view of inquiry and scholarship has been altered from the ones they began with and will, no doubt, influence the kind of work they will want to do in the many other courses they have yet to take.

GRADUATE STUDENTS AS LOCAL CHANGE AGENTS

Because students' views of any given discipline are necessarily limited, students sometimes fail to take risks in their research that faculty might well endorse. Authorized with the experience of this class and supported with its training, it is possible that students will move away from the traditional in the work they do in other graduate classes and thus become agents of change in my department culture. Graduate students have some modicum of power to influence what a department delivers to them in the way of course work—what they enroll in, what they are excited about, what they talk about with faculty. Through this kind of indirect and informal change, this course has the potential to influence local change.

While adapting graduate education to community engagement in my department rests significantly on the will of individual faculty members, a recent addition to our nontenure-line faculty employs service learning in her undergraduate writing courses, as mentioned above. As staffing needs have allowed her to teach graduate seminars occasionally, she takes her awareness of community engagement into those seminars. Since our graduate program is small, the dose of community engagement available to our students through her classes and my own thus has potentially greater effect than it would in a large program. Demand for graduate courses in the last few years has grown so that the director is eager to offer any viable course a faculty member proposes. Thus, in the *place* where I work, in my local, I focus my energies in the nooks and crannies where change is possible, in one graduate course and the academic and nonacademic lives of its students. Whether or not the graduate curriculum changes, these students have. And I will continue to find ways for that to happen, as often as I can.

Appendix A: Reading List

Bazerman, Charles, and Paul Prior. *What Writing Does and How It Does It: An Introduction to Analyzing Texts and Textual Practices.* Lawrence Erlbaum, 2008.

Gold, David. *Rhetoric at the Margins: Revising the History of Writing Instruction in American Colleges, 1873–1941.* Southern Illinois UP, 2008.

Heller, Caroline E. *Until We Are Strong Together: Women Writers in the Tenderloin.* Teachers College Press, 1997.

Kirsch, Gesa, and Liz Rohan. *Beyond the Archives: Research as Lived Process.* Southern Illinois UP, 2008.

Lebsock, Susanne. *A Murder in Virginia: Southern Justice on Trial.* W. W. Norton, 2003.

Logan, Shirley Wilson. *Liberating Language: Sites of Rhetorical Education in Nineteenth-Century Black America.* Southern Illinois UP, 2008.

Lunsford, Andrea, and Lisa Ede. *Singular Texts / Plural Authors: Perspectives on Collaborative Writing.* Southern Illinois UP, 2009.

Miller, Richard E. *Writing at the End of the World.* U of Pittsburgh P, 2005.

Moore, Kathleen Dean. *Riverwalking: Reflections on Moving Water.* Harcourt Brace, 1995.

Moss, Beverly. *A Community Text Arises: A Literate Text and a Literacy Tradition in African-American Churches.* Hampton, 2003.

Sinor, Jennifer, and Rona Kaufman, eds. *Placing the Academy: Essays on Landscape, Work, and Identity.* Utah State UP, 2007.

Sinor, Jennifer. *The Extraordinary Work of Ordinary Writing: Annie Ray's Diary.* U of Iowa P, 2002.
Tram, Dang Thuy. *Last Night I Dreamed of Peace.* Harmony, 2007.

Appendix B: Final Project Assignment

SITES OF WRITING—FINAL PROJECT: IDENTIFICATION AND EXPLORATION OF A LOCAL SITE

BACKGROUND

As someone for whom St. Louis is not home, I am interested in learning as much as I can about it, and you can help me. My guess is that St. Louis and the metro area have a rich diversity of writing sites, historically and currently—well, it's more than just a guess. I'm sure of it.

What sites can you find and what can you learn about them—through personal interviews, primary sources such as the internal documents of a church (e.g., newsletters), other archival sources, secondary sources such as in a library or contemporaneous newspaper accounts of it? I've made a list of possible sites below; you may imagine others. I'll ask you to choose one, learn about it, analyze it, and eventually share your knowledge with the class.

The goal of the assignment is for you to learn as much about the site as you can, to analyze it contextually and rhetorically. As a class, the accumulated projects will showcase St. Louis sites of writing, what they say about what goes on here, what has gone on, what diversity we have, and how much writing sites are embedded in St. Louis culture, life, and history.

PROMPT

As you already know, our class discussions are complicating the definition of "writing site" and looking deeply into multiple ways that writing functions within any given site. Your research into a St. Louis site asks you to investigate it as deeply as you can and use the insights from our class discussions and readings to explore the site and its functions, its reasons for existing, the contexts which influence it, any forces that push against it or support it, reasons for its demise (if it no longer exists), and so on. The end results will be two:

1. A brief presentation to class about the site
2. A written essay, 10–12pp (probably) that analyzes the site

GETTING STARTED

The questions below should help you conceptualize the kind of research you should do. For any given site you choose, you'll have to adapt the questions, of course.

- What is the site?
- Origin of the site—why and how it came into being
- What interests you about the site?
- Who participates in the site?
- What work does writing do at the site?
- Do other things besides writing operate at the site? If so, how do they intersect with writing?

POSSIBLE SITES FOR RESEARCH

1. 19th-century African American newspapers
2. 19th-century German or Irish newspapers and their work
3. Abolitionist newspapers
4. 19th-century African American women's clubs
5. Pre–Civil War African American schools
6. The Women's Sanitation Society, a Civil War women's organization that provided hospital care to injured soldiers. (I'm not sure if that's the exact name or how much writing it involved, but a local resource, Paula Coalier, would.)
7. Some aspect of Harris-Stowe University. What's its origin as an HBCU—when and why? Who were the players in its origins?
8. International Institute of St. Louis, the "area's leading refugee resettlement agency," "Area has rebirth as a hub for immigrants," http://www.stltoday.com/news/local/metro/article_0949bd85-d591-597c-a0fa-ae00699d0e3c.html#Scene_1; "Open Arms Lead to Influx," http://www.stltoday.com/news/local/metro/article_b485327d-7c44-5334-85c9-0a31da42f6aa.html; "Refugee from Iraq Grateful to Have Work," http://www.stltoday.com/news/local/metro/article_23fba0b1-c10f-5501-b809-73afafb4a03a.html. *St. Louis Post-Dispatch,* 9/5/10
9. Vietnamese, Bosnian, et al. literacy sites
10. Ethnic churches
11. Contemporary ethnic newspapers
12. Notable (or not so notable) local diaries

13. Local normal school (?) and its history
14. Veterans for Peace (Korean War: Wilson M. Powell and Zhou Ming-Fu)
15. A faculty member's research—its origins, development, results, e.g. Richard Cook (Kazan biography journals), Sally Ebest (Irish women writers), Wendy Saul (in Asia), Virginia Navarro (in Asia, too, I think), Nancy Singer's, Jody Miller in Sri Lanka
16. The Gender Studies program on campus
17. The Center for International Studies
18. Community literacy centers (Girls Reading, Deborah Maltby)
19. Writing Centers (UMSL's, Meramec's)
20. Sites related to one of the other books I ordered for class: *Women Writing the Academy: Audience, Authority, and Transformation*; *Noise from the Writing Center*; *The Community College Writer: Exceeding Expectations*
21. Something else

Notes

This chapter builds on work previously published in the *Journal of Public Scholarship in Higher Education*. I thank the journal editor, Emily Donnelli-Sallee, for permission to use that work here.

1. In other places, I have written about how conditions, usually institutional, have pressed me into redefining the discipline and our roles in it. See, for example, "Place, Culture, Memory" in Strickland and Gunner and "Skeletons in the Closet, Ghosts, and Other Invisible Creatures" in Enos and Borrowman.

2. I realize that some departments are closer to this tradition and some are further away. Mine happens to be close in many ways; yours may not be. This aspect of my *local* has helped spur my thinking for this essay, and so it is important here. But I hope it does not suggest that I am unaware of how different other departments may be from mine.

3. Ours is an urban institution that serves primarily first-generation college students from the local area. Although undergraduate English majors with an emphasis in composition and rhetorical studies are springing up around the country, they are still rare, and so our graduate students come from undergraduate studies in literature. Additionally, the graduate program offers only the MA, and a sizeable percentage of its students are high- and occasionally middle-school teachers. The student demographics and student purposes for seeking graduate education combine with the department's traditional bent to bring into its graduate programs students with little other than literary training and interests.

4. For over twenty years, I have assigned primary research in many classes, but it was entirely new to my students.

5. The writer has happily given me permission to use her text extensively.

6. My first experience challenging students to new content and methodologies was when Lunsford sponsored our development of a composition course that paired basic writing and honors students and asked them to do ethnographic research. The students most able to do traditional academic work were flummoxed, at least initially, by the unfamiliar—and unmastered—tasks.

Works Cited

Anson, Mirra. "The 1926 Lists." N.d. TS. University of Missouri–St. Louis graduate English course.

Brandt, Deborah *Literacy in American Lives.* Cambridge UP, 2001.

Deans, Thomas. *Writing Partnerships: Service-Learning in Composition.* National Council of Teachers of English, 2000.

Ellison, Julie, and Timothy K. Eatman. *Imagining America: Scholarship in Public: Knowledge Creation and Tenure Policy in the Engaged University.* 2008. http://www.imaginingamerica.org/TTI/TTI_FINAL.pdf.

Enos, Theresa, and Shane Borrowman, eds. *The Promise and Peril of Writing Program Administration.* Parlor Press, 2008.

Klein, Julie. *Humanities, Culture, and Interdisciplinarity: The Changing American Academy.* State U of New York P, 2005.

Miller, Richard E. "Richard E. Miller Responds." *College English*, vol. 59, no. 2, 1997, pp. 221–24.

Spigelman, Candace. *Personally Speaking: Experience as Evidence in Academic Discourse.* Southern Illinois UP, 2004.

Strickland, Donna, and Jeanne Gunner, eds. *The Writing Program Interrupted: Making Space for Critical Discourse.* Boynton / Cook, 2009.

UMSL English Department Master of Arts in English. http://www.umsl.edu/~umslenglish/graduateprograms/masters.html/.

The Vietnam Center and Archive. http://www.vietnam.ttu.edu.

VISUAL RHETORIC, INTERCULTURAL WRITERS
THE UNIVERSITY'S TURN

ALYSSA J. O'BRIEN

> Where writing once meant *print* text—black marks on white paper, left to right and top to bottom—today "writing" is in full Technicolor; it is nonlinear and alive with sounds, voices, and images of all kinds.
>
> —Andrea A. Lunsford, *Writing Matters*

In classrooms everywhere across the country, new pedagogies enable students to analyze *and* compose visual and multimedia texts as forms of writing. Always a visionary and prescient rhetorician, Andrea A. Lunsford identified the seismic changes in what characterizes writing for the twenty-first century when she described it as "in full Technicolor" and "alive" (*Writing Matters*, xiii). Given this shift, Carrie Leverenz, among others, has called for similar seismic changes in academic institutions. In "Remediating Writing Program Administration," Leverenz argues for "the importance of valuing more than a single print-centric literacy, including those literacies facilitated and supported by computer technologies—visual, audio, multi-media, and digital" (38). Amidst her synthesis of professional voices urging writing programs to embrace "new media composing" (39), Leverenz refers to Lunsford's articulation of "secondary literacies" or the way in which the field might redefine "rhetoric and writing as epistemic, performative, multivocal, multimodal, and multimediated" (Lunsford, *Writing Matters* 8). Building on this concept of "secondary literacies," I propose a further advancement of our knowledge of "writing" as both a discipline and a practice. Specifically, I offer a theory of "tertiary literacies" that examines "new media composing" in global contexts made possible by new applications of technologies that extend the reach of writing practices beyond classroom walls and university halls. In this chapter, I argue that not only does the university need to make what rhetoric scholars call "the visual turn," but, more significantly, academic institutions need to foster what I will define as "intercultural writers" who are able to communicate globally and across cultural differences through "multimediated" writing.

To support this contribution to social understandings of writing, I first add to the systemic study of "visual rhetoric" by analyzing disparate global artifacts of early "writing." In the subsequent section, I employ this global perspective to generate new configurations of the composition classroom across time, geography, and culture. I assert that incorporating a "cross-cultural storyboard" within new compositional methodologies allows for the emergence of "intercultural writers" who engage in what Lunsford describes as "multivocal" and "multimodal" rhetoric. Ultimately, I contend, the strategic inclusion of a transnational "shared screen" or "digital page" challenges insular and outdated paradigms of the university as a self-contained entity.

The exigency for this new theoretical and applied understanding of "writing" emerges from the tectonic transformations in the tools that produce today's marks, sounds, voices, and images. As Lunsford and her colleagues Jenn Fishman and Warren Liew explain, "classroom innovations are absolutely necessary to all teaching in the twenty-first century, where technology has multiplied the forms and futures of students' literacy practices" (Lunsford et al., "College Writing" 489). Since writing is indeed no longer simply (an individual's) black marks on (a static) white paper, we therefore need a scholarly investigation into its earliest forms and a theoretical conception of its future potential as a communication media that connects people globally.

Yet writing, Lunsford has argued, is also often an act of violence (*Writing Matters*, xii). This chapter, then, moves from the scholarly analysis of transnational writing activities conducted as part of a large-scale research project to a violent break—the sudden devastating fracture of cross-cultural collaboration. It moves, too, from professional scholarship to a rhetoric record of pain—which spread globally and was only abated by Andrea Lunsford's personal compassion and public fortitude—such that from here forward I will refer to Andrea by her first name. For truly only the wisdom, intellectual optimism, and ethos of care that Andrea shared made possible a return—a turning back again, recursively—to understand writing as a powerful, even positive tool for human connection. Therefore this chapter's concluding call for "tertiary literacies" serves as a tribute to Andrea, and my proposed theoretical conception of tertiary literacies is, fittingly, rhetoric that engages not just the head but also the heart.

WRITING THE VISUAL, OR HOW WRITING IS (ALWAYS) CHANGING

> One of the Western world's oldest technologies, writing—like the art of rhetoric to which it is often linked—is plastic, endlessly adaptable to new situations, challenges, and opportunities, and thus difficult to pin down, to know with certainty.
>
> —Andrea A. Lunsford, *Writing Matters*

The composing practices of each new generation—so well documented by the Stanford Study of Writing that Andrea launched in 2001[1]—reveal that today's university students are "writing more than ever before in history" (Lunsford qtd. in Haven, "The New Literacy"). Andrea's groundbreaking work made visible the many modes through which students communicate and the ways in which student-authored hybrid texts combine the verbal and the visual. By placing today's student texts into historical perspective, my aim is to trace a line back to some of the very first instances of writing, what Andrea calls "one of the...world's oldest technologies" (*Writing Matters*, xi).

From the earliest proto-writing, forms of communication, such as the pictograms of Chinese Jiahu symbols dating back to 6600 B.C.E. or Egyptian hieroglyphs from 4000 B.C.E., the "visual" has been a primary rhetorical mode for signifying meaning or connecting people in "conversation" across time and space. Runes from rural Sweden, carved on rocks or sticks; oracle bones from China, consisting of characters inscribed on turtle shells; and petroglyphs chipped into stone walls by Native Americans all testify to the power of "visual writing" as communicative media for early societies.

Characters in Chinese connote values that extend beyond the translatable content of words: the very shapes signify. Similarly, in illuminated manuscripts such as the Book of Kells from 800 A.D., the visual has purpose and value as communicative matter, not merely as decoration. Early Greek paintings and sculptures personify concepts later spoken or written down in words, such as the 300–400 A.D. limestone relief figures of Kairos and Metanoia described so powerfully by Kelly Myers (17). This century's video games and virtual reality systems, social media and Internet advertisements, image-rich blogs and emoji-studded text messages continue the tradition of "writing" as communicating—and persuading—through a combination of verbal and visual signs.

While scholars across the academy have historically focused on visual texts as objects of study, the more recent coining of "visual rhetoric" as a new field signals the university's turn towards acceptance of multimodality, given that visual rhetoric has emerged at the intersection of a wide range of disciplines (English, art history, film studies, media and communication, journalism, classics, and cultural studies, to name a few).

Perhaps most influential in scholarly attempts to wrestle out specific definitions or taxonomies for "visual rhetoric" was W. J. T. Mitchell's identification—over two decades ago—of what he called "the pictorial turn," an advance on viewing the visual as merely mimetic or subservient to linguistics. However, Mitchell wrote, "We still do not know exactly what pictures are, what their relation to language is, how they operate on observers and on the word, how their history is to be understood, and what is to be done with or about them" (13). Rhetoric and composition scholars David Blakesley and Collin Brooke introduced Mitchell's "picture theory" into academic discussions of "mixed media" and articulations of writing pedagogy (2). Importantly, Blakesley and Brooke also looked back to antiquity, and they noticed that classical rhetoricians—Gorgias, Aristotle, Quintilian, and others—spoke of the power of words in pictorial metaphors or encouraged speeches that would evoke the visual in the minds of audiences. In my own scholarly review of such ancient texts, I discovered that some translations of Aristotle frame his famous definition of rhetoric in visual terms, as "the faculty of *observing* in any given situation the available means of persuasion" (24, emphasis added). Thus any contemporary cultural understanding of "writing the visual" must take into account the historical knowledge offered by such digging into scholarship, namely, that the art of rhetoric has always included the visual.

Despite this recognition of the ubiquitous presence of the visual as a form of "writing," scholars have struggled to generate a common discourse at the theoretical level. Andrea addresses this problem in "Notes on Visual Literacy." She quotes Stephen Apkon's observation, from his book, *The Age of the Image:*

Redefining Literacy in a World of Screens, that people in contemporary society are "not properly cognizant of or conversant with the grammar of visual communication, the coded messages of its style, and the practical components of its production. We are largely, in a word, illiterate." Her profound contribution in the form of her theoretical articulation of "secondary literacies" provides a remedy for this intellectual and cultural crisis. Moreover, Andrea elevates the field of rhetoric and writing studies as the academic home for advancing knowledge through the analysis and production of visual texts.

True to her generous spirit, Andrea then uses the space of "Notes on Visual Literacy" to applaud composition scholars and writing teachers for "the many articles and books our field has produced on the subject over the last ten years or so." She mentions Carolyn Handa's collection, *Visual Rhetoric in a Digital World*, which includes Gunther Kress's early work on visual communication and multimodal literacy. To these texts I suggest we add articles on the visual rhetoric of design by Diana George and Mary Hocks in *College Composition and Communication Online*; Anne Wysocki's mediated work in *Kairos*; Kathleen Blake Yancey's CCCC address, "Made Not Only in Words: Composition in a New Key," and explorations of visual and multimodal writing by Jody Shipka, Cynthia Selfe, and Wendy Hesford, among others.

For the classroom—the site where students might learn "the grammar of visual communication"—innovative textbooks dedicated to visual literacy have emerged as complements to and applications of theoretical approaches. Donald McQuade and Christine McQuade's *Seeing and Writing*; *Picturing Texts*; Anne Wysocki's *Compose, Design, Advocate: A Rhetoric for Integrating the Written, Visual, and Oral*; and even *Envision*—a textbook that my colleague Christine Alfano and I wrote at Stanford University under Andrea's mentorship—provide rich pedagogical applications of scholarship on visual rhetoric and instruct students how to analyze and produce visual arguments. Finally, each revised edition of Andrea's own books—*Everything's an Argument, Easywriter, The Everyday Writer, St. Martin's Handbook, Everyone's an Author*, and *Writing in Action*—offers sophisticated yet accessible chapters on visual rhetoric, multimodal assignments, and document design. Collectively, this work signals not just "the pictorial turn," but also *the field*'s turn to visual rhetoric, and even "the university's turn" to approaching writing as an adaptable technology.

One of the more exciting practical applications of the university's turn to visual rhetoric has been Andrea's seminar on "The Graphic Novel," in which students draw their own panels.[2] Students' textual production for these courses relies on the pedagogical study of the graphic novel and the cast of characters it employs: villains and heroes from *Maus*, gendered narratives in *Persepolis*, social misfits from *Ghost World* or *Jimmy Corrigan: The Smartest Kid on Earth*. The graphic novel also celebrates the archetypal story of triumph over adversity, such as found in Tin Tin, Superman, and Spiderman or, more recently, Marisa Acocella Marchetto's *Cancer Vixen: A True Story* and Allie Brosh's *Hyperbole and a Half*.

In *Writing Matters*, Andrea puts into perspective the significance of these changes in the university curriculum; she cites Peter Schjeldahl's landmark *New Yorker* article in which he asserts that today's students prefer graphic novels over traditional prose books and "drawing pens" over poetry. Given such cultural shifts in the practices of reading and writing texts, Andrea introduces the term "secondary literacies" and theorizes that this rhetorical mode "advances a looser prose style, infiltrated by visual and aural components to mirror the agility and shiftiness of language filtered through and transformed by digital technologies and to allow for, indeed demand, performance" ("Writing, Technologies" 170). Her research through the Stanford Study of Writing "underscores the need for campus-wide pedagogical change of the kind demonstrated by many composition teachers who, for decades now, have been 'flipping' the traditional classroom script by privileging *what students are doing* over what the teacher is saying" ("College Writing" 488, emphasis added).

In these ways, writing and rhetoric studies differ from other disciplinary approaches to visual texts. As Andrea points out, writing instructors take seriously those texts that students create as contemporary acts of writing, such as the blogs, websites, text messages, and video compositions discovered by the Stanford Study of Writing. Through the development and implementation of pedagogical practices devoted to "privileging what students are doing"—namely reading and writing visual and multimodal texts—academics in rhetoric and writing studies are indeed forcing "the university's turn" to embrace pictorial theory and its applications.

But, I would argue, there is one more crucial feature of visual culture in this new century: it is exceptionally and undeniably global, a network of cross-cultural influences and exchanges. What merits greater attention, then, is how the university needs to make yet another turn, this time to look outward and foster intercultural writing practices based on a theory that I identify as "tertiary literacies."

FROM CHALK BOARDS TO SHARED SCREENS, OR HOW CLASSROOMS ARE CHANGING

> The newest "new" rhetoric is one that is deeply mediated, deeply technologized. In fact, writing . . . has consistently transformed itself in relation to new and emerging technologies.
>
> —Andrea A. Lunsford, "What Is the New Rhetoric?"

In *The Global School: Connecting Classrooms and Students around the World*, William Kist stresses the need for "teachers [to] envision ways to help their students survive and thrive in this internationalized world" (1). The new Common Core Standards for primary and secondary education require that students "come to understand other perspectives and cultures. Students [must] appreciate that the twenty-first-century classroom and workplace are settings in which people from often widely divergent cultures and who represent diverse experiences and perspectives must learn and work together" (qtd. in Kist, 2). At the university level, study abroad programs have previously promised hands-on experiences learning cultural differences. Today, however, as financially strapped students reconsider study abroad, and as world events escalate, the responsibility often falls to classroom teachers to use the "new and emerging technologies" mentioned by Andrea in order to meet the need for global citizenship and cross-cultural understanding. Carrie Leverenz explains the impetus for such work: "It is not just the availability of new communication technologies that is pressing us to expand our definition of writing but also the recognition that in an increasingly global society, we need to widen the scope of the kinds of communication available to us as workers and citizens" (39). Consistent with scholarly and pedagogical innovations in "visual rhetoric," writing and rhetoric instructors have stepped up to meet this need.

At Stanford, the work we took on was to design and implement new technologies to radically change the classroom, replacing one physical wall with a screen through which connections could be made with other students around the world. In the process, we provided students with previously unimagined opportunities for synchronous transnational engagement: to analyze and produce multimodal writing collaboratively with students in different countries—students separated by geographic boundaries and time zones, as well as by political ideologies, cultural norms, and lived realities. In this section, I argue that the transition from chalkboards to shared whiteboard screens signals a monumental change in what constitutes "education" and that, if the university completes the "turn" to cross-cultural pedagogical practices at a global level, we might be able to teach student writers the intercultural knowledge and rhetorical proficiency necessary to tackle the increasing national insularity and consequent damaging global effects that are rampant today, in this era of the Anthropocene.

When we started in 2005 with a research grant application to the Wallenberg Global Learning Network, Andrea generated the title, "Developing Intercultural Competencies through Collaborative Rhetoric," which soon became known through its nickname, the Cross-Cultural Rhetoric Project, or CCR. Andrea at Stanford and Brigitte Mral at Örebro University, Sweden, were principal investigators. In a generous act of leadership, Andrea and Brigitte turned over the research design and operations of the project to the instructional team: at Stanford, the team consisted of Christine Alfano and Alyssa O'Brien, along with technology specialists Dan Gilbert and Robert E. Smith. In Örebro, instructors Anders Eriksson and Eva Magnusson, along with technology specialist Stefan Borjeson, formed the team.[3] Together we generated a new curriculum and a methodology of pedagogical practices through which we connected students in real time across a nine-hour difference through video-conference technology.[4] Only a few years ago, this kind of synchronous interactive teaching was revolutionary. Today, we see more and more such connections, especially with the advent of digital platforms such as Skype, Face Time, iChat, and Google Hangout. But when we started in 2005, we were just figuring it out.

Following in Andrea's footsteps, we dedicated hours to collaboration as an instructional team. Our efforts began through online conversations and brainstorming sessions, then evolved into weekly video-conference instructional team meetings at 6 A.M. California time and 3 P.M. Sweden time. As our project progressed, we visited each other's campuses, met each other's families, and developed the bonds that we sought to promote in our students as intercultural communicators and writers. By 2008, our list of university partners expanded across five continents to include the American University in Cairo, Egypt; the National University of Singapore; the University of Sydney, Australia; and Khabarovsk State Academy of Economics and Law, Russia. With each partner, we experimented with new technologies and generated lesson plans in collaborative visual rhetoric production as a means to foster intercultural competencies in our students.[5] We also researched methods for asynchronous connections and developed assignments that asked students to produce and publish collaborative multimodal texts on a blog, a project wiki, various Facebook groups or Twitter sites, as well as a range of university-sanctioned electronic course sites.

The knowledge generated through the research project might be theorized through the lens of Elizabeth Clark: "The future of writing—based on a global, collaborative text, where all writing has the potential to become public—informs our classrooms and forms a new, 'digital' imperative, one that asks how we can reshape our pedagogy with new uses of the technologies that are changing our personal and professional lives" (qtd. in Lunsford et al., "College Writing," 489). This is important work for universities in the twenty-first century: in this shift from static chalkboards to digital screens, students take ownership for their writing as members of a global team. In the early years of CCR, our methodology entailed using a software technology called Marratech that consisted of several significant features: video-conference windows in which participants saw each other, a chat box for written communication, a white board upon which both "sides" could write or draw, and a recording feature that enabled the instructional team to screen capture the entire connection for future review and for research purposes.

The software also allowed for multiple groups of students to connect to one main server such that up to ten or even fifteen separate video-conference boxes appeared on the screen in one column, showing every participant in the virtual meeting and allowing every participant access to the shared whiteboard screen (see figure 5.1). Thus we could break our classes into groups for peer review, rhetorical analysis projects, discussion of key political or cultural issues, and the collaborative production of visual or multimodal texts.

Moreover, by working in teams that were independent from the surveillance of the instructor, the students took control over their learning. These new technologies enabled them to type, draw, photograph, record, vocalize, and otherwise "write" in multiple modalities. What we observed was that student teams turned again and again to visual composition. That is, students decided to draw, rather than just write words of greeting or self-representation. How does the fact that students turn to graphic composition both challenge and inspire our understanding of what it means to write?

For some, visual rhetoric offered a means to bridge the language barrier, such as when students from Sweden or Egypt connected with Stanford students and the conversation started with drawings on the whiteboard. Theoretically, we can view those drawings as forms of writing, a way for students to make their mark, creating a representation of themselves similar to the initials one might carve in a table to show "I have been here. I exist."[6]

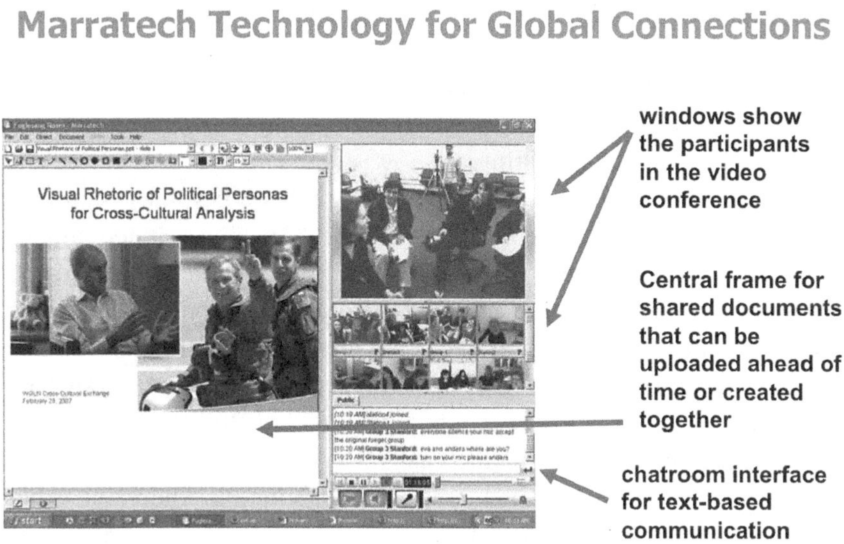

Figure 5.1. Annotated rendering of the software interface for CCR videoconferences, a connection that entailed a visual rhetoric analysis of the media personas of then-national leaders Prime Minister Fredrik Reinfeldt of Sweden and President George W. Bush of the United States.

For others, the act of drawing filled in the gap of absence. During one Stanford-Orebro connection, for example, two Swedish students did not attend the video-conference. Suddenly there was movement as compositionists on both sides of the screen took hold of the pen tool. Students in the United States created stick figure outlines of a girl and boy. Swedish students added a hat to one and a lit cigarette to the other, in order to convey the personalities of their missing colleagues. When they were done, students on both sides looked at the graphic visualization of their missing colleagues. "Now we are all together," said a Swedish student. What merits emphasis is that in this space of two writing classes—on two different continents—joined by video-conference technology, they indeed were all together.

From the perspective of "secondary literacies," if we recognize the doodle not as deviance or distraction but as the creation of a text that enables intercultural communication, we can learn to engage our students as multimedia writers, composers in various genres and modalities. Through this lens, we can reconceive of the whiteboard as a shared blank page that empowers students to express their visual literacy and to produce collaborative digital texts across time, distance, and culture. Thus the visual text produced by the students as a communicative, rhetorical act demonstrates how we need to view writing as "epistemic, performative, multivocal, multimodal, and multimediated" (Lunsford, *Writing Matters*, 8). In other words, the whiteboard stands as evidence that writing continues to change along with the technologies for making writing.

Yet I propose that the power of the drawing extends beyond its signifying function as communicative media; the doodle—drawing as it does missing members of a team—works on the level of affect as well. It provides a space for feelings from the heart to enter the rhetorical situation of an academic, required composition class. By replacing loss with visual presence, these students demonstrate what I term "tertiary literacies": communication competencies that engage "habits of mind" (Council of Writing Program Administrators) or what Janet Bennett calls "the heartset" required for global citizenship.[7] Central to tertiary literacies is collaboration. Andrea, an expert on theories and practices of collaboration in the academy, as well as a generous facilitator of shared projects through invitations and agreements to join scholarly endeavors, articulates the shift to student collaboration as a benefit of new technologies in university classrooms.

> If we look beyond the hand-wringing about young people and literacy today, beyond the view that paints them as either brain-damaged by technology or as cogs in the latest race to the top, we will see that the changes brought about by the digital revolution are just that: changes. These changes alter the very grounds of literacy as the definition, nature, and scope of writing are all shifting away from the consumption of discourse to its production across a wide range of genre and media, away from individual "authors" to participatory and collaborative partners-in-production; away from a single static standard of correctness to a situated understanding of audience and context and purpose for writing. ("Our Semi-literate Youth?")

If we change our conceptual lens and view these students as "collaborative partners-in-production" who draw with the purpose of involving their absent peers, we might then see how visual rhetoric makes possible writing across a wide range of genre and media.

What, then, are the features of visual rhetoric that connects writers across cultural divides? In other words, what exactly happens in the shared writing space of the whiteboard? Does it serve as *connective tissue* between multiple cultures or as a *barrier* between them? Does each "side" inscribe their views upon its surface as partners in participatory culture or is the writing competitive, even combative, and inherently marked by difference?

These questions are worth asking of the artifacts students produced during the years when the CCR instructional team launched a series of "wild experiments" as lesson plans for each connection.[8] For example, we asked students to make a collaborative collage: to take clip art, images from ads, and drawings to serve as a visual argument. We challenged students to create brochures and publicity materials for imaginary companies involving all team members. We required them to produce ads that appealed to radically different cultural values across countries. Ultimately, we created a lesson plan in which we turned to the resources of the graphic novel to ask students to perform that most important task: collaborative learning in the generation of a "cross-cultural storyboard."

TRANSNATIONAL COLLABORATION BY INTERCULTURAL WRITERS: FRAMING IDEAS AND AFFECT THROUGH THE STORYBOARD

> Young people . . . face huge challenges, of course—challenges of access and of learning ever new ways with words (and images). What students need in facing these challenges is not derision or dismissal but solid and informed instruction. And that's where the real problem may lie—not with student semi-literacy but with that of their teachers.
>
> —Andrea A. Lunsford, "Our Semi-literate Youth?"

For our lesson on visual literacy involving storyboarding, we set up a videoconference for a three-way connection among student teams in the United States, Sweden, and Egypt. The groups had been connecting regularly for two months. For this class meeting, we had each team analyze two short films and break down the films in terms of panels, arrangement, argument, and rhetorical situation. Then, we asked them to transfer the learning from their analysis to a collaborative activity in which they would create their own storyboard on the shared screen. The prompt for the activity was as follows:

Task: Storyboard your learning

ADDRESS THE FOLLOWING QUESTIONS: Is this kind of videoconference worth doing? What specifically do you learn about rhetoric, writing, research, and cultural values from these activities that you would not learn otherwise? Together, draw your argument in the form of a cross-cultural storyboard.

Figure 5.2. Storyboard composition area

> INSTRUCTIONS: As a team, discuss the questions above. Develop an argument, collaboratively, to share with the class and then storyboard your answer. As shown in the boxes (see figure 5.2), a storyboard is an outline in graphic format; it helps people visualize the content of a film, a dramatic script, an animation, an ad campaign, or even an essay. It is a feature of the graphic novel.
>
> PROCESS: Using the shared whiteboard, draw in sketches / words for the argument you want to make about your group's response to the questions above regarding video-conference learning. Use simple drawings to begin with. Once the story or argument is in place, you can add more to it. Then, select two people to present the storyboard argument to other groups, and one person as "blogger" to create a post on the Cross-Cultural Rhetoric Project blog. Copy your work to the blog in order to "publish" it for a wider audience. Be sure to include everyone's names in the blog post and words of explanation about your storyboard argument.
>
> TIME ALLOWED FOR THE TASK: 20 minutes

As formidable as this activity sounded to us, as instructors, all the groups completed it with time to spare. They just buckled down and got to work. Their "composition speed" was remarkable—faster than it had been for writing words out in response to previous collaborative activities. Moreover, the students all seemed completely comfortable in the realm of graphic representation.

So what happened and how can we understand its significance for writing pedagogy, for the theoretical space of the shared whiteboard, and for contributions to knowledge about visual rhetoric, media communications, and affect in collaboration? One group's work provides a lens through which to answer these questions. As shown in figure 5.3, this group used no words, only pictorial representation. Their methodology encompassed several steps. First, they visualized the intercultural conflict experienced at the initial contact with strong red jagged lines that depicted the discord of group members trying to work together (figure 5.3). Their negative experience and its visual rhetoric depiction correspond to what Mary Louise Pratt calls the "perils of writing in the contact zone" (37). But subsequently, these students used visual rhetoric to indicate how they met on common ground through a love of music. The next panel represented their process of synthesizing their differences to come together as a team—not through assimilation of difference into one dominant culture or worldview, but through positive affect and recognition of shared passions. Notably, they represented their identities in terms of circles of various shapes and colors. In the final panel, each colored shape remained distinct, not merged into one, and yet their shapes were connected through a multicolored line encircling the group that was, at last, working as a team.

Figure 5.3. Storyboard of the self-titled team "Cultural perceptions"

From a theoretical perspective, the writing panel as a shared collaborative text for this global team does function as connective tissue between different students. But the tissue is red and raw with chafing in places. It takes work to come together as a team. Initially, the whiteboard as blank page allows for the expression (or writing) of conflict and tension, such as shown in the big red splotch. Yet the composing process is also generative. It enables students to move beyond conflict to a change in perception. Through visual rhetoric, the team communicated this transformation.

An unexpected benefit of this wild experiment of storyboard-writing is that in their composing, students created a distinct argument, set up their panels according to a specific arrangement of that argument, and designed the graphics to signify each student's persona. In this way, the production of visual rhetoric made possible deep learning about writing practices. There is obvious attention to invention, arrangement, and style in the storyboard. There is effective use of evidence. There is an introduction, a body, and a conclusion in which distinct parts come together. By facilitating such activities in the classroom, we argued, instructors can promote transferable skills in composing—from multimodal writing to writing an essay about their experiences, using the same concepts of invention, arrangement, style, evidence, and argument. These practices are especially essential when digital technologies connect students from disparate composition classrooms across the globe in a single virtual classroom. Using the shared whiteboard as a blank page for "writing" enables collaboration, creativity, spontaneity, and a sense of ownership over the learning in the twenty-first century.

The storyboard thus reveals a deep level of intercultural competence, or what theorists Guo-Ming Chen and William Starosta call "an individual's ability to develop a positive emotion towards understanding and appreciating cultural differences in order to promote appropriate and effective behavior in intercultural communication" (408). By "intercultural competencies," I refer also to Carl Lovitt and Dixie Goswami's early theorization of the ability to "develop sensitivity to and consideration for others from diverse cultural contexts" (1). In the drawings, conflicts are enacted and resolved, fighting individuals are reconciled, other cultures are viewed through new lenses, and the beauty of each individual is celebrated visually. Can the ultimately positive outcome of this activity be seen as an instance of tertiary literacy? I think so, and to me, the most heartening aspect of such transnational, cross-cultural pedagogy is that it will always be pioneering new forms of writing, new incarnations of texts produced by students working in global teams. I contend that as educators we face a moral imperative to foster "intercultural competencies" in our students. After thousands of video-conference connections, the team argued that if universities might make a turn to support innovative global pedagogies, then we might be able to take one step forward in combating the violence and rising tide of hate that divides people from different contexts and cultures.

GRAPHIC FRACTURES

> Young people today are aware of the precarious nature of our lives. They understand the dangers that await us.
>
> —Andrea A. Lunsford, in Cynthia Haven, "The New Literacy"

Suddenly and without warning, the project experienced fierce fractures and then a violent end. Seismic shocks of a different nature shook the foundations of our research. We were severed from our resources. Global events broke communication with our partners. We encountered the precarity of human existence, as the shadow side of human relationships came into view.

At Stanford, we lost our classroom spaces—the small conference rooms we used for videoconferences, where we had set up whiteboard screens as windows on the world. It felt like a rupture, a forceful extraction, as if we were being carved out of a site in which we had made our home.

On the other side of the world, our partners in Egypt, at the American University of Cairo, faced the crisis and chaos of the Arab Spring. The university cancelled classes and closed the campus as demonstrations brought transportation to a standstill, and we lost communication with our colleagues. Videoconferences were no longer possible. Rolling brown-outs thwarted digital connection. We strained to decipher the shimmering static images—protests in Tahrir Square, the fierce clash of citizens living in Cairo, and women attacked in the middle of the city.

Worst of all, in Sweden, Eva Magnusson, our colleague and friend in Orebro, whose family we knew and whose theory of "bonding" had contributed to the first publication of the project, went missing. Her ebullient presence, which we had seen every Tuesday via video-conference for years, disappeared. The whiteboard went dark. Suddenly illiterate, we could not make sense of Swedish newspaper accounts and police reports. We started feeding news stories into Google Translate and relied on our Danish colleague at Stanford, Helle Rytkønen, to share with us any scrap of information. It felt like trying to read scratches on rocks, and we did not have the legend.

As the accounts became increasingly graphic and unthinkable, it was as if the media technologies that used to connect us now showed us only fragments of the truth, pieces we tried to assemble into some kind of story that might make sense.

And then we learned a terrible word—an intercultural language lesson that we never expected and could not comprehend: "styckmord." A shocking death. One of our own had murdered another one of our own. Stefan Börjesson, the project's technology specialist, was arrested, confronted with evidence of his crime, and left alone in jail where he hung himself with the shoelaces of his sneakers.

RE-VISION

> Writing is a way to get a sense of power.
>
> —Andrea A. Lunsford, in Cynthia Haven, "The New Literacy"

When interviewed about the Stanford Study of Writing, Andrea emphasized the transformative nature of writing for today's students: "Good writing changes something. It doesn't just sit on the page. It gets up, walks off the page and changes something" (qtd. in Haven). This collection is a means to honor Andrea, her incredible contributions to rhetoric and writing studies, her accomplishments as a visionary teacher and generous colleague, and her influence upon students and scholars across multiple generations. In rereading her words, written over so many years, three beautiful aspects of her character shine through above all: her optimism, her determination to make change, and her ethos of care. When there is injustice, she gets up and changes something. Where there is suffering, she extends a wise word and a caring hug. This ethos of care extends to her theoretical view of writing: "Where there is language there will always be rhetoric, and that rhetoric will inevitably renew itself with each succeeding generation" ("Key Questions for a New Rhetoric").

A year after Eva Magnusson went missing, Brigitte Mral, the principal investigator of our CCR project in Örebro, convened a symposium in Eva's honor. Andrea and I flew over, along with colleagues Cheryl Glenn and Robert E. Smith. We presented words and images that sought to rally us against hateful acts; we presented stories from the history of feminist rhetoric against violence. We sought renewal, a rewriting of the recent past. We visited Eva's mother, and although we could not communicate in words across the language barrier, we spent moments of gazing at photos of Eva and let those images in some small way begin to fill the absence. We tried to replace our last imaginings of Eva with those of the love and kindness of her family. We made dinner and shared wine with Eva's three grieving sons, connecting through ritual rather than through words. And we planted a flowering tree at Eva's small hut by the lake, lifting stones and placing them in piles to signify the meaning of our visit. The precarity of life transformed through rocks arranged in rhetorical acts of remembering and revision.

In "Thoughts on Graduate Education in English," the last chapter of *Writing Matters,* Andrea concludes with these words: "Can we rethink the PhD in ways that will make our programs more open and inclusive, more truly diverse, more responsive to the dreams and desires of our students, more connected to emerging definitions of reading and writing, more collaborative, more engaged with issues close to the hearts of our communities? *Of course we can*" (71). The sentences—and the sentiment—speak to the force of writing as "a way to get a sense of power."

The original argument of this chapter was that the collaborative production of visual texts promotes deep learning writing practices across cultures and enables students to develop as "intercultural writers." For this possibility to become reality, the university must make "the turn" to allow graphic texts as legitimate forms of academic writing and to provide opportunities for global communication and connection. But, as the process of writing is generative, I see now in writing this, my argument is not about the university at all. It is about creating human connections, about daring to care and to show compassion, daring to be present and visible in times of conflict or even tragedy. It is, ultimately, about relationships—and relationships in turn are at the heart of tertiary literacies. I believe that I've learned it through working with and knowing Andrea.

"There is no rhetoric without relationship," Marvin Diogenes, associate director of the Program in Writing and Rhetoric at Stanford when Andrea was faculty director, once told me. This focus on relationships—the affective collaboration across differences, the act of connecting with the heart as well as the head—is actually the reform most needed in universities today.

If we take inspiration from Andrea's words in *Writing Matters*, we can celebrate writing as a living art—much as those runes and oracle bones and wall etchings remain as testaments to communities and people bonded together in the past. Then, we might be able to revise our histories and heal our hearts. We might see writing and visual rhetoric as possibly preserving the sounds, voices, and images of those in our communities, in both our "public and private lives" to use the subtitle of her book. Perhaps it is by carrying on such work that we will best honor Andrea's charismatic teaching, ethos of care, and wisdom.

Notes

1. The Stanford Study of Writing (ssw.stanford.edu), a longitudinal examination of undergraduate writing practices, entailed the collaboration of colleagues Marvin Diogenes, Jenn Fishman, Erin Krampetz, Paul Rogers, and Laurie Stapleton, among others, as well as 189 students of the Stanford class of 2005.

2. Andrea subsequently advised Stanford instructors in the creative writing program on the launch of a popular course dedicated to the publication of a class-composed graphic novel. *Shake Girl* and *From Busan to San Francisco* were the first two graphic novels produced by the students.

3. The history of the project, as well as links to syllabi, lesson plans, student projects, and more can be found on the project website: http://ccr.stanford.edu. For details on the project's innovations in technologically mediated pedagogy, see O'Brien and Alfano, "Connecting Students Globally through Video-Conference Pedagogy."

4. For a discussion of the project's theoretical / scholarly foundations, research questions, quantitative and qualitative outcomes, and implications for global learning, see O'Brien and Eriksson.

5. Specifics on how we experimented with different digital technologies to accommodate the access and institutional parameters of our partner universities can be found in "Tech Travels: Connecting Writing Classes across Continents" by Alyssa O'Brien and Christine Alfano.

6. In *Writing Matters*, Andrea frames the power of writing one's name as an act of claiming identity, but she also examines writing in some ways as an act of violence.

7. Bennett calls for a threefold set of requirements for global citizenship: *the mindset*, or cognitive competencies, *the skillset*, or behavioral competencies, and *the heartset*, or affective competencies composed of a set of attitudes that include "curiosity, initiative, risk taking, suspension of judgment, cognitive flexibility, tolerance of ambiguity, cultural humility, and resourcefulness" (20). Further analysis of this concept can be found in O'Brien, "Global Citizenship and the Stanford Cross-Cultural Rhetoric Project."

8. See http://ccr.stanford.edu/digrep.htm for links to many of these lesson plans and course materials.

Works Cited

Alfano, Christine L., and Alyssa J. O'Brien. *Envision: Persuasive Writing in a Visual World.* Longman, 2005.

———. *Envision: Researching and Writing Arguments.* Pearson, 2014.

Aristotle. *Rhetoric.* Translated by W. Rhy Roberts. Introduction by Edward P. J. Corbett, Modern Library, 1984.

Bennett, Janet M. "On Becoming a Global Soul: A Path to Engagement during Study Abroad." *Developing Intercultural Competence and Transformation: Theory, Research, and Application in International Education*, edited by V. Savicki, Stylus, 2008, pp. 13–31.

Blakesley, David, and Collin Brooke. "Introduction: Notes on Visual Rhetoric." *Enculturation* vol. 3, no. 2, 2001. http://enculturation.gmu.edu/3_2/introduction2.html.

Chen, Guo-Ming, and William Starosta. "Intercultural Communication in the University Classroom." *Intercultural Communication: A Reader*, edited by Larry Samovar and Richard E. Porter, Wadsworth, 2000.

Clark, J. Elizabeth. "The Digital Imperative: Making the Case for a 21st-Century Pedagogy." *Computers and Composition*, vol. 27, 2010, pp. 27–35.

Council of Writing Program Administrators. 2000. *WPA Outcomes Statement for First-Year Composition.* http://wpacouncil.org/files/wpa-outcomes-statement.pdf.

Diogenes, Marvin, and Andrea Lunsford. "Toward Delivering New Definitions of Writing." *Delivering College Composition: The Fifth Canon*, edited by Kathleen Yancey, Heinemann/Boynton Cook, 2006, pp. 141–55.

Faigley, Lester, Diana George, Ana Palchik, and Cynthia Selfe. *Picturing Texts.* W. W. Norton, 2004.

Fishman, Jenn, Andrea A. Lunsford, Elizabeth McGregor, and Mark Otuteye. "Performing Writing, Performing Literacy." *College Composition and Communication*, vol. 57, no. 2, 2005, pp. 224–52.

George, Diana. "From Analysis to Design: Visual Communication in the Teaching of Writing." *College Composition and Communication*, vol. 54, no. 1, 2002, pp. 11–39.

Haven, Cynthia. "The New Literacy: Stanford Study Finds Richness and Complexity in Students' Writing." Interview of Andrea Lunsford. *Stanford Report*, October 12, 2009. http://news.stanford.edu/news/2009/october12/lunsford-writing-research-101209.html.

Hocks, Mary E. "Understanding Visual Rhetoric in Digital Writing Environments." *College Composition and Communication*, vol. 54, no. 4, 2003, pp. 629–56.

Jewitt, Carey, and Gunther Kress. Introduction. *Multimodal Literacy*, edited by Carey Jewitt and Gunther Kress, Peter Lang, 2003, pp. 1–18.

Kist, William. *The Global School: Connecting Classrooms and Students around the World*. Solution Tree, 2013.

Kress, Gunther. "'English' at the Crossroads: Rethinking Curricula of Communication in the Context of the Turn to the Visual." *Passions, Pedagogies, and 21st Century Technologies*, edited by Gail E. Hawisher and Cynthia L. Selfe, Utah State UP, 1999, pp. 66–88.

Leverenz, Carrie. "Remediating Writing Program Administration." *WPA: Writing Program Administration*, vol. 32, no. 1, 2008, pp. 37–56.

Lovitt, Carl, and Dixie Goswami. *Exploring the Rhetoric of International Professional Communication: An Agenda for Teachers and Researchers*. Baywood, 1999.

Lunsford, Andrea A. "Key Questions for a New Rhetoric." *What Is the New Rhetoric?*, edited by Susan E. Thomas, Cambridge Scholars Publishing, 2007, pp. 4–15.

———. "Notes on Visual Literacy." 2 Nov. 2013. http://andrealunsford.com/.

———. "Our Semi-literate Youth? Not So Fast." Nov. 2010. https://ssw.stanford.edu/sites/default/files/OPED_Our_Semi-Literate_Youth.pdf republished 26 June 2013. http://andrealunsford.com/.

———. *Writing Matters: Rhetoric in Public and Private Lives*. U of Georgia P, 2007.

———. "Writing, Technologies, and the Fifth Canon." *Computers and Composition*, vol. 23, no. 2, 2006, pp. 169–77.

Lunsford, Andrea A., Jenn Fishman, and Warren M. Liew. "College Writing, Identification, and the Production of Intellectual Property: Voices from the Stanford Study of Writing." *College English*, vol. 75, no. 5, 2013, pp. 470–92.

Mitchell, W. J. T. *Picture Theory: Essays on Verbal and Visual Representation*. U of Chicago P, 1994.

Myers, Kelly A. "Metanoia and the Transformation of Opportunity." *Rhetoric Society Quarterly*, vol. 41, no. 1, 2011, pp. 1–18.

McQuade, Donald, and Christine McQuade. *Seeing and Writing*. Bedford/St. Martin's, 2000.

O'Brien, Alyssa. "Global Citizenship and the Stanford Cross-Cultural Rhetoric Project." *Journal of the National University of Singapore Teaching Academy*, vol. 1, no. 1, 2011, pp. 32–43.

O'Brien, Alyssa, and Anders Eriksson. "Cross-Cultural Connections: Intercultural Learning for Global Citizenship." *Locating Intercultures: Educating for Global Collaboration*, edited by Mara Alagic and Glyn Rimmington, MacMillan, 2010, pp. 29–50.

O'Brien, Alyssa, and Christine Alfano. "Connecting Students Globally through Video-Conference Pedagogy." *Journal of Online Learning and Teaching*, vol. 5, no. 4, 2009, pp. 675–84.

———. "Tech Travels: Connecting Writing Classes across Continents." *Transnational Writing Program Administration*, edited by David Martins, Utah State UP, 2015, pp. 48–71.

Pratt, Mary Louise. "Arts of the Contact Zone." *Profession*, vol. 91, 1991, pp. 33–40.

Schjeldahl, Peter. "Words and Pictures: Graphic Novels Come of Age." *New Yorker.* 17 October 2005. Accessed June 2011. http://www.newyorker.com/archive/2005/10/17/051017crbo_books1.

Shipka, Jody. "A Multimodal Task-Based Framework for Composing." *College Composition and Communication*, vol. 57, no. 2, 2005, pp. 277–306.

Wysocki, Anne Frances. "Monitoring Order: Visual Desire, the Organization of Web Pages, and Teaching the Rules of Design." *Kairos*, vol. 3, no. 2, 1998. Accessed 12 June 2002.

Wysocki, Anne Frances, and Dennis A. Lynch. *Compose/Design/Advocate: A Rhetoric for Integrating the Written, Visual, and Oral.* Longman, 2006.

Yancey, Kathleen Blake. "Made Not Only in Words: Composition in a New Key." *College Composition and Communication*, vol. 56, no. 2, 2004, pp. 297–328.

PUSHING GENERIC BOUNDARIES IN RHETORIC AND COMPOSITION
THREE SITES, ONE READER'S RESPONSE

MELISSA A. GOLDTHWAITE

> Discourses, academic or otherwise, do not remain constant; figures (that is, conventions of discourse) change over time through an accumulation of nuance and inflection. People write. Boundaries blur. We shape language even as language shapes us.
>
> —Thomas E. Recchio, "On the Critical Necessity of 'Essaying'"

What is the expected ethos for a writer of academic discourse? How does a writer's choice of form, stance, and style shape and position audience—and affect reader response? What do experimental forms do for readers of academic prose? In this essay—constructed, in the spirit of this inquiry, in a hybrid of traditional academic writing and an alternate style and form—I visit three sites of published work in the field of rhetoric and composition from which writers "push against the boundaries of what is acceptable in traditional academic discourse, bringing in personal experience, colloquial language, other languages and dialects, and direct address" (Lunsford, *Writing Matters* 31). Although I have drawn these examples from the past three decades of publications, I do not present them in chronological order but, rather, in a continuum of genres arranged from the traditionally informal to formal: comment and response, the pedagogical essay, and the research report. When a writer chooses to push against the traditional generic conventions that usually mark these forms of academic writing, he or she may risk being dismissed or not taken as seriously, but stylistic play and expanded options for presenting oneself, one's ethos, can also help audiences engage new questions or see what was once familiar in a new way.

SITE ONE: COMMENT AND RESPONSE–HE SAID, SHE SAID

Two pieces in the Reader Response section of the 20.2 volume of *JAC* (2000) illustrate in a microcosmic way the pushing of traditional generic boundaries in academic discourse: Cynthia Selfe's "To His Nibs, G. Douglas Atkins—Just in Case You're Serious about Your NotSoModest Proposal" and G. Douglas Atkins's "Art and Anger—Upon Taking up the Pen Again: On Self(e)Expression." This exchange pushes the boundaries of what counts in academic discourse as an acceptable tone (both Selfe and Atkins make use of direct address, name-calling, hyperbole, and colloquial language), and it brings to the forefront questions concerning what methods and tools a writer should use.

The Message, the Medium, and the Valuing of Work: Selfe's Response to Atkins

> I am tired of essay writers who think that all the strength and vigor and pain of language could ever be contained in a single genre, in one holy form, in one blessed medium. That's nuts."
>
> —Cynthia L. Selfe, "To His Nibs, G. Douglas Atkins—Just in Case You're Serious about Your NotSoModest Proposal"

In "To His Nibs, G. Douglas Atkins—Just in Case You're Serious about Your NotSoModest Proposal," Cynthia Selfe responds to, or more accurately rails against, Atkins's personal essay "On Writing Well; Or, Springing the Genie from the Inkpot: A Not-So-Modest Proposal" published in the 20.1 issue of *JAC*. In his essay, Atkins lays out five beliefs he holds strongly: "Writers know best how to write"; "writing workshops are the best place to learn both how to write and how to teach"; "we write best about what we know firsthand and what we care about"; "writing students should be reading"; "rather than composition theory or textbooks," they should "read Cynthia Ozick" (74, 75). Simply put, Atkins wants students to read and write essays (a particular kind and class of essay—"mellow" and "beautiful" are his tastes), to be taught (if they should be taught at all, and on this point he's ambivalent) by writers, and he wishes to argue the following points: "that with which you work, your tool, your implement, your writing instrument matters" (76), and "the pen is the instrument by which writing is best made" (77).

If Atkins were just a man fancying his pens, his essay might seem quaint but not necessarily offensive; however, in the course of penning his point, he does offend, pitting his understanding of "good writing" against the writing that he finds in composition theory and textbooks. In praising William Zinsser's writing, Atkins states,

> Being so readable, it is quite unlike the weighty rhetorics, monstrous "readers," leaden "composition books," and arcane writings about writing, composition theory, culture and composition—what you have to slog through these days and somehow know about if you're going to teach writing. . . . With some exceptions, these ponderous tomes are as unhelpful as they are unreadable, examples of how *not to* write in the guise of teaching how *to* write. (74)

This statement appears in *JAC*, a journal whose audience is largely composed of composition teachers and theorists, an audience of people who teach and write the books he, without specific example, disparages. What's puzzling about Atkins's critique (as well as his counsel—"rather than composition theory or textbooks, let them read Cynthia Ozick" [75]) is that composition readers and textbooks do contain the types of essays Atkins admires. And as Lynn Z. Bloom's research on the essay canon indicates, composition classrooms are one of the few places in the academy where essays (particularly the kinds Atkins admires—though those are certainly not the only kinds of essays that have value) are actively taught and seen as model forms of writing.

In his essay, Atkins is not just pointing his pen at compositionists, but also at computers. He implies, through a quotation by Barry Hannah, that those who write with word processors write generic prose (76); he assumes that Cynthia Ozick could not have crafted the "glorious sentences" he quoted of hers "with anything but a pen" (78), and claims that "the computer breeds prose neither comely nor muscular" (81). Even in his litotic attempt not to "bash the computer," Atkins makes his disdain quite clear:

> Although I am computer-illiterate and blissfully so, I admit that the computer is not without value. On occasion I have encouraged offspring, friends, even students to expedite my quest for books through our labyrinthine library system or from Amazon.com. And although I have not

> (yet, at least) advanced to the point of dictaphone as intermediary for my hieroglyphics, I've certainly reaped the benefits of Lori Whitten's [his secretary's] skill in using WordPerfect. (77)

For Atkins, it seems, the value of the computer rests solely in its convenience as a tool for his offspring, friends, and students to use to secure books for him, or for his secretary to use to type for him. Consider Cynthia Selfe's response.

She's *mad:*

> I am tired of pissing contests.
>
> I am tired of literary scholars and nonfiction writers who scorn composition teachers.
>
> I am tired of blusterers who pronounce prose written with the pen to be purer, more finely crafted, more "comely" than the words and images created on a computer screen. (405)

Apparently, Selfe couldn't care less about the "comeliness" of Atkins's words: "You give good words, G. Doug. But your heart is small and your mind is dark" (406).

Comeliness—with its connotations of beauty, delicacy, seemliness, and decorum—won't allow Selfe to word process her response; she needs words like "cool," "stink," and "diss" to confront what she terms Atkins's "terminal elitism" (408); "You must think you're better, G. Doug. You must think you're superior" (406). She turns the superiority around, confronts Atkins with his own implements: "you Levenger man, you nib licker, you essay pimp" (408).

To support her claims, Selfe draws attention to those teachers, writers, and students who are left out of Atkins's constructed world of pen-loving privilege, those who operate "outside the field of [his] not-so-modest vision" (409). In using examples of her own colleagues, friends, and students—Randy Freisinger, Marilyn Cooper, Anne Wysocki, Vicki Crenshaw, Zhigang Wang, Nancy Barron, and others—Selfe advocates not one genre, but many; not one literacy, but many; not one tool, but many (408, 409). And in this cry for multiplicity, Selfe commands: "Keep your pens and your essays. Move the hell over" (412).

And then she apologizes.

No more G. Doug. Now "Professor Atkins." And the claim that she is not writing to him but in response to his proposal and the collective strains of established scholars—usually, but not always, men; usually, but not always, literary scholars—who imply that the work composition teachers do, with or without computer technology, is work to be dismissed, work that is done better, done smarter, by literary scholars or nonfiction writers or just about anyone else. (413)

The coda, an apology and explanation, doesn't take away the sting of words already written. But it does provide a broader context for the response: collective strains of dismissal, a devaluing of work. Selfe's response brings up questions concerning what types of work are and should be valued in the academy. Her call for multiplicity encourages readers to think about the ways the form of her response makes an implicit argument about the range of forms that can be used productively in differing settings. (What expressions of anger, beyond the veiled anger of condescension, are acceptable in academic settings?) And her response also brings up questions concerning the boundaries of what can be named "good writing": who defines what it is and can be?

Atkins states that Selfe's "greatest indulgence" appears in her "embrace of, shall I say, *free prose*" (418–19). And while he marks Carole Maso's "Rupture, Verge, and Precipice / Precipice, Verge, and Hurt Not" (Selfe's model for response) as more successful than Selfe's piece, he does not know how to categorize it; he refers to Maso's piece as a prose poem and then qualifies that categorization with the parenthetical "(I suppose that's what it is)" (419). The qualifications—"shall I say" and "I suppose"—display a kind of disdain, the very disdain that seems to provoke Selfe's anger.

Atkins Pens "On Self(e)-Expression"

> What I object to is not experimentation per se . . . but indulgence, although experimentation with genre succeeds only when one is thoroughly familiar with, and sufficiently skilled at, the form being pushed to its boundaries.
>
> —G. Douglas Atkins, "Art and Anger—Upon Taking up the Pen Again: On Self(e)Expression"

In "Rupture, Verge, and Precipice / Precipice, Verge, and Hurt Not," Carole Maso writes, "You think me unladylike. Hysterical. Maybe crazy. Unreadable. You put me in your unreadable box where I am safe. Where I am quiet. More ladylike" (165). It seems only appropriate to begin a discussion of Atkins's response to Selfe with a quotation from the essay that Selfe takes as her model and inspiration, for Maso's words seem to foreshadow Atkins's response. He appears shocked by Selfe's response, "a piece full of phrases that [he finds] uncivil, offensive, and unquotable" (414). And disconcerted: "Never before have I encountered such vituperation, replete with name-calling, as disfigures Selfe's piece" (415). But due to the public, sometimes violent, nature of the comment / response format, he cannot put Selfe or her response in the "unreadable box." He can, however, mark both Selfe and her response as suspect:

> Although tempted, I will not speculate on any personal problem, apart from the obvious anger, that prevails in the Selfe-expression—a Freudian might have a field day! The lack of control spilling out into the opening sentence deteriorates soon into gratuitous name-calling. But, of course, the greatest indulgence appears in Selfe's embrace of, shall I say, *free prose.* (418–19)

In the "perennial struggle (or warfare)" of comment and response, Atkins declines pacifism (415). He, in an interesting rhetorical move, enlists—through his use of sources—an army of feminist writers to support his points: Jeanette Winterson, Jane Tompkins, Virginia Woolf, and others. He writes, for instance, "Winterson's fondness for signed first editions resonates with the passion for pens I share with writers and collectors" (417). And a paragraph later, Atkins quotes Winterson's comments on T. S. Eliot's work, observations about self and poetry, and he claims—without detailing the connections—these "asseverations apply directly to Selfe" (417). Seeking to contrast Selfe and Winterson, Atkins praises Winterson as a "careful and balanced reader as well as writer," implying that Selfe is neither careful nor balanced (417). Atkins's use of Winterson's work—both in an epigraph and two long quoted sections—is surprising, for the book from which he quotes, *Art Objects: Essays on Ecstasy and Effrontery*, contains words and arguments Atkins might find, as he found Selfe's response, "uncivil and unquotable." Consider the following excerpts:

> No one asks Iris Murdoch about her sex life. Every interviewer I meet asks me about mine and what they do not ask they invent. . . . What is it about? Prurience? Stupidity? And as Descartes didn't say, "I fuck therefore I am."? (104)

and

> Forget the copycat girls who wouldn't know the end of a dildo from a vacuum rod. They are only chintz dipped in mud and we are after real material. What is forbidden is scarier, sexier, unnightmared by the white-collar cataloguers of crap. (114)

I quote these sections not simply to shock, but to draw attention to the ways Atkins's choice of quotations and his use of them—for example, his extending of Winterson's professed love for books to his love for pens—tames

Winterson's work. How would Atkins respond to other sections of Winterson's book, ones that seem more applicable to Selfe's argument and form? For example, how might Atkins incorporate Winterson's discussion of Gertrude Stein, her contention that what Stein was critiqued for was trespassing "gender as well as social niceties and literary convention" (53)? What does he make of Winterson's comment, "Most of what masquerades as literary criticism is a mixture of sexism and self-importance" (53)?

Such accusations of sexism and self-importance are implicit in Selfe's response, and they are criticisms that the many feminists Atkins quotes have made of others at other times. It seems, then, appropriate to acknowledge such critiques rather than to ignore them or to dismiss them by accusing Selfe of being "a wolf in sheep's clothing, the Devil in the self(e), the *soi-disant* oppressed taking on the filthy mantle of the alleged oppressor" (420).

Atkins contends that writers write their character (420), but in the genre Atkins and Selfe are scripting, they write caricatures of others in their attempts to compose themselves. Atkins is angered by Selfe's anger, name-calls her name-calling: "So uptight is the Selfe we find on display" (420); "What we find in Professor Selfe's response is not just anger spilling over and inciting carelessness and error but also the narrowness of which she (falsely) accuses me" (420); "the ways of the self(e) are wily and treacherous, determined and committed ultimately to its own interested ways" (420). The self, or ethos, Atkins seems to value, and at times in his essay composes, is one that is controlled, poised, marked by equanimity. These are the values he attributes to the forms of writing he admires as well.

The back-and-forth wrangling of this comment and response positions readers as witnesses to an argument, pressed either to take sides or to play the role of referee. Or, perhaps, readers find humor in the hyperbolic caricatures. The use of hyperbole and name-calling lessens the possibility of finding common ground, but it also provides an opportunity for readers to consider and question what genres, styles, and presentations of self and others are and should be valued in academic settings. Unlike more controlled academic debates, this comment and response highlights the ways writing is a performance, ethos involves choices, and style can reinforce or undermine one's argument. In making an argument for the benefit of multiple genres, literacies, and tools, Selfe refuses to be confined by the expectation of controlled equanimity. The fact that this exchange was published in a composition journal at the turn of the twenty-first century shows that, perhaps, the field of rhetoric and composition was opening to the very multiplicity Selfe champions.

SITE TWO: THE PEDAGOGICAL ESSAY–TEACHER AS STUDENT

> I think "how-to" or "how-we-did-what-we-did" essays are unfortunately undervalued these days, perhaps because they are often written in a conventional, predictable style. By changing the assumed shape of a how-to essay, I aim to recuperate and open up this genre for your consideration.
>
> —Wendy Bishop, *Teaching Lives*

In 1999 and 2000, I interviewed three writers / teachers / researchers in rhetoric and composition who were pushing against traditional boundaries in their published academic discourse. When I interviewed Nancy Sommers, Lynn Z. Bloom, and Wendy Bishop, I did so with the belief that form constructs audience. As Mary Jo Reiff writes in "Rereading 'Invoked' and 'Addressed' Readers through a Social Lens: Toward a Recognition of Multiple Audiences,"[1]

> "Audience" is an unstable referent, a floating signifier. The term can refer to a construct in the writer's mind—the "imagined," "intended," or "invented" audience. Or it can refer to a textual presence—the audience "implied" by textual cues or "inscribed" in the text. Audiences can also refer to "real" people—the actual readers who exist either apart from and prior to the text (as "addressed" readers) or those who exist as part of the community in which the text is produced.

This complex understanding of audience shaped the questions I asked these three writers. One of the questions was this: "What kinds of readers do you think your work constructs, invites, or hails?" Wendy Bishop seized the question, pointing to a reader who is interested in both style and content. She explains, "I know it has to invite a playful reader, a reader who's not set in linear expectations" (Interview 7/2000). She continues, reflecting on being a reader of her own work, saying,

> When I go back and read some of my stuff, I'm surprised by the person that's there sometimes. I am embarrassed about gaps and leaps I've made. Some of them are when I've lost attention; some are because I'm trying stuff that I can't quite pull off. And so I see those seams. And I'm pretty sure some of those seams show in my texts because I know those are the things that irritate certain reviewers.

Bishop discusses the constructed reader in her texts by both positioning herself as reader (one surprised by the constructed writer) and by drawing from the responses of actual readers (in this case reviewers), illustrating the connections among different audiences. She then reflects on her process of writing as a way of anticipating the kind of reader hailed by her texts: "It's not like I get more fluency in a text and it gets more and more seamless. It seems like the more I write about sentences and structure, the more excited I am as a writer to try to push those things. So, the ride is bumpy. So, people have to be willing to have a certain kind of bumpy ride." She expresses a desire to be in conversation with readers, saying, "If they'll just hold on and go with me, we'll hopefully get there by the end of the piece." As she reflects on her writing, Bishop points to a constructed reader who is willing to give, but who also gains something in return: "And what I hope they get back is a constructed voice that's doing surprising but interesting things."

Bishop recognizes that readers bring differing expectations to texts, acknowledging that someone "who wants a kind of certainty in the text and an authority" might be irritated by her style: "Sometimes I think it looks intentionally sloppy. Sometimes I think it looks superficial." As she teases these connections between production and reception, she looks away, as if trying to think things through, then talks more about her style and goals for writing, the textual features evident in her texts. She then circles back to my question: "So what would that reader be? Oxymoronically, really serious but not really serious. I'm deadly serious about what I'm doing, but I don't want us all to feel serious." She pauses and looks at me. "Does that make sense?" she asks, then laughs; "You have to say 'yes.'"

In order to explore the ways constructions of readers enable particular kinds of writing and response and inhibit other ways, I present a reader response to one of Bishop's pedagogical essays. Her use of form invokes and positions a particular kind of reader, encouraging pedagogical reflection. Even as I make this claim, however, I recognize that reading experience is not fully determined by the text and encourage others to reflect on their own processes of reading in order to better understand the complicated ways form positions readers and readers position themselves in relation to form.

In "Grammar Test: A Personal Look at the Problem(s)," Bishop enacts through form the pedagogy she values, inviting readers to reflect on pedagogy as well, to consider their own values as teachers, writers, and readers. Her essay, written as a test in a question / answer format, started as an invited talk for a TA training class at the University of Long Island. Bishop asked the organizers of the event what they would like her to talk about; she explains,

> They told me that, because they have a lot of basic writers, one of their concerns was teaching grammar and basic writing. . . . And it kind of made me freak out because I didn't really want to talk about grammar. And I didn't in any way think of myself as a specialist to talk about grammar. (Interview, July 2000)

In reflecting on the form she chose for the essay, Bishop comments, "I think it came from panic over having to give a talk"; as well, she wanted her audience to write about the issues, so the question / answer format was useful. In preparing the talk, Bishop started with a basic principle she learned from one of her professors, Pat Hartwell: that it's possible to make anybody a basic writer. She tells me that "any time you're taking exams, you're like a basic writer," so in this sense, too, she used form—a test—to position her readers and to support her argument.

The reading of "Grammar Test" I offer here is one more attentive to the questions Bishop asks than to the answers she provides. In this reading, I take seriously the invitation Bishop presents toward the end of her piece: "I trust you will examine your own grammatical and ungrammatical past in order to tell your stories, explore your test results, undertake your own teaching self-evaluations, on the way to helping your students become better writers, and grammatically fluent writers at that" (39). She ends with the questions that structure her essay. I answer these questions here.

> *Please write down your exact response to the words "Grammar Test." What physical response did you have? What memory response?*
>
> I'm in junior high—taller, more developed than the other girls. We write with purple ink, circling the correct answers in our grammar workbooks. The wrong options amuse me, especially "et" instead of "ate." Or "John learned / taught Suzie how to ride a bike." I wonder who would confuse the two. Though I think the exercises are ridiculous, I'm good at them and take some pleasure in being right.
>
> We diagram sentences on the chalkboard. The sentences have no context. We don't pull them from stories, even paragraphs. They have nothing to do with us, but we dissect and label them. It's a form of control: simple, compound, complex. My favorite: compound-complex.

As a writing teacher, I once arrived late for class because I lost track of time in my office while diagramming a sentence for fun.

As an administrator, I observed a college-level business writing class. The day I visited, the teacher handed out punctuation exercises: a sheet on commas and one on semicolons. The class went through the answers sentence by sentence. I thought I was back in junior high, though now no taller than the other students. The exercises still seemed ridiculous, but I still liked being "right."

List the first five rules of grammar that you follow that come to mind.

1. A verb should agree with its subject in number and person.
2. When three or more items appear in a series, they should be separated by commas.
3. Use apostrophes to signal possessive case.
4. Use quotation marks around titles of poems.
5. Use a comma after an introductory clause.

List the first five rules of grammar that you regularly break that come to mind.

1. Don't use contractions in formal writing.
2. Use *who* and *whom* appropriately.
3. Do not place a modifier between *to* and the verb of an infinitive.
4. No fragments.
5. And don't begin a sentence with a conjunction.

List three ways you've tried to teach grammar and the results of each.

1. A quiet blonde always sat in the second row of my forty-five person introduction to poetry class. Her papers were mostly strong in terms of argument, but they were riddled with grammatical errors. On her first paper, wanting to encourage her, to draw her out, I wrote nearly all positive comments. I also marked patterns of grammatical error (narrowed them to three concerns) and tried to mention delicately in my end comment that she might want to be attentive to these concerns on her next paper. Still wanting to encourage, I gave her an overly generous A-, thinking she'd be relieved. The day

I returned the papers, she stayed after class, red-faced and livid. She wanted to discuss her grade: "You said all good things! Why didn't I get an A?" I agreed to read her paper again. Defensive in my rereading, I started counting errors: seventeen in a four-page essay. I wrote a long letter, explaining in considerable detail not only the patterns of error but each particular error she made. I copied pages from a grammar handbook. I invited her to come and talk with me, not about the grade (that would stand, though I secretly wished I could lower it) but about how to work on these issues. I gave her the phone number for the writing center.

And I lost her in my need to be right.

She sat through the remaining classes with lips pressed tightly together, eyes down. She continued to hand in papers with the same errors. I continued to type long responses to her papers (while the other students received my handwritten comments), rereading my own responses to make sure my tone was controlled and that there were no visible errors in my letter. I gave each subsequent essay a still-generous B+. I stopped writing directly on her papers and, instead, photocopied the originals and my responses. I kept the copies in a folder. She's the one student (okay, maybe there are two or three) I hope never to run into on campus again. If she were the one grading, I have no doubt she'd give me less than a generous B+.

2. After reading and commenting on a stack of drafts, I make a list of the grammatical errors that show up again and again. At the start of the next class, before returning the drafts, I transfer my list to the whiteboard or project it using a document camera. I then go through the list casually, explaining each error and how to correct it. I give an example of each. Maybe half the students take notes; the others stare blankly. Some of the note-takers will hand in new drafts where they've made changes. I'll stare blankly at many of the barely revised drafts, marking the same sentences, transferring my whiteboard list back to individual papers. I'll think of Sisyphus.

3. After I proofread a paper for a friend, she asked me, "Did I make less mistakes this time?"

"You made *fewer*," I answered, laughing.

The next day, I told her, "Ohio State won Penn State in football."

She answered, "They *beat* Penn State?" We go back and forth that way, teaching and learning.

When you're at a party and someone asks what you do and you say "teach writing" and they say, "I never was good at English grammar," what do you think and say?

I think "Oh lord" but say nothing. I smile politely, sometimes change the subject: "And what do you do?" I'd much rather hear about installing fences or selling insurance. It happens more on airplanes than at parties.

But once I was at a party in Florida. Spring break from college, visiting a friend's aunt. Everyone raved over the poached salmon. I hadn't yet learned the art of small talk. When one of the aunt's friends asked me what I liked to read, I answered truthfully: "Annie Dillard and Sylvia Plath." The aunt came up behind me and scolded, "Say someone he knows." I searched for a more appropriate answer: Thomas Hardy?

What is the (socially, rhetorically) appropriate answer to "I never was good at English grammar"?

1. "Me neither."
2. "How did your teachers teach it?"
3. "Too bad the grammar checker on my word processor isn't any good either."
4. "Your grammar sounds fine to me."
5. "Huh. I was never any good at _________ (installing fences, selling insurance, molecular biology, surgery). Guess we chose the right professions."

When was the last time you felt like a basic writer?

Today. I keep writing and deleting sentences.

Please write a sonnet. You have five minutes.

You've got to be kidding. Immediately, I think: Shakespearian sonnet, three quatrains and a couplet (fourteen lines). I know the typical rhyme scheme (*abab cdcd efef*) and meter (iambic pentameter). What on earth does this have to do with grammar? I get Bishop's point: she wants me to feel like a basic writer. I know the rules but just can't implement them to my satisfaction in five minutes. Give me five hours, and I'll give you a sonnet. Is this what it means to be a basic writer? I doubt it. What does grammar have to do with it?

When you read a large pile of student papers and realize that writers in this class, too, are producing writing that has many sentence-level errors, what do you most want to say to: the class, the teacher educator who trained you, the department or university administrator who suggests you / your program is not teaching grammar well enough?

To the class, I want to say, "These are the patterns of error I'm seeing in your papers. What can we do to improve? Which of these issues are you most interested in discussing?" To the teacher educator who trained me: "I use your handbooks almost every day." To the department or university administrator: "Give me the staff, time, and resources to do so, and I will."

What is a gerund?

All I know is this: a gerund ends in *ing*.

Thinking about grammar makes some students crazy. "Thinking about grammar" is a gerund phrase, I think.

What grade do you give yourself as a teacher of writing and why?

B+ because it's the grade I give for good work, significant effort, and room for improvement.

One of the reasons I claim that the form of "Grammar Test" encourages pedagogical reflection is that if asked what I focus on as a writer and teacher, grammar and punctuation would have been on the bottom of my list, for—trained as a writing tutor—I've internalized a hierarchy of concerns:

1. Subject, audience, purpose
2. Organization
3. Paragraphing
4. Sentences
5. Grammar and punctuation

My responses to Bishop's grammar test, however, expose my grammatical concerns. When I respond to student papers, I do mark grammar and punctuation—not to "take off points" or to shame—but simply because the surface matters to me, because there are times I can't get beyond the surface to consider subject, audience, and purpose until I make changes. I mark grammar on students' texts for myself more than for them, so I can read on.

As a teacher, it's useful for me to be aware of my own habits, habits so internalized that they were invisible to me until I compared my own answers to Bishop's grammar test with hers. Because of the form she chose and the questions with which Bishop ends the piece (the same questions that structure the essay), I focus more on my response than her answers to the same questions, and I am reminded:

1. There are productive and nonproductive writing rules, and depending on the setting / situation / piece, these change.
2. Think *grammars* instead of *grammar.*
3. Form is not simply a container for ideas; it's a vehicle. The writer may start in the driver's seat, but sometimes the reader takes the wheel.

SITE THREE: THE RESEARCH REPORT—A FORM FOR COLLABORATIVE PLAY?

There are those special books, articles, songs, or other forms that somehow seem life-changing. Perhaps the timing of the encounter is just right. Decades later, you remember exactly where you were when you heard that song or read that text. Robert Connors and Andrea Lunsford's "Frequency of Formal Errors in Current College Writing, or Ma and Pa Kettle Do Research" is one such article for me. I first read it in December of 1994 when I was a graduate student pursuing an MFA in creative writing. It was this essay—its collaborative playfulness and allusions to (once-) popular culture—that drew me to the field of rhetoric and composition and made me believe in the possibility of collaboration, of creative attention to form in academic discourse, of being simultaneously playful and serious with and about research.

Near the beginning of the article, Connors and Lunsford describe their relationship as both research colleagues and friends: "The labyrinthine project of which this research is a part represents an ongoing activity for us, something we engage in because we like to work together, have a long friendship, and share many interests" (395). They then continue by making a surprising comparison: "As we worked on this error research together, however, we started somewhere along the line to feel less and less like the white-coated Researchers of our dreams and more and more like characters we called Ma and Pa Kettle—good-hearted bumblers striving to understand a world whose complexity was more than a little daunting" (395). Although this comparison has the potential to undermine their position as serious researchers, it, instead, functions as a self-deprecating remark that makes them more likable, demonstrating a sense of humor almost always lacking in research reports.

The depth and specificity of the research project they undertake and the results they present in one of the field's most prestigious journals undermine any comparison to the uneducated—even foolish—characters of the 1940s / 1950s Ma and Pa Kettle film series. Their ethos as researchers is not compromised by this allusion, for Lunsford and Connors then ground their playful approach to form in both classical rhetoric and French literary theory: "Being fans of classical rhetoric, *prosopopoeiale*, *letteraturizzazione*, and the like, as well as enthusiasts for intertextuality, *plaisir de texte*, *differance*, etc., we offer this account of our travails—with apologies to Marjorie Main and Percy Kilbride" (395). With humorous section headings such as "The Kettles Smell a Problem" (395), "Ma and Pa Suck Eggs" (398), and "The Kettles Say, 'Aw, Shucks'" (402), Lunsford and Connors demonstrate not only the pleasure of intertextuality but also the fun of collaboration. They present themselves as "good-hearted bumblers" (395), even as the attention to history and their carefully presented findings show the irony of their playful self-deprecation.

Another way in which this article pushes the boundaries of a traditional research report is in Lunsford and Connors's attention to the material conditions of carrying out large-scale research. They describe the real work of research with a close attention to setting:

> It was a grueling Friday and Saturday. We trained raters to recognize error patterns all Friday afternoon in the dusty, stuffy old English Library at OSU—the air of which Thurber must have breathed, and probably the very same air, considering how hard the windows were to open. On returning to our hotel that night, we found it occupied by the Ohio chapter of the Pentecostal Youth, who had been given permission to run around the hotel giggling and shouting until 3:30 a.m. In despair, we turned our TV volumes all the way up on white-noise stations that had gone off the air. They sounded like the Reichenbach Falls and almost drowned out

> the hoo-raw in the hallway. After 3:30 it did indeed quiet down some, and we fell into troublous sleep. The next day the Pentecostal Youth had vanished, and Ma & Pa had research to do. (401–02)

The background story of research—the frustrations, the humor, the sheer exhaustion involved—is often left out of the report. Perhaps such textual silences help readers focus on the results of the research, but the inclusion of this background information contributes to Connors and Lunsford's ethos; they are researchers, yes, but the process of a large-scale research project is rarely, if ever, smooth. (And how else can a writer get the word "hoo-raw" into *CCC*?)

Two decades later, many years after Connors's untimely death, Andrea and Karen Lunsford undertook a similar collaborative research project. The findings were just as significant as the ones two decades before, but the presentation of that research bore only traces of the earlier playfulness and humor—a nod to the earlier study embedded in the first footnote and a description of the less than glamorous conditions for coding research. Like the opening of the earlier study, the footnote of the later study creates a certain ethos, acknowledging the humor of the 1988 article and the friendship between Lunsford and Connors:

> Connors and Lunsford published several essays resulting from this study, including "Frequency of Formal Errors in Current College Writing, or Ma and Pa Kettle Do Research." This essay, which attempted a bit of humor—a try at what is now called "alternative discourse"—was huge fun to write. The loss of Bob Connors in a motorcycle accident in the summer of 2000 has left the field of what he termed composition-rhetoric without one of its best (and often funniest) spokespersons. We dedicate this essay to his memory. (804)

The "huge fun" of writing "Ma and Pa Kettle Do Research" is presented as a memory, yet within the body of the text of the study published in 2008, there is an echo of the earlier attention to setting; though the coders have changed, their work remains grueling:

> Armed with stacks of coding rubrics, most coders worked in two large classrooms we had reserved; some retreated to their nearby offices; all read at a diligent pace. Occasionally they returned to the conference room, where fresh papers awaited them along with a smorgasbord of snacks, lunch, and the soothing, continuous burble of two Mr. Coffees and one rescued-from-an-attic Mrs. Tea. (791)

The coders who "all read at a diligent pace" as Mr. Coffee and Mrs. Tea burble on seem far more professional than Ma and Pa Kettle turning up the volume on their hotel room TVs to drown out the "hoo-raw" of the Pentecostal youth, yet such attention to setting and sound provides a welcome echo of the earlier study.

Perhaps the most interesting part of Lunsford and Lunsford's 2006 study, at least for the purpose of this essay, is that they found "little evidence of what has come to be called—perhaps in homage to Winston Weathers's charming and important *An Alternate Style*—alternate or alternative discourse" (799). They found, instead, that most of the papers they "examined stuck resolutely to what Weathers dubbed Grammar A: traditional usage, organization, and style" (799). I paused when I read this because I had noticed how Lunsford and Lunsford's 2006 study seemed far more traditional in style and ethos than the earlier Connors and Lunsford study. The results of the later study are no less important, yet—as a reader—I miss the sense of playfulness evident in the earlier research report. Ironically, humor and playfulness may prime readers for reflection on serious topics, making the results of research more memorable.

CONCLUSION

> If we come to composition with options, open-mindedness, adaptability, we not only fulfill ourselves the more but we obviously are capable of giving more to others.
>
> —Winston Weathers, *An Alternate Style: Options in Composition*

Alternative discourses, in and of themselves, are not necessarily better than traditional genres. What Winston Weathers termed "Grammar A" and "Grammar B" depend on one another. That is, one cannot push boundaries if there are none; one cannot disrupt audience expectations if there are none. And disruption is not, in and of itself, productive. Writers and readers need guidance, forms, and expectations; they also—as Weathers asserts—need "options, open-mindedness, adaptability" (55).

Generic expectations in disciplinary discourse can be useful, providing guidance both for composing and for audience response, but they can also be limiting, especially when arguments—whether they're about differences among factions in English studies or about grammar and error—become entrenched. By experimenting with form, ethos, and style—by pushing generic boundaries and engaging in serious play—writers and scholars can expand not only their own rhetorical options and tools but also open up new spaces for reader response, reflection, and appreciation.

No matter what traditional generic conventions usually mark academic forms as diverse as comment and response, pedagogical essays, and research reports, it's possible to push productively against boundaries in all of these genres. Showing adaptability in ethos and tone, a usually kind and measured Cynthia Selfe can boldly and humorously challenge a more traditional position about what genres and tones and tools should be valued in rhetoric and composition. A teacher, like Wendy Bishop, can show through her use of a playful form that teachers also need to be learners—and she can ask the kinds of questions that lead to reflection and understanding. Researchers like Robert Connors and Andrea Lunsford can show the pleasure of collaboration and the not-so-glamorous aspects of research, even as they provide and analyze important data. Although these examples are different in form, style, and ethos, they all show writers and scholars willing to engage in serious play for pedagogical or scholarly purposes, expanding options and genres and expectations for a new generation of writers and scholars.

Note

1. Reiff's article is a response to Lisa Ede and Andrea Lunsford's 1984 article "Audience Addressed / Audience Invoked: The Role of Audience in Composition Theory and Pedagogy."

Works Cited

Atkins, G. Douglas. "Art and Anger–Upon Taking up the Pen Again: On Self-(e)-Expression." *JAC*, vol. 20, no. 2, 2000, pp. 414–26.

———. "On Writing Well; Or, Springing the Genie from the Inkpot: A Not-So-Modest Proposal." *JAC*, vol. 20, no. 1, 2000, pp. 73–85.

———. Personal interview. 29 July 2000.

———. "Places to Stand: The Reflective Writer-Teacher-Writer in Composition." *College Composition and Communication*, vol. 51, no. 1, 1999, pp. 9–31.

———. *Teaching Lives: Essays and Stories.* Utah State UP, 1997.

Connors, Robert J. and Andrea A. Lunsford. "Frequency of Formal Errors in Current College Writing, or Ma and Pa Kettle Do Research." *College Composition and Communication*, vol. 39, no. 4, 1988, pp. 395–409.

Ede, Lisa, and Andrea Lunsford. "Audience Addressed / Audience Invoked: The Role of Audience in Composition Theory and Pedagogy." *College Composition and Communication*, vol. 35, no. 2, 1984, pp. 155–73.

Lunsford, Andrea A. and Karen J. Lunsford. "'Mistakes Are a Fact of Life': A National Comparative Study." *College Composition and Communication*, vol. 59, no. 4, 2008, pp. 781–806.

Lunsford, Andrea A. *Writing Matters: Rhetoric in Public and Private Lives.* U of Georgia P, 2007.

Maso, Carol. *Break Every Rule: Essays on Language, Longing, and Moments of Desire.* Counterpoint, 2000.

Recchio, Thomas. "On the Critical Necessity of Essaying." *Taking Stock: Reassessing the Writing Movement in the 90s*, edited by Lad Tobin and Thomas Newkirk, Boynton / Cook, 1994. pp. 219–35.

Reiff, Mary Jo. "Rereading 'Invoked' and 'Addressed' Readers Through a Social Lens: Toward a Recognition of Multiple Audiences." *JAC*, vol. 16, no. 3, 1996, pp. 407–24.

Selfe, Cynthia L. "To His Nibs, G. Douglas Atkins–Just in Case You're Serious about Your Not-So-Modest Proposal." *JAC*, vol. 20, no. 2, 2000, pp. 405–13.

Weathers, Winston. *An Alternate Style: Options in Composition.* Hayden, 1980.

Winterson, Jeannette. *Art Objects: Essays on Ecstasy and Effrontery.* Jonathan Cape, 1995.

PART 3
THE POLITICS OF RHETORIC, COMPOSITION, AND WRITING IN THE ACADEMY

CITIZENSHIP, RHETORIC, AND PEDAGOGY

GERARD A. HAUSER

The Franklin D. Roosevelt memorial is out of the way, located along the cherry-tree walk on Washington D.C.'s Tidal Basin in West Potomac Park; the memorial does not have an iconic monument to rivet the eye and impose itself on America's collective memory. The Washington, Jefferson, and Lincoln monuments are iconic. Practically every American schoolchild can recognize them and recite the lore that is each president's legacy. Still, the absence of an iconic monument, and the surrounding shade trees that make the site easy to miss, are overmatched by the memorial's distinctive design. The Roosevelt memorial is designed to be experienced and experiencing it is unforgettable.

President Clinton dedicated the site on May 2, 1997, more than fifty years after FDR died. Roosevelt's disability inspired a design that would make the memorial accessible to visitors with impairments. It is spread over 7.5 acres (30,000 square meters), and invites visitors to participate in twelve years of U.S. history by walking through a sequence of four outdoor rooms, each of which contains tactile reliefs with braille writing for those who are blind. It uses metaphors of water, sculptures that depict representative scenes, friezes, and memorable words from FDR's speeches to engage sight, touch, and sound. It places the visitor into moments of Roosevelt's America and, in those places, invites an experience of the American democracy he had enkindled in a beleaguered and embattled nation. It engages its visitors with these Americans' dreams and possibilities.

Perhaps most significant for this experience is the way the memorial commemorates the struggles of ordinary citizens. The site recaptures their dignity through sculptures depicting scenes from the Great Depression. One shows a man listening intently to a fireside chat, another has men bent over with despair waiting in a bread line, a third renders an Appalachian farm couple fallen on hard times standing outside their barn. The memorial also features displays dedicated to public works projects such as the Tennessee Valley Authority, which was essential to the economic recovery of a region lacking affordable electrical power and frequently devastated by floods. The New Deal is widely understood as a series of federal programs intended to stimulate the economy and provide relief to millions of Americans suffering through the Great Depression. Its economic basis notwithstanding, the genius of the New Deal, which is captured by the memorial, was its inspiring sense that Americans owned a stake in their country through performances of public work.

Letters from the public to the president offer eloquent expression of the ordinary citizen's awakened sense of ownership. For example, the public's voluminous correspondence in 1940 regarding whether FDR should seek a third term gives explicit expression to ordinary citizens' sense of earning their own keep. No matter how down and out they may have been, they did not want a handout; they wanted their dignity. They appealed to Roosevelt's sense of noblesse oblige; he was needed because he was the only one who understood their needs, who gave them a voice at the table (Hauser 232–67). These 1940 expressions of Roosevelt's America are of a piece with those contained in Robert McElvaine's collection *Down and Out in the Great Depression* and interviews in Studs Terkel's *Hard Times*. The public's correspondence is remarkable for what it tells us about the importance of having an investment in a nation, about how a citizen understands an obligation and an opportunity to participate and make a difference, about the difference between charity and opportunity, and, through the public's appeals and observations, about what it means to be a citizen.

MODELS OF CITIZENSHIP

Perhaps every age must redefine what it means to be a citizen. Certainly that seems to be a preoccupation of the current age, as it casts about to make sense of issues such as immigration, the obligations and limits of the government as it intersects with the private lives of its citizens, and the obligations and roles of citizens in support of their government. For many in the United States, citizenship is understood as duties, obligations, liberties, and rights. This conception fashions the citizen as meeting obligations to pay taxes and obey the laws, exercising the right to vote, and guaranteed those liberties set forth in the Constitution and the Bill of Rights. It conceptualizes the citizen as a repository of sorts and often leaves him or her in a passive role unless those rights are either challenged by the citizen's relationship with the state, such as through taxes, or through claims by outsiders to the same privileges. Much of the current rhetoric of the Tea Party movement on such hot-button issues as undocumented immigrants and same-sex marriage seems to rest on this conception.

Another understanding, more active in its fundamental modeling of the relationship among citizens, considers citizenship as community engagement. This ideal frames citizenship as exercising an active role in shaping the community, including speaking out to influence public policies; participating in community activities; bringing one's knowledge, skills, and values to bear on public problems; and in general molding the quality of life in the community. Community engagement fashions the citizen as an active agent who considers the social problems of the community to be, at least in part, his or her own; as open to considering the moral issues involved in these problems in order to make informed moral judgments; and as an active participant in helping to address them in a way that helps the community prosper. This model often portrays the citizen as attempting to do good through community service. Citizenship grows from a moral base.

A third model, reflected in the letters written to Franklin Roosevelt by the down and out, fashions citizenship as public work. Political scientist Robert Boyte refers to ordinary citizens as "builders of the commonwealth" (270). This model considers citizenship in terms of public work and represents a different civic tradition, one based on respect for the productive potential of everyone, regardless of income or education. The emphasis is on work, not service. The men and women participating in public work programs, such as the Works Progress Administration and the Civilian Conservation Corps,[1] acted out of practical self-interests, not high ideals. They wanted jobs. But such work also carried a distinctively civic tone. As people made a commonwealth of public goods, they became a commonwealth of citizens, able to apply civic muscle to public projects.

Each age can be defined by a public task. During the Civil War, Abraham Lincoln held that the task was to keep intact one nation "of the people, by the people, for the people." During the 1940s, the great public project was the war against fascism. During the 1960s, it was the struggle to dismantle segregation in the South, expressed in Martin Luther King Jr.'s description of the civil rights movement as "bringing the whole nation back to the great wells of democracy" (14).

Today, our democracy's challenge is to overcome the forces of radical individualism, unbridled special interests, and bitter division along economic and racial lines. These are problems that arise from difference. They define a chasm between large segments of society that develops when each in its own way frames difference as a threat rather than an opportunity. Our struggle is to create a new commonwealth of shared purposes and public goods capable of reducing the threat of difference. Until that happens, disparities of privilege, power, and wealth that rock the possibilities of community will continue to grow. Higher education will play a significant role in meeting this challenge. If that role is to engender a sense of citizenship as producing commonwealth, the graduate and undergraduate rhetoric curriculum will be pivotal to such a project. Indeed, I wish to argue, rhetorical education offers our age its best hope for reducing the threat of difference.

CHALLENGES TO CREATING THE COMMONWEALTH

Creating a commonwealth of shared purposes and public goods is not an easily met challenge. Besides the attitudinal commitments of radical individualism, unbridled special interests, and bitter division along economic and racial lines, this project faces at least four major challenges.

1. *Bowling alone.* At the end of the last century, sociologist Robert Putnam famously argued that the United States was suffering from a state of fragmentation and isolation, which made community difficult to achieve. His catchy label for this societal condition, "bowling alone," reflected the rising number of bowlers in the United States during the waning years of the twentieth century despite the declining number of bowling leagues. Although more people were bowling, they were bowling alone. Putnam argued that we had stopped being a nation of joiners; fewer of us belonged to secondary associations, such as bowling teams and the leagues they comprised. The diminishing contact with strangers that followed made it more difficult to establish civic ties and community relations.

Putnam's thesis, which placed a good deal of blame on the Internet, drew a firestorm of criticism for its denigration of the Internet's virtual communities and for its communitarian bias. However, many of his critics miss the point of Putnam's book, namely that there is no substitute for direct, face-to-face involvement with other members of the community for creating a sense of community, civic obligation, and civic trust, on which community life depends. Although new media may foster widespread networking, in some cases facilitate coordinated activity, and can offer connection to and involvement with far-flung persons and problems otherwise difficult, if not impossible, to attain, virtual communities are no substitute for the demands of time, physical and psychic energy, and modes of appropriate response that pulse through the iterative relations of physical communities where personal involvement in the lives of others throbs in the experience of direct physical encounter of face-to-face exchange.

2. *The problem of trust.* The decline of membership in secondary associations has meant that most people have fewer opportunities to encounter and engage difference than earlier generations of joiners. This goes beyond class to include differences of ethnicity, religion, race, values, and beliefs. Although some younger adults show greater degrees of tolerance for groups previous generations have stigmatized, such as ethnic minorities and the LGBTQ community, the fact remains that once student days end, without membership in secondary associations the circle of interaction contracts to coworkers, neighbors, family, friends, and networked others on social media. Without participation in secondary associations, social circles often lack opportunities for the types of interaction that demand understanding, tolerance, and accommodation of those whose circumstances of life and perspective exhibit significant differences from our own and, in fact, may require sacrifice for a common good. At the same time, the public problems that intersect our lives are seldom confined to our reference group and more often involve individuals and groups who are marked not only by their diversity but also by their mutual dependence.

For example, the health care system in the United States is not really about health and is not a system; it is a chaotic mix of doctors, nurses, insurance and pharmaceutical firms, laws, patients, patents, interests, and lawyers held together by marketplace conditions pertaining to illness. It does not encourage health and actually rewards those who do not take care of their health by attempting to provide "miracle" cures at extraordinary costs that are paid for by insurance companies and, ultimately, the insured who pay premiums. Moreover, when insurance companies refuse to fund exorbitant costs for drugs with limited efficacy, they are vilified by those who have been denied.

The political debate, which focuses alternately on containing costs and the free enterprise system, bears little resemblance to the realities that bear on health and distract from recognizing where mutual dependencies reside. The employee and the employer, for instance, have a shared interest in wellness, which can promote health, increased productivity, and reduced insurance premiums. Although 90 percent of firms employing more than 75 persons have some sort of wellness program, most are of the information-only variety. Only 28 percent of employers offer health risk assessments, with less than half (43 percent) of these offering them annually. Only 42 percent of all employers offer financial incentives and disincentives to promote good health. Relatively few employers offer comprehensive workplace programs to promote health and of those that do the average expenditure is sixty dollars per year per employee compared to forty-three hundred dollars per employee spent for annual health insurance premiums (Duncan 246). Instead, the debate centers on differences, with political parties caricaturing each other as socialists and profit mongers. How can citizens deliberate, much less have dialogue, with those whose values, beliefs, and goals seem so antithetical to their own?

The emphasis on difference over mutual dependence has contributed to our society's endemic distrust of those who are different.[2] Writing in the 1920s, John Dewey diagnosed the problem of the public as its proliferation and fragmentation. Dewey thought publics were too finely differentiated by special interests of region and class leading to too many publics for the voice of the people to have a meaningful impact on the state. The proliferating stress on identity politics over the past fifty years has only exacerbated our sense of difference and distance between our beliefs and those of others we perceive as different from us, and our suspicion that these differences are irreconcilable. It is difficult to have vibrant debate with partners whose values and objectives are framed as irrevocably at cross-purposes with our own and to build community with them when we seem to share little in common. When recognition of mutual dependency is trumped by emphasis on difference, it is difficult to pursue solutions that will depend on trust for them to succeed. With a loss of trust in those who are our deliberative partners has come a loss of trust in the process of public deliberation as a means for resolving public problems (Hauser and Benoit-Barne).[3]

3. *Missing face-to-face associative structures.* In the not-so-distant past we had structures of secondary associations that fostered interaction with strangers in face-to-face contexts. Participation in church, community, leisure, and volunteer groups, among others, allowed us to encounter those

with whom we might otherwise have never come in contact and to share an activity of mutual interest. Importantly these were face-to-face contexts of interaction, which facilitated taking advantage of opportunities to socialize with these otherwise strangers. Quite apart from the expressed purpose of these associative structures, the opportunities they offered to socialize with new acquaintances served the important function of taking the threat out of difference. Through sociality, people learn of the interests and life circumstances they share in common. For this awareness to occur among those who are dissimilar from one another requires structures that bring people together and encourage social interaction. When we have countervailing information of likeness, difference is framed as but one feature among many that defines the Other. Interacting with difference helps us establish trust. Regrettably, these structures are in decline. The proliferation and power of virtual communities is undeniable, as is witnessed by the role of the web and blogs in the United States during the 2008 Democratic presidential primary and then the national presidential election,[4] or, more recently, the use of tweets by Donald Trump during the 2016 presidential campaign and his presidency to control the news cycle in ways that also energize his base. But these communities tend to be of the like-minded; blogs may root out and banish interlopers; and each, along with 140-character tweets, arguably, tend to intensify difference as threatening.

4. *Missing contexts for trustworthy acts.* To develop a sense of being a stakeholder in something larger than ourselves and making a difference because of what we can contribute, we need a context in which trustworthy acts can be performed for the greater good. In an earlier publication, Chantal Benoit-Barne and I identified five defining characteristics of trust.

1. Trust surfaces in conditions of uncertainty. If one knows for sure, one does not need to trust.
2. Trust emerges in situations in which a choice between alternatives is required.
3. To trust one must rely on beliefs about others to form expectations about their behavior and use these expectations to make choices.
4. To trust one must rely on the familiar to anticipate the unfamiliar in the sense that one uses the available repertoire of experiences to form expectations.
5. Trust relationships are self-stabilized by establishing an obligation to honor trust.

These characteristics suggest two important dimensions of trust germane to this discussion. First, there must be contexts in which we are compelled to collaborate with those who are, in some important way, strangers to us. Whether the salient aspects of strangeness are cultural, ideological, racial, or economic, if we never find ourselves in collaborative contexts with strangers, distrust of difference, and therefore the threat it poses, cannot be addressed, much less overcome. Second, the conditions of trust are based on relationship. Social scientists point out that trustworthiness in relationships with strangers is a reflection of social capital and point to social structures as the vehicle for creating it. However, the evidence they provide suggests it is the interactions occurring within these structures—the social conversation of formal and vernacular exchanges within civil society—that generate the social capital, on which, in turn, trust depends (see Fukuyama; Gambetta; Luhmann, *Trust and Power,* "Familiarity"; Misztal; Putnam, *Making, Bowling;* Seligman; Warren; and Wuthnow). The evidence points to trust as rhetorically constructed.

These problems pose important questions for generating a sense of citizenship as building the commonwealth: How can we create such contexts for developing trust? What rhetorical skills are developed in these contexts? What role does rhetoric's pedagogy play in developing such citizens? I wish first to elaborate on how participation in secondary associations develops rhetorical skills and then to consider the implications of civic participation for pedagogy.

TRUST AND SECONDARY ASSOCIATIONS: THE ITALIAN STATES

The concept of citizenship as public work entails ordinary citizens becoming involved in their community, which, in turn, entails a sense that their involvement matters. Against the mantra of apathy commonly invoked to describe ordinary U.S. citizens, there is evidence to the contrary. Whether looking at Bellah and associates' classic study of American political values, *Habits of the Heart,* in which ordinary citizens are depicted as wanting a robust public life but lacking a vocabulary of comparable richness as that to describe their private lives, or Karen Tracy's *Challenges of Ordinary Democracy,* published a quarter century later, in which local citizens attending school board meetings hotly contest actions of the board, the teachers, and the views of their neighbors, scholars suggest that ordinary citizens care passionately about local issues and become involved in myriad ways, or at least wish to do so. In this regard, Robert Putnam's less frequently discussed (than *Bowling Alone*) but more enlightening project for a discussion of rhetorical education and capacitating students to practice citizenship as public work is his longitudinal study of the Italian states, *Making Democracy Work.*

The Italian central government had a poor track record of balancing Rome's bureaucratic central administration with accommodations necessary to take account of Italy's considerable regional economic and cultural differences. These same differences also led to a dysfunctional legislature marked by factionalism and filibusters that made legislating problematic if not impossible. In 1970, Italy invoked an overlooked constitutional provision to reorganize the government into fifteen regional councils with legislative and budgetary authority within the constraints of the Italian constitution. In 1975, five additional special regional councils were created. Starting in 1970 and over the next eighteen years, Putnam and his associates conducted interviews with ordinary citizens, political party members, and members of the regional councils to answer the question: "*What are the conditions for creating strong, responsive, effective representative institutions*" (6). They hypothesized that the answer would lie in the extent to which the region had participated in the industrial revolution. Those that were more prosperous would run more responsively and effectively than those that were not. At the conclusion of their fieldwork, however, they found that this hypothesis could not explain the variance between the successful and unsuccessful regions. To their surprise, a better explanation was found in a series of correlations between what I call "rhetorical competencies" and "civic community."

The first finding, later developed in the bowling alone studies, was *a positive correlation between participation in secondary associations and civic involvement.* They found that if people belong to sports clubs, singing societies, literary guilds, philanthropic groups, commercial associations or clubs of any sort, they also show a greater tendency to participation in the civic affairs of the region. Importantly, the relationship has nothing to do with membership in a political party or participation in a political organization. Rather, the positive correlation is with participation in a community activity that gathers citizens who, otherwise, have no reason to congregate.[5] As Putnam notes, a person who participates in secondary associations is more likely to develop skills in cooperation as well a sense of responsibility for collective enterprises (90). In rhetorical terms, these would include such skills as rhetorical sensitivity, audience adaptation, ability to reframe issues, skill at listening to understand the other's point of view, willingness to compromise in order to find reasonable solutions, and means for establishing and sustaining identification.

Secondly, *high civic involvement correlates with a high incidence of newspaper readership, whereas in locales with low involvement the opposite is true.* Since newspaper readers are better informed than nonreaders, they are better equipped to participate in civic discussions. More obviously, people who read newspapers are more likely to discuss what they read, which means they are more likely to raise current civic concerns in their conversations.

Although the intervening 30 years since Putnam's Italy study have seen newspaper readership decline, the proliferation of digital alternatives keeps alive the prospect of ordinary citizens being informed on events that intersect with the community's life. Even if those sources do not have their facts straight, they nonetheless have had an energizing effect on civic conversation. Moreover, while digital news sources also increase the opportunity for and accelerate the distribution of false- or dis-information, which, in turn, can stymie understanding, those facts only underscore the importance of being accurately informed to constructive dialogue.

Here we move into the realm of vernacular rhetoric where local discourse constitutes a rhetorical region of micropractices that extends rhetoric's scope to include the ordinary exchanges of the everyday. We find *vernacular rhetoric* in the interaction within a discourse community that depends on localized knowledge, concerns, meanings, modes of arguments, value schemes, logics, traditions, and the like. These ordinary citizens neither act in any official civic capacity nor have an elite status that offers entrée to established power, yet their everyday discourse can make their views matter on outcomes that affect their civic lives. Elsewhere I have developed in more detail the rhetorical salience of vernacular expression that gives ordinary expression significance beyond mere chitchat (*Vernacular; Attending; Prisoners*). Importantly in this context, it involves the constitution of a dynamic public sphere that is interactive and inclusive of readers, but also points to the failure of pubic spheres to materialize when ordinary citizens are uninformed, misinformed, or dismissive of inconvenient facts. The power of immediate local interests to skew interpretations of counterveiling information, even when pursuing those interests may prove deadly, cannot be underestimated (see Hochshild).

Putnam's data also showed *voter turnout for referenda is higher when the dominant organizational pattern for resolving individual concerns is horizontal, lower when it tends to be vertical.* The reason for this tendency is not difficult to fathom. Talking to peers to resolve concerns, rather than appealing to an authority figure such as the parish priest, produces experience that reinforces confidence in your ability to have a direct effect on the problems you confront. On the other hand, organizing your social life vertically, again by going to the parish priest to get a problem resolved, produces experience that reinforces reliance on an authority figure who has the power to fix things.

This pattern of turning either to peers or to authority figures based on whether the community is organized horizontally or vertically correlates with the outcomes of vernacular rhetorical practices. Everyday discourse is a primary mode of rhetorical influence, forming bonds of identification, fostering communal coordination and concerted action, and constituting a communal world that ascribes meaning and value to persons and events. Those with vernacular fluency share identity as a community, whether they are neighbors, a class, or any other signifying group. *Horizontal* organization calls for a rhetoric that establishes *peer* relationships and requires give and take to reach a commonly acceptable solution; *vertical* patterns rely on the vernacular rhetoric of appeal to a *patron* to solve a problem—priest, professor, parent, political leader, or some other authority figure with power to intervene on the individual's behalf.

The link among vertical or horizontal organizational patterns and voting to "rhetorical competence" and involvement in "civic community" were clarified when Putnam analyzed differences in the quality of talk between citizens in civic communities and those in less civic regions. By exploring who talks to whom (99–107), he found, once again, vertical and horizontal organizational patterns matter. Citizens in "civic communities" do not contact their representatives as much as those in nonrepresentative ones, and when they do make contact, it is to discuss policy rather than patronage. In other words, when citizens are in a "civic community," their associative bonds produce greater confidence in fellow citizens than a political leader to assist in addressing their needs. They develop *trust* in their fellow citizens to obey laws, to act in responsible ways, to be sensitive to legitimate needs. Even in communities where economic, educational, social, and political differentiation is high, Putnam found this to be so. Equally, leaders in regions where there is a "civic community" tend to support grassroots participation, are relatively honest, are predisposed to compromise with their political adversaries. In sum, these communities value solidarity, civic engagement, cooperation, and honesty (82–120). These values emerge through formal and vernacular rhetorical engagements. *These engagements depend on and contribute to rhetorical competencies.*

PUBLIC TRUST, PROFESSING RHETORIC, AND RHETORICAL EDUCATION

The research of Putnam and his Italian colleagues suggests the importance of trust to civic community and, more importantly, to the performance of citizenship understood as public work. Building civic community from the horizontal organization of a region went beyond civic engagement to construct the commonwealth of a political culture. Civic communities that fostered cooperation across differences, that encouraged involvement through actively seeking news, that underscored the significance of voter participation through referenda on important public issues, and that emphasized personal responsibility for addressing public issues through informed discussion and deliberation produced the commonwealth of shared norms and basic competencies essential to a vibrant public sphere. Finally, this research suggests that building commonwealth requires rhetorical competencies that engender trust and, moreover, that trust is a rhetorical construction. I wish now to take up the relation that pedagogy in rhetorical studies bears to citizenship modeled on production of commonwealth.

Putnam's study of Italy's regional governments points to civic communities' critical need for contexts in which trustworthy acts can occur. Among existing structures that can serve in this capacity, colleges and universities stand out as places where (mostly) young adults develop basic attitudes and skills that can contribute greatly to a sense of citizenship as public work. Traditionally, universities have played an important part in developing a sense of student responsibility through their many organizations, which are student governed and which have budgets to assist in achieving their missions. Student organizations also must perform myriad communication tasks from group meetings to publicity to engaging the university community in actions supportive of a collective goal. They involve negotiations over means and ends, including several levels involving budgets. They are hotbeds of secondary associations—structures that emphasize diversity, and set rewards and penalties that are linked to rhetorical skill in dealing with difference, including community sanctions when their actions and / or advocacy are decidedly unaccommodating of difference.

Rhetorical education is central to capacitating our students in this regard. By helping them to develop rhetorical competence, rhetorical education also plays a major role in helping students understand civic responsibility, act responsibly, and, we hope, grow in performances of citizenship as public work. This claim may seem a traditional bromide that repeats a shared value among those who teach rhetoric. However, teaching and learning rhetoric occurs in a number of contexts that belie the simplicity of obvious claims about studying how rhetoric capacitates students for citizenship, or what an instructor is doing when teaching rhetoric, and can modify understanding of how rhetorical education and citizenship are linked.

Rhetorical education begins in a civic context in which the problem of trust extends to the professoriate. The profession of professors is to profess and, as every other profession, requires public trust. This need exists not just in public education, where citizen trust can have consequences for public financing, but beyond that to the social capital of the professoriate at large as a voice of knowledge on public issues.[6] The relation of trust to a profession is not something we normally invoke to explain what any given profession is, but its essential relationship to the profession becomes evident when trust fails, such as in law, medicine, or accounting. Our trust is that law, medicine, or accounting will regulate itself without regard for its practitioners' private gain and in a way commensurate with the public good. Quite apart from disciplinary norms, which set standards for research, tenure and promotion, selected course contents, and even curriculum in some cases, professors also must meet norms of *civic professionalism,*[7] which entails public trust.

Civic professionalism borrows norms from medicine and engineering: *do no harm* and *is it safe?* It also has a third norm: *advance the public good.* Civic commitment is not an inherent part of the disciplines; it comes from regard for the intersection of disciplinary practices with the well-being of those in the larger communities they touch. Whether and how we accomplish this end is very much a matter of education, which raises a central dilemma of contemporary rhetorical studies. We seem to be caught in that institutional form of schizophrenia I first experienced as a graduate student at Madison, where rhetoric was not only taught, but also where it was taught with the expectation that those in its graduate program were being prepared for the role of sustaining and advancing the rhetorical tradition within the discipline, in the academy, and in society. As I have argued elsewhere, the question was, which tradition, precisely, were we to sustain and advance: that of *paideia*—the tradition of citizenship with roots in Athens, or that of *Wissenschaft*—the tradition of research with roots in Berlin ("Teaching")?

The rhetorical tradition begins with teaching students to speak and write effectively. It shares the Athenian concern with *paideia*—the *formation* of young students by developing their capacity to function as responsible citizens. The goal of teaching for civic virtue was both public and political: instilling *phronêsis* in the student who, as an adult, would require the political skills necessary for a self-governing democracy to function and thrive. Importantly, while Isocrates sought to capacitate his students for responsible political and public action, he acknowledged that this could not be taught directly; civic virtue had to be apprehended. Observing the practice of exemplary leaders, reading important historians, poets, and the speeches of statesmen, and engaging in exercises that brought the student from technique to the *kairos* of *praxis* suited to the demands of the situation were schooling by indirection. The student had to be receptive to these cultural texts, submit to them, and internalize their practical relevance through practice in order to learn what a rhetorical education had to teach. Students had to appropriate the wisdom of "masters" and acquire their own sense for its translation into *phronêsis*. In this model, teachers exist for students.

The Athenian model of educating for *paideia* is at odds with the context in which much, perhaps most, rhetorical (and liberal arts) education occurs today. During the nineteenth century, the German research institute was established with a remarkably different set of goals from those of Athens. It assumed that students would learn well-established and no longer problematical knowledge—the cultural texts—in their secondary education. By contrast, research universities, in Wilhelm von Humboldt's words, "always treat knowledge as an as yet unresolved problem, and thus always stay at research" (cited in Fallon 16). This vision promulgates a bipolar model that stresses two quite different but interrelated enterprises: orderly, disciplined critical research, or *Wissenschaft,* and professional education. The Berlin model establishes a relationship of the student to knowledge and to the teacher based on an apprenticeship that is not focused on the student's personal growth but on the discovery of knowledge. The student aims at learning how to conduct research by asking researchable questions that can produce verifiable answers via repeating the same investigative procedures. Berlin's hallmark is the academic freedom to pursue one's research interest.

At the graduate level, this model seeks to train students to become professionals who will continue to conduct research. At the undergraduate level it emphasizes learning objective facts and acquiring the basic investigative methods of the discipline in order to put them in service to the technical demands of the professions for which students are preparing. *Wissenschaft* provides for critical rigor; professional education prepares for the application of theory to practice. In this model, teachers do not exist for their students.

They are researchers for whom students are needed to help achieve the goals of their research projects. Consequently, their teaching method depends on communicating their results directly to their students in order to keep them focused on the research project, which sits at the center of the students' study, but has little concern for their *formation*. The Berlin model, which came to the United States with the founding of Johns Hopkins in 1876 as its first graduate university, introduced a culture of Enlightenment intellectual values that continues to dominate American higher education, with the PhD degree, a research degree, as normative of excellence.

Although the values of Berlin are at odds with those of Athens, there is no gainsaying its accomplishments, including those in rhetorical studies. We may be especially proud of our intellectual histories, critical studies, and theoretical contributions to knowledge about human discourse and its consequences for society. The dilemma is not one of displacing Berlin within the framework of Berlin, but to restore Athenian values in a way that they can survive in Berlin, which has little concern for the *formation* of the student and has pushed concerns for citizenship to the margins.

Relevance in the World

The relevance of rhetorical studies to civic education depends less on the world understanding the relevance of rhetoric than on students in rhetoric classes learning to think and act in ways that embrace the values of rhetoric—invention, *kairos*, using language for identification and influence, resolving problems through effective communication, establishing agency, and so forth. Citizenship as public work starts with change agents—we hope our students—who are rhetorically competent, which means that gaining competence in rhetoric first needs to be relevant to our students as a way of thinking and doing before it can be made relevant as a way of being in the world.

For our pedagogical practice to live up to the ideals of civic responsibility, we can start to address this dilemma of an Athenian discipline situated in Berlin-like institutions by recalling that rhetoric is a practical discipline. It alone among the liberal arts has not abandoned praxis for the exclusive pursuit of theory and critique. Commitment to praxis is important because it continues to define the discipline as practical, as a discipline concerned with doing as central to human experience. It also means that rhetorical pedagogy has an abiding concern for how rhetoric is practiced in public life. Yes, it is true that communication generally and spoken and written communication specifically are not exclusively concerned with public life, but it also is true that citizens engage one another through public life, which is inherently a rhetorical engagement. Finally, the practical character of rhetoric also significantly shapes our pedagogy. The great writings of Greek and Roman antiquity that addressed rhetoric instruction—Isocrates, Cicero, Quintilian, even Plato's dialogues in opposition—were predicated on the assumption that students learned by doing.

We still share that assumption, and our instruction is informed by classical principles of rhetoric insofar as our pedagogy stresses *experiential learning*. This was an informing element in the apprenticeship of a student to a person of accomplishment (recommended by Isocrates) as well as the use of *suasoriae* and *controversiae* in the ancient Roman schools. The use of experiential learning then and now recognizes that rhetoric is not another form of philosophy or literary criticism, that students internalize its theory—a practical theory—not only through practice but also by observing the theory manifested in practice. An experientially based pedagogy involves more than experiencing the text. It also involves experiencing *action*—performances in the world that have productive power to initiate, sustain, and transform human reality. In the context of citizenship, this is the experience of producing commonwealth.

Modest Proposals

I have three modest proposals for beginning to restore Athenian values in the research university and to center rhetoric in capacitating our students for citizenship as public work. I will paint them in broad strokes.

First, and perhaps foundational, we must *rethink the professional part of graduate education* in rhetoric to reclaim rhetoric's tie to citizenship and its identity as one of the practical liberal arts—a process that is already under way in a number of programs.[8] Rather than adapting graduate preparation in rhetoric entirely to higher education's prevalent model of *Wissenschaft*, wherein rhetorical education loses its distinctive union of theory and practice and risks coming under fire for being no more than "research lite," I suggest we pay conscious attention to developing programs of study that emphasize the theory / praxis union. In order to recenter rhetorical studies on *paideia*, we must prepare future members of the professoriate to teach courses and perform research concerned with *paideia*. This may be as simple as, at one end, including public advocacy as part of the courses our graduate students take and teach to, at the other, more formal preparation through broadening their understanding of theory to include viewing the rhetorical situation as theory producing (rhetoric and composition has much to teach communication here). In line with attention to rhetorics' role in building public work, a broadened understanding of theory must ensure that our graduate students' understanding of rhetorical materials includes the voices of vernacular rhetoric and the data disclosed by ethnography in addition to exemplary expressions that nurture skill in reading and models for performing citizenship.

Second, we need to *expand opportunities for graduate and undergraduate students to engage in public rhetoric.* For example, in the University of Colorado Boulder's Introduction to Rhetorical Theory course—a most Berlin-like offering enrolling 75 to 150 undergraduates—I have used the city-as-text assignment for the students' semester project (see appendix). City-as-text asks students to analyze the rhetoric of a local issue in light of our city's rhetoric about itself. They discover that local rhetoric, of Boulder in our case, inflects public discussion in ways unique to the community. *Phronêsis* and *kairos* in Boulder are not identical with that in their hometowns. Early on I discovered that students were more eager to advocate than analyze. To get them back on track, I changed the assignment to require that they use their analysis as the basis for crafting a public appeal to an official, governance body, local media, or some other audience that matters in shaping public policy.

Equally, and beyond the model of community involvement afforded by civic engagement or other courses that link to a community partner—an expert practitioner—rhetoricians might bring their expertise to community workshops that meet the rhetorical needs of various groups and connect these workshops with undergraduate courses. A good example is Stephen Hartnett's communication workshops taught in prisons, where student prisoners are writing autobiographies and poetry and learning to debate. He conducts these workshops with his on-campus students who, in conjunction with his course on "Communication, Prisons, and Social Justice," accompany him to prison each week. According to Harnett:

> One of the real joys of this process is watching the students who go to jail with me become ambassadors back to the campus and community, where they inevitably become advocates for the imprisoned men and women they have come to know and sometimes love. Driven by what they have seen in the prison, these students write stories for local newspapers and blogs; they host events; they testify in class; they quickly become not only better poets and public speakers but excited and tireless activists—going to prison fills them with purpose, it energizes them. (22–23)

Experiential learning of this sort helps students to translate rhetorical concepts into rhetorical practices. They emulate the Isocratic ideal of cultivating *phronêsis* through experience.

Third, we need to give *greater and a different form of attention to the canon of American democracy,* such as the Declaration of Independence, Abraham Lincoln's Gettysburg Address, Susan B. Anthony's "Women's Right to the Suffrage," Martin Luther King Jr.'s "Letter from Birmingham Jail," and so forth, by encouraging students to "submit" to them as living documents on national ideals of citizenship. Asking the student to internalize these texts in new ways and extend them into the present can bring them alive as relevant for present realities.[9] Rather than simply historically interesting statements of who we were, they can connect our sense of ourselves as citizens with that of our forebears, often with new and unanticipated outcomes. The point of such assignments is not to pass an exam but to produce ideas for living. At their core, they are about interpreting who we are as a nation, about how to think old ideas and meanings into new contexts, about their productive power for advancing commonwealth, about cultivating habits of thought that support developing the *paideia* of thinking new meaning when certainty is gone, and about tempering such public thinking with the dicta: *do no harm, is it safe,* and *advance the public good.*

Each of these proposals seeks to advance rhetorical education's trademark as engaging in the *civic professionalism* our country and our students need. I do not claim that instruction along these lines will remove the tension between Athens and Berlin, but it need not lead the student into dazed schizophrenia or into abandoning *Wissenschaft* for *paideia.* Instead, it is true to the ideals of Isocrates and Protagoras, whose goal as teachers of rhetoric was the formation of their students' character as citizens.

Appendix: City-as-Text Term Project

THE ASSIGNMENT

I was introduced to the concept of "city as text" at a workshop on pedagogy sponsored by the National Collegiate Honors Council. Each year NCHC supports an honors semester, which is offered at a host institution and integrates classes on a theme peculiar to the local place. For example, a semester offered at Iowa State University, in Iowa's corn belt, might schedule courses in economics, literature, sociology, political science, and agronomy that focus on food. Students write a final research paper on a topic relevant to the theme that integrates what they have been studying during the semester.

The city-as-text assignment adapts this pedagogy to the rhetoric class. It assumes that each community has local issues and, importantly, local ways for communicating about and dealing with them. A central part of the pedagogy is observation and "critical-incident" reporting. At key points in the semester, students are assigned to venture into the local community (let's say Ames) to observe natural state events related to the problem that is the semester's focus (let's say food) in light of what they are studying in class. The instructor assigns students to observe places, persons, groups, interactions, and events germane to an issue that an individual student or group of students has decided to study for a final project. Students make periodic "incident reports" of specific issue-relevant rhetorical phenomena they have personally observed. These reports ask students to distinguish between observations (what they objectively witnessed), inferences (what they believe was taking place), and interpretations (what they believe to be the significance of what they witnessed). These "incident reports" can become the basis for a final paper that develops a rhetorical analysis of the issue as it plays out on the local scene. The term paper assignment is intended to facilitate conducting focused research at a basic level. It affords students the opportunity to deepen their understanding of rhetoric and to keep their work concrete.

Early on I learned that students tended to slip from analyzing the rhetoric on a local issue to personal advocacy on it. They wanted to take a stand, which was not the purpose of the assignment. However, their personal involvement was a sign that the issue mattered to them, which I wished to encourage, so I included an "advocacy" element. The paper assignment thus became a rhetorical analysis of the City of Boulder in terms of a local issue, to investigate how Boulder communicates messages about itself through the public issues it raises and the ways it addresses them. It also asked them to develop a public advocacy statement on this issue.

All cities have unique meaning communicated through formal and informal means and distinguishing them from one another. A city communicates with formal documents, such as ordinances or development plans or buildings and spaces. And it communicates in vernacular ways through the things that take place there, its neighborhoods and customs, and the myriad enactments of community values. Every city has its own identity in terms of its *civitas*—its way of participating in public life and the civic virtues it extols and that define what it means to be a good citizen. In addition to formal efforts, every city tries to create an impression of its quality of life, community values, economic vitality, and citizen involvement through self-referencing messages that serve as forms of persuasion influencing local impressions of what the city stands for. These vernacular expressions occur in the types of people and businesses a city attracts, its relationship to nature and local natural resources, institutions, organizations, neighborhoods, nightlife, tax structures, the topics that predominate community discussion, and the like. Each of these is part of the city as a text that we learn to read and use as a basis for our understanding of its meaning and our relationship to it.

As Aristotle observed, rhetoric is concerned with the way discourse leads us to form judgments. These vernacular and formal elements of city as text play an important role in this process of arriving at judgment: in the way public issues are framed, deliberated, and resolved. In the case on my campus, the assignment asks students to reveal Boulder's uniqueness as reflected in its public discourse on important public issues (features that lead the rest of Colorado, for instance, to refer to the city as the "People's Republic of Boulder").

CRITICAL INCIDENT WRITING (HANDOUT)

Critical incident writing consists of your observation and analysis of a recent communication event (i.e., it occurred since the beginning of this course, preferably within a week or two of submission) that you personally observed, and that employs concepts developed during the current unit of the course. It could be a public or private transaction, but it must be one that you believe is distinctively informative about how rhetorical behavior influences local citizens and social life. You may use this assignment to further your work on the city-as-text project, but you need not. A critical public incident might include a meeting of a public assembly when it considers an important or controversial matter (e.g., a meeting of the Boulder Faculty Assembly, the Arts and Sciences Council, UCSU, an undergraduate association, City Council, etc.), a public address (e.g., a public statement and public responses on an issue of local significance to social life, such as a press conference or a statement by a concerned citizen before the school board, etc.). It also might be an interaction on the street or at a private gathering that you witness, such as an interaction among two or more individuals (roommate negotiations, department store sales interactions, etc.), or other real-time interactions where influence is being exerted through the management of verbal symbols and in a way that suggests it supports an inference (or at least a strong implication) about how rhetorical behavior influences people and social life. The essential aspects of critical incident writing are (1) that it be of a current communication event that has occurred since the course began, (2) that you observed outside of class, and (3) that you use concepts we are currently considering in the course to guide your remarks.

What is included in critical incident writing?

CIW must include three steps:

1. Describing the incident so that you and any other reader will know what happened
    - Where did the incident occur?
    - What were the important circumstances surrounding this incident that are shaping it: place, occasion, social contexts, time of day, weather, etc.
    - Who were the people (include significant factors that relate to the incident): e.g., their position in relationship to you, their age, occupation, sex, attitudes, behaviors, opinions.
    - What were the circumstances or events that led up to this incident (this helps to provide a context for the reader)?
    - Describe the situation itself. Explain briefly what happened, including the conversations of those involved and the activities that occurred.
    - Emphasize what was said and done during the incident, including anything you did and said.
    - Be sure to explain what was at issue in this incident: was there a problem to be solved, a decision to be made, an action to be taken, a mission to be accomplished, a controversy to be settled, an opinion to be arrived at, an agreement to be reached?
    - What was the outcome of this incident?
2. Analyzing the incident, using a unit concept(s), in terms of its impact on those involved, including you
    - What is the relevant rhetorical concept(s) that applies to this incident?
    - Why do you think the other people behaved as they did during this incident? What were their motives? What were they trying to accomplish?
    - Why did you behave as you did during this incident? What were you trying to accomplish? What would you do the same or differently next time? Why?
    - In terms of the rhetorical features you observed, why do you think things turned out the way they did?
    - Have other incidents like this occurred before in your experience? How did you think and feel about those? Can you generalize about incidents like these?

- Does this incident have any relationship to other things you are learning this semester? Briefly state what you think you have learned from this incident.
- How has your perspective on yourself been changed and / or reinforced? Where do you go from here?
- What other insights or understanding did this incident stimulate? Did any values or goals become clarified for you?

3. Relating the incident to unit concepts, ideas, abilities, and skills
    - What skills or abilities do you think are needed to perform effectively in situations like this one?
    - Did any concepts or ideas guide you during the incident? Do any concepts or ideas occur to you now about the incident? If you were going to assist a person new to such a situation in handling it, what principles would you emphasize?
    - Can you relate any of these principles to your assigned reading? To discussions in the seminar? To conversations with other students?

Notes

1. By 1938, 372,000 women held WPA jobs, while more than three million were unemployed and another two million could not find more than part-time work. There were eighty-five hundred women in the Civilian Conservation Corps before Congress eliminated the women's section in 1937. The WPA and CCC each employed more than three million men at their peak in 1938.

2. A 2010 Pew Research Center survey showed trust in government near record lows, at 24 percent compared to nearly 80 percent in 1960. Given partisan discord, this result is not surprising. More alarming with respect to building commonwealth, trust in others has declined markedly between the 1970s and today among American adults and among twelfth graders, as shown in a study by Twenge, Campbell, and Carter. For example, from 1976 to 1978, 32 percent of twelfth graders agreed "most people can be trusted," but by 2010 to 2012 that figure had sunk to 18 percent. The decline of trust in others among late adolescents is especially alarming because it suggests America is becoming a nation of distrusters. Although the data are too complex to fix the cause for this decline on a single variable, the authors find this decline consistent with "lower concern for others and civic engagement found among Millennials and with the higher individualism among both individuals and the culture in recent years" ("Declines" 10). Interestingly, the data do not support the hypothesis that networking

with others via social media, prevalent among millennials, compensates for their declining physical participation in secondary associations with respect to establishing the social capital on which interpersonal trust depends. See also Clark and Eisenstein.

3. An Esquire–NBC News survey of October 2013 (Dokoupil) offers an ironic proof of the problem engendered by the tone of political rhetoric circa 2013. Although political parties at this time seem irrevocably divided and promulgate a polarizing rhetoric that accentuates division, this survey suggests there is expanding common ground. It showed that despite widespread perceptions among Americans that they are a nation divided, there is growing evidence that a majority of Americans (51 percent) actually share political views that gravitate toward the middle. At the same time, however, the partisan rhetoric of political parties distorts perceptions of public sentiment by extreme representations of issues and opponents that perpetuate an impression of an unbridgeable value gulf that stymies dialogue by making it appear futile.

4. There were exceptions to this. For a discussion of serious Internet deliberation about the vice-presidential candidacy of Sarah Palin in 2008, see Sanprie.

5. The lone exception to this pattern was membership in Catholic church organizations, which, given the institutional authority the church has traditionally held in Italy, carries ideological meaning that tends to encourage a political stance with strong allegiance to the church.

6. A recent *Scientific American* ("In Science We Trust") poll, for example, showed that although Americans trust scientists as a group, trust wanes when it comes to specific topics. Although when not tied to a specific topic, scientists were regarded as trustworthy, when asked about fifteen specific topics within the domain of scientific expertise, respondents were much more ambivalent, regarding scientists as trustworthy on only three. On issues such as stem cells, nuclear power, climate change, the causes of autism, genetically modified crops, and flu pandemics, public trust slides toward neutral.

7. The concept of *civic professionalism* was advanced by Thomas Bender. He wished to reenergize a healthy tension between scholarly work and public needs more common a century ago than today. Civic professionalism is a helpful way for thinking about how universities of the twenty-first century can relate to their publics in terms of the public good of intellectual work. It contrasts with disciplinary professionalism, often detached or even un-public-minded in its impenetrable jargon and isolation from the work of building commonwealth, and often a source of public distrust of scholarly work.

8. Some noteworthy examples include the community outreach dimension of the University of Arizona's doctoral program, work on literacy in learning disabled communities that occurs at Carnegie Mellon, work with rural and farming communities at Arkansas and at Iowa State, specific links to industry and government at Virginia Tech, and the University of Maryland. Also in this vein is the emphasis on digital communication within scientific and technical communities, such as at the University of Minnesota, and expanding embrace of ethnographic rhetoric by doctoral programs offering a specialization in rhetoric, such as at the University of Illinois at Chicago and the University of Colorado Boulder. Too often, however, these programs are associated with the work of a specific faculty member rather than curricular design, which limits their impact and threatens their sustainability.

9. Certain texts are sacred documents of the American political and social experience. My short list includes the Declaration of Independence, Madison's Federalist Paper No. 10, Frederick Douglass's "The Hypocrisy of American Slavery," Lincoln's Gettysburg Address and Second Inaugural, Anthony's remarks after being convicted of voting in the 1872 presidential election, Franklin D. Roosevelt's "First Inaugural," John Kennedy's "Address to the Greater Houston Ministerial Association," and King's "Letter from Birmingham Jail" and "I Have a Dream." The longer list available to the instructor makes selection as dependent on the students' sociopolitical awareness as on course objectives.

Works Cited

Bellah, Robert N., Richard Madsen, William M. Sullivan, Ann Swidler, and Steven M. Tipton. *Habits of the Heart: Individualism and Commitment in American Life.* U of California P, 1985.

Bender, Thomas. *Intellectual and Public Life: Essays on the Social History of Academic Intellectuals in the United States.* Johns Hopkins UP, 1993.

Boyte, Harry C. "Building the Commonwealth: Citizenship as Public Work." *Citizen Competence and Democratic Institutions*, edited by Stephen L. Elkin and Karol Edward Soltan, Pennsylvania State UP, 1999.

Clark, April K., and Marie A Eisenstein. "Interpersonal Trust: An Age-Period-Cohort Analysis Revisited. *Social Science Research*, vol. 42, no. 2, 2014, pp. 361–75.

Dewey, John. 1927. *The Public and Its Problems.* Swallow, 1954.

"Distrust, Discontent, Anger and Partisan Rancor: The People and Their Government." Pew Research Center. 18 April 2010. http://www.people-press.org/2010/04/18/about-the-survey-10. Accessed 9 Feb. 2015.

Dokoupil, Tony. "The New American Center: Why Our Nation Isn't as Divided as We Think." NBC Politics on NBCNEWS.com. 15 Oct 2013. http://nbcpolitics.nbcnews.com/_news/2013/10/15/20960588-the-new-american-center-why-our-nation-isnt-as-divided-as-we-think. Accessed 5 Dec. 2013.

Duncan, Ian G. *Managing and Evaluating Healthcare Intervention Programs.* ACTEX, 2008.

Fallon, Daniel. *The German University.* Colorado Associated UP, 1980.

Fukuyama, Francis. *Trust: The Social Virtues and the Creation of Prosperity.* Free P, 1995.

Gambetta, Diego. "Can We Trust Trust?" *Trust: Making and Breaking Cooperative Relations*, edited by Diego Gambetta, Basil Blackwell, 1988, pp. 213–37.

Hartnett, Stephen. "Speaking with the Damned: Prison Education, Social Justice, and Communication as a Human Right." Public Address Conference, Pittsburgh, PA. 2 Oct. 2010.

Hauser, Gerard A. *Vernacular Voices: The Rhetoric of Publics and Public Spheres.* U of South Carolina P, 1999.

———. "Teaching Rhetoric, Or Why Rhetoric Isn't Just Another Kind of Philosophy or Literary Criticism." *Rhetoric Society Quarterly*, vol. 34, no. 3, 2004, pp. 39–54.

———. "Attending the Vernacular: A Plea for an Ethnographical Rhetoric." *The Rhetorical Emergence of Culture*, edited by Felix Girke and Christian Meyer, Berghahn Books, 2011, pp. 157–72.

———. *Prisoners of Conscience: Moral Vernaculars of Political Agency.* U of South Carolina P, 2012.

Hauser, Gerard A., and Chantal Benoit-Barne. "Reflections on Rhetoric, Deliberative Democracy, Civil Society, and Trust." *Rhetoric and Public Affairs*, vol. 5, 2002, pp. 261–75.

Hochschild, Arlie Russell. *Strangers in Their Own Land: Anger and Mourning on the American Right.* New Press, 2016.

"In Science We Trust: Poll Results in How You Feel about Science." *Scientific American*, Oct. 2010. http://www.scientificamerican.com/article.cfm?id=in-science-we-trust-poll.

King, Martin Luther, Jr. "Letter from Birmingham City Jail." Philadelphia: American Friends Service Committee, 1963.

Luhmann, Niklas. *Trust and Power.* John Wiley and Sons, 1979.

———. "Familiarity, Confidence, Trust: Problems and Alternatives." Gambetta, pp. 94–107.

McElvaine, Robert S., ed. *Down and Out in the Great Depression: Letters from the Forgotten Man.* U of North Carolina P, 1983.

Misztal, Barbara A. *Trust in Modern Societies.* Polity, 1996.

Putnam, Robert D. *Bowling Alone: The Collapse and Revival of American Community.* Simon and Schuster, 2000.

Putnam, Robert, with Robert Leonardi and Raffaella Y. Nanetti. *Making Democracy Work: Civic Traditions in Modern Italy.* Princeton UP, 1993.

Sanprie, Virginia. "Sarah Palin, Live and on the Web: The Critical Analysis of Online Texts." Unpublished doctoral dissertation. University of Colorado, 2009.

Seligman, Adam. *The Problem of Trust.* Princeton UP, 1997.

Tracy, Karen. *Challenges of Ordinary Democracy: A Case Study in Deliberation and Dissent.* Pennsylvania State UP, 2011.

Twenge, Jean M., W. Keith Campbell, and Nathan T. Carter. "Declines in Trust in Others and Confidence in Institutions among American Adults and Late Adolescents, 1972–2012." *Psychological Science*, vol. 25, no. 10, 2014, pp. 1914–23.

Terkel, Studs. *Hard Times: An Oral History of the Great Depression.* Random House, 1970.

Walker, Jeffrey. "On Rhetorical Traditions: A Reply to Jerzy Axer." Alliance of Rhetoric Societies Conference, Evanston, IL, September 11–14, 2003, pp. 1–12.

Wuthnow, Robert. "The Role of Trust in Civic Renewal." *Civil Society and Democracy, and Civic Renewal*, edited by Robert K. Fullinwider, Rowman and Littlefield, 1999, pp. 209–30.

Warren, Mark, ed. *Democracy and Trust.* Cambridge UP, 1999.

WHO, THEN, IS THIS RHETORIC MAJOR?

JOHN J. RUSZKIEWICZ AND DAVIDA CHARNEY

In a plenary address at the 2008 Council of Writing Program Administrators Conference in Denver, Andrea Lunsford expressed some reservations about the increase in the number of undergraduate writing programs and majors: "What worries me most is that the new majors, programs, and departments seem to be proliferating without what I'd call a center of gravity—it's kind of like what Gertrude Stein said of Oakland, California—that 'there's no *there* there.'" Not for the first time, Lunsford had identified a concern of importance to scholars in a field with theoretical and pedagogical stakes in everything from sophist orators to video games and social media. Given that diversity, as well as the institutional circumstances from which many of these programs were emerging, it is not surprising that they might, initially, seem muddled. But it is important, we think, that new departments be shaped by some congruence between the needs of students today and the disciplinary claims of a field with roots planted more than two millennia ago.

Perhaps the problem is that one can't have gravity without mass: independent programs in writing and rhetoric may only just be reaching the point where they can begin to define their *there.* Despite a half-century of innovative work by scholars willing to identify themselves with the teaching of language, writing, and rhetoric, the field today still remains tied by complex intellectual, academic, and administrative entanglements to traditional departments of

English—which, we could argue, are also having significant problems these days defining proper subjects, interests, methodologies, and goals for their undergraduate literature programs. What we consider a landmark event for programs in writing and rhetoric was the appearance in 2010 of perhaps the first scholarly book on the subject of undergraduate majors in rhetoric and writing: Greg Giberson and Thomas A. Moriarty's *What We Are Becoming: Developments in Undergraduate Writing Majors*. In that same year, the Conference on College Composition and Communication reported that seventy-two majors and tracks in writing were currently being offered at sixty-eight different institutions, of which more than a dozen had been created since 2006.

Of course, the whole notion of an undergraduate major in rhetoric and composition is not new; as early as 1975, *College Composition and Communication* published a proposal for such a program by several faculty at Texas Christian University (George Tade, Gary Tate, and Jim Corder), who declared that "rhetoric is an effective model for university education." A decade later, Maxine Hairston famously called for teachers of writing to rethink their relationship with English departments in her 1985 Chair's Address to the CCCC, pointing out that "rhetorical studies held the center of humanistic studies until the seventeenth century, and were a major component in American departments of English until early in the twentieth century" (280). Yet until recently, most efforts in the discipline continued to be focused on developing graduate programs at the master's and doctoral levels. In 2004, Kathleen Blake Yancey used the occasion of her Chair's Address to CCCC to urge fellow compositionists to acknowledge a "tectonic change" in literacy that puts within their bailiwick all the modes, genres, and occasions for communicating that students use today, most of them "outside of school" (298–300). While the textual focus of traditional English departments, Yancey argues, makes them anachronistic in an era of screen and digital literacy, programs in rhetoric and writing "*already* inhabit" this new environment and so face great opportunities (307–08), one of them the development of new majors in composition located in whatever sites will have them: "English department, writing studies department, rhetorical studies program" (321). The steady rise in the number of programs across the country attests to the readiness of those in our field to seize these opportunities.

However, despite the recent flurry of activity, most of the articles and reports on undergraduate writing majors treat the students themselves only indirectly or instrumentally. In the literature, the term "writing major" refers much more often to the programs than to their students. After all, faculty and administrators who offer rationales for (or against) new academic curricula or units are typically responding to disciplinary issues or administrative needs. Tade, Tate, and Corder, for instance, in their pioneering proposal for a major in rhetoric describe a field more interested in processes of inquiry and self-discovery than in offering specific knowledge:

> Many major programs are predicated upon the assumption that the entering student already knows and has accepted many of the terms and directions of the study. Many are predicated, too, on the assumption that the student has already understood the occasion and the need for the study he is embarking upon. We do not choose to make either of these assumptions, claiming instead that a major program needs to establish its occasion, the possibilities it offers, and its capacity to deliver value. (22)

Indirectly, the authors are outlining the task that advocates of writing concentrations and majors have faced in arguing for such innovations at their institutions.

Disciplinary and administrative issues are foremost to Hairston too in her call for new academic configurations: she is obviously aware that her manifesto will have consequences for students, but her primary interest is in assuring that the teaching of writing "become[s] a recognized and respected intellectual discipline" (281), a professional concern that resonates throughout the literature on stand-alone writing programs. Yancey similarly focuses on the disciplinary opportunities that the current historical moment offers to faculty in rhetoric and composition—though she is particularly mindful that current modes of teaching writing may not suit "members of a writing public" who daily encounter changes in genres, media, and textual sites (311). As Yancey depicts students today, they seem to be the ones who know something is happening to writing and composing—and it's now up to academics in the field of composition to figure out exactly what *that* is and to seize opportunities for disciplinary and institutional reform.

For the administrators developing most of the programs listed in the 2009 report of the CCCC Committee on the Major in Writing and Rhetoric, the question is not overly complicated: most of the programs (60 percent) promise to train students for careers as technical and professional writers. Many others pair composition with journalism or creative writing. Only ten programs promote rhetoric as a key area of humanistic study rather than primarily as a practice (Ball State, Clemson, Georgia Southern, Georgia State, Mount St. Mary's [in its Department of Communications], Syracuse, Texas Christian,

Rhode Island, Texas at Austin, and Winnipeg). The list that the committee updated in 2015 is greatly expanded with a total of 137 writing programs, of which 30 percent specify training in technical / professional writing and 30 percent use the term rhetoric.

Yet the question remains: Who are these students signing up as writing majors, often in surprising numbers, and what is it they are hoping to learn in their new concentrations or departments? What might they find appealing in a subject described by a philosopher no less eminent than Socrates as devoid of content? Are they, indeed, interested primarily in technical and professional training? Students presumably choose to major in English because they like to read literature, pursue psychology because human behavior intrigues them, follow a business curriculum to learn how to manage portfolios or businesses. What motivates rhetoric majors? Where do they come from, what do they expect to learn, and what do they hope to do?

This essay examines the rationales that students at the University of Texas at Austin offer for majoring in rhetoric and how their self-reported college experiences compare with those of other students in the liberal arts. We draw on data from a departmental "Survey of the Rhetoric Major," administered in 2008 and 2011, a 2014 alumni survey of rhetoric and writing majors, as well as a 2016 update of both. We also draw on literacy narratives from two courses across a period of three years looking for unprompted anecdotal reports of students discussing their choice of major. Our findings suggest that students may be seeking a major more aspirational than those driven chiefly by job market skills—important as they are. They appreciate the intellectual skills and perceptions that a broad-based, intellectually challenging program in writing and rhetoric provides.

INSTITUTIONAL HISTORY OF UT AUSTIN'S RHETORIC AND WRITING MAJOR

Most accounts of rhetoric programs and students, it seems, must begin, as Jessica Yood has observed, "with institutional histories" (173). And this one is no exception. In 2005, the Department of Rhetoric and Writing at the University of Texas at Austin finally put its own major on the books, the pathway to that goal as tortuous as most such program developments in academia tend to be.

Few if any faculty or administrators had majors in rhetoric and writing on their minds when on September 1, 1992, William H. Cunningham, on his last day in office as president of the University of Texas at Austin, authorized the creation of a Division of Rhetoric and Composition. Officially, President Cunningham was implementing a recommendation made by his Committee on the Undergraduate Experience, which, in a wide-ranging fifty-five-page report entitled "Enriching the Undergraduate Experience," offered six suggestions for improving writing instruction, the most significant being the final one:

> —that a Division of Rhetoric and Composition be established in the College of Liberal Arts that would be responsible for the administration, staffing, and teaching of first-year and advanced composition classes. (Bean 13953)

Unofficially, in embracing the recommendation, Cunningham had decided that a divorce was the only way to end years of conflict between faculty within the English department with vastly different views about the role that writing instruction should play in undergraduate education. The battles had earned the university much unwanted national attention, first during a mid-1980s dispute over an upper-division writing requirement (which eliminated business writing and technical writing from the department's purview) and, just a few years later, in a widely publicized shoot-out over the content of the first-year writing course—E 306, Rhetoric and Composition.

The Committee on the Undergraduate Experience report said little else about the proposed Division of Rhetoric and Composition (DRC), other than it should "oversee a first-rate computer laboratory devoted to the teaching of basic writing skills" and be responsible for teacher training and supervision. Over the next year, faculty members from the Department of English and the future DRC negotiated the terms of the split, divvying up resources, faculty lines, graduate student appointments, and so on. It became evident that the DRC would be a reasonably well-funded academic unit empowered to hire at the tenure-track level, promote its own members, and develop an undergraduate curriculum.

Yet when the Division of Rhetoric and Composition opened its doors on June 1, 1993, it had a serious identity problem. Although President Cunningham had insisted that the new unit be genuinely independent from the Department of English, its courses continued to carry an English prefix; faculty and graduate students in the DRC taught *English* 306, *English* 309K, *English* 325M. Just as confusing to students, university staff, and faculty, its identification as a "division" suggested that the DRC remained the property of English. Contributing to that view, all but one member of the regular faculty maintained joint appointments with English, teaching both upper-division undergraduate and graduate classes in that department, where the highly successful doctoral concentration in "rhetoric and writing" remained. Without faculty, students, or a major of its own, the DRC operated initially as the university had envisioned it: as a service unit with a primary mission to teach and supervise lower-division composition courses.

Some faculty members appreciated from the outset that a major would be the key to the unit's identity and long-term survival. However, delaying a push for a departmental status was strategic. With just six tenured or tenure-track faculty and two adjuncts, the new unit was in no position to staff a major in 1993 or for years afterward. Nor did faculty have time to create such a program as it scrambled to build the DRC into a sustainable enterprise. Other needs were immediate and more pressing: creating a writing center, revamping the training of writing instructors, reviving lower-division elective writing courses, establishing new upper-division offerings, building networked computer classrooms, hiring and promoting DRC faculty, and, not least, achieving peaceful co-existence among faculty weary after two decades of strife.

In some ways, working "under the radar" had its benefits as the DRC delivered up a string of tangible achievements throughout its first decade. The new Undergraduate Writing Center quickly proved its worth, growing to handle more than eleven thousand consultations per year. The Computer Writing and Research Lab prospered, becoming a major center for digital media research as well as fostering innovative teaching. Just as important, the revamped and carefully supervised writing courses offered by the DRC proved extremely popular with undergraduates, who used them to satisfy a two-class "substantial writing component" (SWC) requirement. Undergraduate courses included Magazine Writing, an award-winning Advanced Expository Writing class, and an internship for prospective writing center consultants. Most popular of all was 309K, Topics in Writing, its sections designed by graduate student assistant instructors after teaching 306, the required first-year course, for a year. Their topics were often timely, and the instructors were inventive and enthusiastic: The Rhetoric of Religious Dissent, The Rhetoric of Cartoons, The Rhetoric of Globalization, Arguing the Digital Divide, and so on. Finally, in Spring 2001, these writing courses gained a distinctive rhetoric prefix (RHE 306; RHE 325M).

Significantly, the DRC proved able to hire very well at all levels right from the start. While prominent faculty retired (James Sledd, Maxine Hairston, and James Kinneavy), others with backgrounds in rhetoric, composition, and computers and writing were routinely hired, tenured, and promoted. The

Department of Rhetoric currently has eleven tenured / tenure-track faculty, only two of whom retain partial appointments with English. With allied faculty in English providing coverage of medieval and Renaissance rhetoric, the DRC could claim expertise across the history of rhetoric, contemporary theories and technologies, as well as gendered and comparative rhetorics. A key attraction for prospective faculty remained the doctoral concentration in rhetoric. Though still housed in the Department of English, the concentration enabled DRC faculty to teach graduate seminars in their areas of expertise. However, at the undergraduate level, when more specialized upper-division classes in rhetoric failed to attract an anticipated number or quality of students, these new hires added their voices to those who yearned for an undergraduate major that would also confer departmental status on the DRC: we wanted students of our own.

The opportunity finally arose in April 2002 when the dean of the College of Liberal Arts asked the DRC to prepare a detailed plan for enhancing student writing throughout the college. The plan the DRC offered in January 2003 included, among its many components, the establishment of a major in rhetoric and writing. The dean approved the plan in its entirety, and the DRC pressed forward with both the liberal arts writing initiative and the undergraduate major. Shortly after the major was approved in 2005, the unit officially changed its designation to the Department of Rhetoric and Writing (DRW).

DESCRIPTION OF THE MAJOR IN RHETORIC AND WRITING

Conceptually, the proposed major was conservative and workable, yet flexible. The initial degree plan required just twenty-fours hours of coursework in rhetoric and composition, including a foundations course and at least one upper-division course in each of three general areas (history, theory, and digital media / technology). Additional electives (such as proposal writing, magazine writing, and technical writing) had been on the books for a long while as SWC courses. The degree program subsequently grew to include a writing course requirement and an honors thesis opportunity. The simplicity of the degree, faculty hoped, would appeal to students and enable us to use available resources while enabling faculty to design courses reflecting their areas of expertise.

The shape of the major clearly reflected these areas of expertise. While the faculty included authors of best-selling composition textbooks and a few who had taught and published in technical communications, neither professional writing nor composition per se seemed central. The decision may have gone otherwise had the DRW been responsible for offering courses tailored to engineering or business majors. Rhetoric also seems more appropriate than composition to place at the center of the major. Rhetoric's dual focus on analysis and production led naturally to the objective that majors become adept at both skills. Rhetoric's long history and the evolution of rhetorical theory gave substance to the content that majors were expected to learn.

The foundations course, Principles of Rhetoric, was designed to introduce major terms, issues, and approaches in the theory and practice of rhetoric and writing. To allow faculty to represent the field from their different perspectives, the syllabus for Principles of Rhetoric was not fixed; over the years, course texts have included Crowley and Hawhee, Jasinski, and Bizzell and Herzberg.

The three upper-division area courses—Advanced Studies in Digital Rhetoric, History of Rhetoric, and Rhetorical Theory and Analysis—were fashioned as topics courses to allow maximum flexibility for both faculty and students. Faculty members are free to develop new topics, and students may take more than one version of the courses. Below are sample offerings for each area course.

Media / Technology RHE 330C	Rhetorics of Cyberculture Multi-Media: Remaking Invention User-Centered Design Rhetoric and Serious Games Digital Monumentality Writing and Photography
History RHE 330D	Classical to Modern Rhetoric Sophistry and the Invention of Rhetoric Rhetoric Invented, Revis(it)ed, Retold African-American Rhetoric: 1950–Present Kairos and the Rhetorical Situation Rhetoric in the English Renaissance
Theory RHE 330E	Democracy and the Media Pathos Demagoguery Rhetoric of Science in Popular Media Comparative Rhetoric Psychology of Writing

Allowing the topics to vary and designating all the courses as having a substantial writing component was a way to hedge our bets; students in government, economics, philosophy, and so on seeking an upper-division writing course might be drawn to rhetoric courses and then decide to double major to burnish their writing credentials. We also offered a rarity at a major research institution: an undergraduate course of study in which almost every class had fewer than twenty-five students and most required classes were taught by tenured / tenure-track faculty.

Still, in designing the program, faculty were pretty much guessing about the character, motives, and needs of their future constituents. Could we offer them an appealing program that would serve them well? The rough transcript of a faculty meeting on the major includes numerous comments like the following:

> We don't know what comes first: do we build the courses first and then get the major, or design the major and then build courses?
>
> What do the students want? There is a tension between that question and our sense of what they ought to want. Ideally, I think the way to go is get the kids in the door to show them what's waiting for them and have them so enchanted that they say, *oh, what else is here?* Then they get into theory, classical rhetoric, to balance out their practical courses.
>
> One reason business is such a dominant major is that so many students are job driven. They are scared that they will spend $$$ and there will be nothing there for them when they get out. I think that there needs to be a balance between theory and practice. We need to pay close attention to what they want. They have a right to be concerned with the practical considerations.
>
> We can grow in ways like cross-cultural rhetoric. Stretch students a little bit. I'm only slightly moved by what students *think* they want.

Underlying all these ruminations was the unspoken question of numbers. In the hallways, we joked: What if we gave a major and *nobody* came? The initial projection in 2004 was modest: fifty students within five years. But what happened if we get ten, or five or none? Nobody quite knew.

In fall 2005, the paperwork for a major in rhetoric and writing went forward and, with some speed, the plan was approved at all administrative levels, along with a secondary proposal to rename the unit the Department of Rhetoric and Writing (DRW). By fall 2006, we were in the major business.

Oddly, as the program was rolled out, shepherded by the associate chair of the department, Diane Davis, most of the department's energy was absorbed by the preparation of new courses and the politics of the dean's writing initiative in the college. There was neither energy nor time to attract students to the new major: no special programs, websites, speakers, or outreach. Yet at almost every departmental meeting Davis dutifully reported unexpected news about additional students signing on to the major. The numbers continued to rise, semester by semester, amusing faculty at first, then delighting them, and finally worrying them. The program had enrolled twenty-one majors in January 2007, 140 majors in October 2008, and 214 in September 2010. The department soon was concerned about its ability to staff its suddenly robust upper-division offerings in rhetoric and writing. Just about every section was oversubscribed—and many had waiting lists. In 2015–16, majors dropped to a manageable 150, but by 2017 the number again stood at more than two hundred. Why had all these students selected us?

DEMOGRAPHICS OF RHETORIC MAJORS

To gain information about rhetoric and writing majors, we conducted surveys of students and made use of assigned literacy narratives from several classes. The surveys were conducted using Survey Monkey in 2008 and 2011 and Qualtrics in 2016. In each case, about 40 percent of majors responded, 62 of 140 majors in 2008, 85 of 213 majors in 2011, and 97 of 218 majors in 2016. One of the authors of this chapter requires students to share a literacy narrative online at the beginning of each term in both an Advanced Writing class and a writing center internship course. Neither class is restricted to rhetoric and writing candidates, but once the major was in place students in the program regularly (and without prompting) began discussing their motives for choosing their field of study. Quotes from students are used with permission.

GENDER. The rhetoric and writing major has increasingly attracted women: 53.8 percent in 2008, 58.4 percent in 2011, and 74 percent in 2016.

SEMESTER STANDING. Most respondents have been seniors (59 percent) or juniors (23 percent); the remainder have been evenly divided between first-year and sophomore standing.

COLLEGE WRITING PREPARATION. In 2011, most respondents (59.7 percent) placed out of the RHE 306 requirement; even more reported receiving AP credit (66.2 percent). A substantial number fulfilled the requirement at a two-year or community college (15.6 percent) or a different four-year college (19.5 percent). In 2016, far fewer placed out by exam (13 percent), but a substantial number earned dual credit while in high school (12 percent). A substantial proportion still satisfied the requirement through AP credit (42 percent).

DOUBLE MAJORS. In 2011, just over half the respondents (54.1 percent) reported rhetoric and writing as their only major; the rest reported a double major: one-third (34.1 percent) were double majoring with another program in the College of Liberal Arts (COLA); a small percentage (9.4 percent) were double majoring with a program outside the Liberal Arts; 2 percent were currently minors. In 2016, the proportion of single majors increased to 62 percent, with 17 percent of respondents double majoring in other liberal arts disciplines and 21 percent in majors outside the COLA. It is notable that since 2008, the university initiated several changes to reduce time to degree that also reduced the flexibility of many majors. These changes may be responsible for the increasing prevalence of single majors.

PATHWAY TO THE MAJOR

Both the literacy narratives and the surveys suggest that students have three reasons for choosing to major in rhetoric. On the pragmatic level, students see the major contributing to their future career goals. On the personal level, students see the major allowing them to do what they love—writing and arguing. On the social level, students at this huge public university appreciate the unique features of the program: small classes and close contact with tenured / tenure-track faculty. While career goals are among the highest scoring reasons for both years, love of writing is strong—even exceeding career goals in both 2011 and 2016. (See Appendix A.)

In their literacy narratives, many students tie their inclination to the major to specific experiences. Sometimes a particular course inspires them—it can even be the required first-year course or one of the RHE 309K topics courses taught enthusiastically by a graduate student. Just as frequently, majors mention a notably cogent book, a challenging or passionate teacher, a demanding parent, or some compelling engagement with the political process that has made them appreciate effective arguments and seek to emulate those who can wield them. Linking the field of rhetoric to personal inclinations often comes through a process of discovery.

> After a few months of indifference in many fields of study, I finally realized that I enjoyed writing. I enjoyed the structure, syntax, style, and rhetorical arguments in everything I read. I found myself searching for more than just the required analysis in my classes. At that point, I realized that I wanted to do something along the lines of rhetoric.

The diversity of rationales offered for choosing a writing major is not unexpected and, in fact, roughly parallels the paradigmatic rhetoric students, identified as Kerry, Joe, and Ashieka, that Jennifer Courtney, Deb Martin, and Diane Penrod construct in their discussion of majors at Rowan University (253–55). That our Texas students mention argumentation more and discuss careers less than do their colleagues in New Jersey may measure a conceptual difference between majors labeled "Rhetoric and Writing" and "Writing Arts."

CAREER GOALS

Based on statements in the literacy narratives, it is clear that a significant number select the major because they are interested in becoming nonfiction writers—conceived as professionals who do important work in the world. A good many students choose rhetoric as an alternative when the traditional English major doesn't quite fit.

> I have always loved writing, so I started out as an English major. I became a Rhetoric and Writing major because I wanted to focus on good composition and the practical applications of writing rather than analyzing literature.

A former science major describes her change of major in more detail.

> I spent my freshman year at UT as a biology major. I've never really been a creative writer, and I don't write "beautifully," but the kinds of writing I had to do for my natural science classes that year were painfully dry for me. Something I did like to do, oddly enough, was going over my roommate's various essays and pointing out spelling mistakes, fixing grammar, and improving sentence structure. As I realized that I wouldn't be satisfied with a future in the natural sciences, I also missed being able to challenge myself with writing assignments and textual analyses. Eventually, I found the Rhetoric and Writing major, which has so far been just my cup of tea.
>
> Studying rhetoric has immensely changed my knowledge of writing and arguments, and I've applied this more mature way of thinking to

> the world around me as well. I know now that writing encompasses so much more than just grammar and writing good individual sentences. There are people who can articulate it better than I can, but I see writing as a medium for people to communicate their ideas, and I want to know more about the process. Although I'm definitely not as well-read as I'd like to be, I'd love to be able to combine my interests in writing with the enjoyment I get out of helping people.

Knowing how to write helps make students engaged or accountable citizens able to express ideas well and reach significant audiences. Cicero would have understood.

Majoring in rhetoric enables students to exercise the valuable reading and analytical tools taught in English classes on a wider playing field. (One student even argued in his narrative that training in rhetoric is the best pathway to understanding and composing poetry, a claim that would make perfect sense to writers from the European Middle Ages and Renaissance.)

When asked more specifically about their career goals on the survey, students were also pragmatic, indicating that their most likely next step would be an entry-level job or further graduate training. Professional training and graduate school were mentioned much more by seniors than by the group of respondents as a whole. In open-ended comments, eleven students mentioned law school. Seven mentioned writing-related goals, in journalism, public relations, technical writing, or an MFA. The other responses included the ministry, business, and the foreign service. (See Appendix B.)

So it seems, not surprisingly, that rhetoric majors want to learn how to analyze persuasive arguments and how to produce them themselves, and they are pleased now to find a college degree that supports those aspirations. Some claim to be good at argument already and eager to raise natural talents to a professional caliber. Some even express a love for grammar, mechanics, and usage.

ATTITUDES TOWARD THE RHETORIC MAJOR

The survey indicates that students in the major are satisfied customers who again express appreciation for working closely with faculty members. On the whole, the scores for 2011 and 2016 are even higher than they were in 2008. (See Appendix C.)

When asked about specific ways in which they felt they were gaining from their major, students were again very pleased; no item on this question scored below a 3.0 on the four-point scale. Majors seem especially satisfied with their training in writing and the identification and use of rhetorical strategies. (See Appendix D.)

In open-ended comments, students elaborated on their gains in terms of other academic experiences and even worldview.

> On a personal level, my experience as an undergraduate in Rhetoric and Writing has also instructed me on how to engage critically with my own thoughts. Before I studied Rhetoric there were times when, quite frankly, I felt trapped by the worldview I had inherited as a child. Studying rhetoric gave me the freedom to not only ethically and logically challenge the positions of others, but also to ethically and logically challenge my own ideas.

> [Courses offered by the DRW provide excellent training in:] Using concise, clear means to communicate. Understanding how context alters meaning. Making thought, speech, and writing more articulate. Understanding how language shapes our thoughts and perception. Learning how to deconstruct anything laden with meaning (texts, images, art, speech) to understand its properties and effectiveness. Learning to construct meaning and communicate meaningfully with others.

> [The rhetoric major has] also helped me to build confidence when presenting ideas, both written and oral, in other classes.

By spring 2014, we were in a position to explore how well alumni of our program were doing after graduation. We were pleased to discover that they remain satisfied with their majors after leaving the University of Texas. We surveyed 175 alumni, receiving responses from 67 for a response rate of 38 percent. All reported being employed, with 22 percent in professional or graduate school, 70 percent employed full-time and 15 percent part-time. The most frequent types of employment were legal, educational, technology, and marketing / sales. Over three-quarters reported writing frequently or very frequently on the job and over half gave oral presentations frequently or very frequently. Over 80 percent of respondents strongly agreed that majoring in rhetoric and writing increased their ability to read critically, write clearly, and write persuasively. Over two-thirds said it helped them figure out how to write in new situations. Some of the skills they considered most important on the job were writing to different audiences, acknowledging and responding to opposing positions, finding and using evidence to support claims, collaborative writing and revising, editing their own and others' texts, and organizing ideas into coherent paragraphs and sections. Over half of alumni rated their training as excellent in all of these skills (except for collaborative writing that came in at 49 percent). Over half also reported receiving excellent training in recognizing and deploying rhetorical strategies and critiquing print and online texts.

The alumni survey was updated in summer 2016 with a response rate of 31 percent from a current total of 323 alumni. Respondents remain exceedingly happy with their training. They also report considerable success in their careers: 22 percent of alumni who graduated before 2013 earn annual salaries of more than $100,000; another 18 percent earn more than $75,000. Even more pleasing are comments that reference rhetorical skills:

> From day one on the job (and in life post-graduation), the emphasis that the rhetoric department puts on understanding your audience has been the greatest tool I've used. Understanding my audience—whether it be needy clients, overbearing attorneys, or bothersome coworkers—has helped me do my job competently. I've often received praise for handling different situations uniquely from my peers, but I feel I can give major credit to my Rhetoric degree and the critical thinking and analysis skills I learned in my Rhetoric classes. The more senior I become in my job, the more I find that I rely on tools I learned as an RHE major. Even now, as I find myself studying for the LSAT after all these years, the critical thinking skills and appreciation for varying perspectives have helped me tremendously in my studies.

This comment was echoed by several other alumni.

CONCLUSION

Students examining and then entering our program have a sense that the new major in rhetoric and writing we have created has purpose and focus. Clearly, there is a *there* for them in the field of study. Indeed, in retrospect, the success of the new program at UT-Austin now seems almost predictable: students made rational choices to select a major offering subject matter and experiences not readily available elsewhere on campus, even in a department of English. And it may be argued that no current major so attentively maps the skills that academics and professionals routinely report as what all undergraduates should demonstrate as a result of higher education: critical thinking, analytical reasoning, and effective written communication (Arum and Roska). Moreover, students quickly perceived that rhetoric and writing complemented a number of more familiar fields of study, including philosophy, journalism, government, economics, and, of course, English.

In retrospect, the flexibility of the program has served the faculty well, allowing faculty to develop new topics as their interests have changed or as it becomes attractive to recruit students in other majors, such as psychology. By working closely with advising staff, we have learned how to get our courses to meet arcane general education requirements, negotiated the shoals of new college software that makes it nigh impossible to cross-list courses, and dealt with policy imperatives for speeding up time to graduation that reduce students' ability to experiment with electives.

Surely students at the University of Texas at Austin are not unique in seeking a major that sharpens their abilities to think, analyze, and communicate and enables them to build a portfolio that documents these skills. Our success suggests that undergraduate programs in rhetoric and writing need not be tied to specific professional tracks such as technical writing nor to other popular kinds of writing such as fiction or journalism. While institutional peculiarities shape the constraints on and opportunities for program development, we believe the time is right for rhetoricians to teach rhetoric.

In doing so, we will in fact be addressing another of Andrea Lunsford's concerns. In an online interview in 2003 with the National Council of Teachers of English's Beth Hewett, Lunsford and the late Professor Michael Leff of the University of Memphis discuss the prospects of a nascent Alliance of Rhetoric Societies (ARS). Toward the end of the interview, Hewett asks, "What is the relationship between the academy and the public where rhetoric is concerned?" After some back and forth, Leff observes, "One thing that needs to be done is to get some serious rhetorical analysis out to the public. I don't mean dealing with this or that point (*did Bush tell the truth*), but more about how his rhetoric works." And Andrea responds, "One obvious answer is that rhetoricians need to be out in public more often—on editorial pages, on the radio, and so on. Our problem is how to position ourselves in such a way that it is not always just one person (like Kathleen Hall Jamieson) who gets asked to comment on matters rhetorical."

We would suggest that a way to assure that rhetoric gains greater public notice is to give the field the status that a major ineluctably confers within academic communities. Students who decide to pursue physics, petroleum engineering, or business at the University of Texas may not be tempted by the rhetoric and writing option, but they now understand that the field exists and describes a specific and demanding course of study. By leading major campus organizations, staffing the tables during liberal arts events, identifying their major on frequent newspaper op / eds or letters to the editor, and simply walking across the stage at graduation, our hundreds of rhetoric majors give the field a presence on our campus that it never previously had. In the long run, growing numbers of graduates will establish the usefulness and potency of the discipline to people establishing careers in business, media, government, and law. If rhetoricians do not play public roles today, it may be simply because the public at large does not realize what exactly the discipline has to contribute to public discourse and professional lives. That, we are confident, will change.

Appendix A

I enrolled in course(s) in Rhetoric and Writing this semester because:

	2008	2011	2016
It's relevant to my career goals	3.50	3.47	3.35
I love to write	3.38	3.71	3.62
I got hooked by taking a previous RHE class	3.35	3.17	2.84
Classes are small	3.30	3.29	2.94
Instructors are full-time faculty	3.20	2.91	na
I love to argue	3.11	3.32	3.04
The requirements for degree are flexible	2.94	2.91	2.37
Class members have diverse backgrounds	2.78	2.74	2.43
My advisor recommended it	2.60	na	na
A friend recommended it	na	1.93	2.28
I needed an upper-division SWC class	2.37	1.94	na

The responses presented in all appendixes are averages on a four-point scale, with a higher score representing "strongly agree."

Appendix B

Within 1–3 years after graduating from the University of Texas at Austin, I plan to:

	2008	2011	2016
Attend a graduate school	2.96	2.57	27%
Apply for an entry-level job	2.90	3.03	23%
Join a volunteer or service program	2.54	2.36	4%
Travel / take time off	2.49	2.37	Na
Attend a professional school	2.42	1.88	9%
Teach in a K12 school	1.77	1.51	Na
Other			38%

Appendix C

I would rate my experience with the Department of Rhetoric and Writing as follows:

	2008	2011	2016
Quality of instruction	3.55	3.65	3.34
Relationship with instructors	3.45	3.69	3.28
Advising toward degree completion	3.24	3.42	3.23
Interesting array of classes	3.20	3.36	3.20
Workload of classes	3.14	3.30	3.19
Resolution of complaints	3.04	3.25	3.19
Opportunities to meet other majors	2.68	2.95	2.86
Opportunities to do an internship	2.62	2.81	Na
Advising toward career opportunities	2.58	2.91	Na
Computer facilities	na	na	3.35

Appendix D

Classes offered by the Department of Rhetoric and Writing provide excellent training in:

	2008	2011	2016
Finding and using evidence to support claims	3.54	3.59	3.73
Editing my own and others' texts	3.41	3.58	3.64
Identifying rhetorical strategies	3.60	3.55	3.75
Writing to different audiences	3.39	3.54	3.54
Organizing ideas into coherent paragraphs and sections	3.63	3.50	3.75
Dealing with conflicting positions on an issue	3.49	3.49	3.36
Deploying rhetorical strategies in my own texts	3.44	3.46	3.76
Collaborative writing and revising	3.47	3.43	2.97
Critiquing print and online texts	na	3.39	3.60
Applying conventions of standard written English	3.49	3.36	3.34
Achieving an effective prose style	3.48	3.36	3.61
Engaging in ethical and effective advocacy	3.16	3.35	3.45
Learning the history of rhetoric as a discipline	3.25	3.25	3.25
Using new media for communication	3.21	3.24	2.90
Identifying historical figures in the history of rhetoric	3.18	3.24	2.96
Writing in different genres	3.05	3.24	3.02

Works Cited

Arum, Richard, and Joseph Roksa. *Academically Adrift: Limited Learning on College Campuses.* U of Chicago P, 2011.

Bean, Frank D., et al. "Report of Committee on the Undergraduate Experience." Documents and Proceedings of the University Council. University of Texas at Austin. 21 Jan. 1992, pp. 13916–979.

Bizzell, Patricia, and Bruce Hertzberg, eds. *The Rhetorical Tradition: Readings from Classical Times to the Present.* 2nd ed., Bedford / St. Martin's, 2000.

CCCC Committee on the Major in Writing and Rhetoric. "Writing Majors at a Glance, Fall 2015." CCCC, http://www.ncte.org/library/NCTEFiles/Groups/CCCC/Committees/2015ListofMajorsWritingRhetoric.pdf. Accessed 4 February 2017.

———. "March 2010 Update." CCCC, http://www.ncte.org/cccc/committees/majorrhetcomp. Accessed 11 July 2011.

———. "Writing Majors at a Glance, January 2009." http://www.ncte.org/library/NCTEFiles/Groups/CCCC/Committees/Writing_Majors_Final.pdf. Accessed 11 July 2011.

Courtney, Jennifer, Deb Martin, and Diane Penrod. "The Writing Arts Major: A Work in Process." Giberson and Moriarity, pp. 243–58.

Crowley, Sharon, and Debra Hawhee. *Ancient Rhetorics for Contemporary Students*, 5th ed., Pearson, 2012.

Giberson, Greg A., and Thomas A. Moriarty, eds. *What We Are Becoming: Developments in Undergraduate Writing Majors*. Utah State UP, 2010.

Hairston, Maxine. "Breaking Our Bonds and Reaffirming Our Connections." *College Composition and Communication*, vol. 36, no. 3, 1985, pp. 272–82.

Jasinski, James L. *Sourcebook on Rhetoric*. Sage, 2001.

Lunsford, Andrea A. "The Future of Writing Programs—and WPAs." Plenary Address. Conference of the Council of Writing Program Administrators. Grand Hyatt, Denver. 10 July 2008.

Lunsford, Andrea A., and Michael Leff. "The Alliance for Rhetoric Society." Interviewed by Beth Hewett. *Kairos*, vol. 8, no. 2, 2003. Accessed 14 Mar. 2012.

Mattingly, Rebecca de Wind, and Patricia Harkin. "A Major in Flexibility." Giberson and Moriarty, pp. 13–31.

Ruszkiewicz, John, Davida Charney, Peg Syverson, and Rosa Eberly. "DRC Strategic Plan: 2000–2004." 12 Dec. 2000.

Tade, George, Gary Tate, and Jim Corder, "For Sale, Lease, or Rent: A Curriculum for an Undergraduate Program in Rhetoric." *College Composition and Communication*, vol. 26, 1975, pp. 20–24.

Yancey, Kathleen Blake. "Made Not Only in Words: Composition in a New Key." *College Composition and Communication*, vol. 56, no. 2, 2004, pp. 297–328.

Yood, Jessica. "Revising the Dream: Graduate Students, Independent Writing Programs, and the Future of English Studies." *A Field of Dreams: Independent Writing Programs and the Future of Composition Studies*, edited by Peggy O'Neill, Angela Crow, and Larry W. Burton, Utah State UP, 2002, pp. 170–185.

NETWORKED FEMINISM
MENTORING IN THE NEW ECONOMY

ROXANNE MOUNTFORD AND CHERYL GLENN

> What stands out to us in reviewing the history of mentoring and the current literature surrounding it is how limited we are in our ability to talk about our experience of mentoring and being mentored.
>
> —Jenn Fishman and Andrea Lunsford

> I would so help me tell you if I could
> how some great teacher
> came to my side and said:
>
> *Let's go down into the underworld*
> —the earth already crazed
> *Let me take your hand*
>
> —Adrienne Rich, "Terza Rima"

When we arrived at the Ohio State University to begin graduate degrees in English (Cheryl as a PhD student, Roxanne as an MA student), there were very few women professors—graduate seminars in rhetoric and composition were taught primarily by Ed Corbett and Frank O'Hare. It was not until the fall of 1986 that Andrea Lunsford was hired and the building of a legendary program began in earnest. The English department was decidedly masculine, still fragrant with stories of wild parties in the 1970s. Mr. Corbett, as he was known to us, subscribed to *Playboy* magazine. Male faculty dated students, so we learned early that mentoring in such an environment was, well, a little "crazed."

In some ways, we were lucky, because such a dodgy environment illustrated the value of the feminism we were just beginning to embrace. In those early days, we learned the value of building the network of mentoring and teaching that has sustained us throughout our careers as scholars and teachers of rhetoric and writing. Our network consisted of women graduate students, including our friend Kris Ratcliffe, along with several other remarkable women (including Jamie Barlowe, Jeanne Colleran, Pat Sullivan, Maria Gonzalez, Becky Rickly, and Molly Travis). When Andrea arrived, she brought shape, focus, and energy to the program and encouraged us in our feminist studies of rhetoric. In many ways, she served as a traditional mentor (in the "mentor / apprentice" model), and like the ancient rhetoricians, attracted new students who clustered around her. So it has taken many years for the two of us to recognize that the network we had developed prior to Andrea's arrival was as powerful to us as her mentorship. Intuitive if not proclaimed feminists when we started, over the years, we have passed on the mentorship we created and received, only recently understanding that the most revolutionary and lasting element of our Ohio State experience was the networking we did outside of our faculty relationships.

In 2008, Roxanne published *Women's Ways of Making It in Rhetoric and Composition* with Michelle Ballif and Diane Davis, a book partly inspired by her positive experiences of being mentored by Andrea. Andrea and Cheryl are profiled in the book, which answers the question, "What does it take to succeed as a woman in the field of rhetoric and composition?" Intended to augment existing mentoring relationships that women graduate students and faculty may already have or to substitute for a missing mentor, the book draws on the literature, qualitative survey data, and the profile interviews to answer this question, organizing the information by epochs of a professor's life, from graduate school to retirement.

Women's Ways was published in 2008, only a few months before the housing market collapsed, sending the entire economy—including private and public colleges and universities—into free fall. In real terms, the profession that we have known has changed. In 2007, the year that Roxanne and her husband, Bill, applied for new positions, the number of jobs in rhetoric and composition and in scientific and technical communication were the highest in two decades; in 2008–09, there was a sharp drop in positions, and in 2009–10, an even steeper drop. Universities shed 30 percent of their total positions in all areas of English studies, positions they have not yet recovered. In addition, the job market has changed. Contracts are signed before the MLA and continue to be signed well beyond the end of the academic year. Once upon a time, almost all the positions were posted in the October MLA Job Information List (JIL). Now, many jobs are listed in the December and February JIL. Few graduate faculty are prepared to comfort a student or colleague on the market with these words: "Well, I'm sorry you have so few interviews by MLA; keep in mind your dream job may not be listed until February or even April." The situation on the ground has moved too fast for most faculty to keep up. And the ground is going to keep shifting for a while. With federal stimulus dollars gone, states are continuing to cut higher education. How do we mentor—or find mentoring—adequate for the world the great recession has left us? What does feminist mentoring look like in this new economy?

In this essay, we focus on traditional feminist models of mentoring, noting the extent to which each of them offers a generative and sustainable system of professional development for graduate students and faculty in the new economy. These models are implicit in such sources as *Women's Ways*. While deeply grounded in a feminist ethic and complicating of the traditional master-apprentice relationship, some models rely too much on the knowledge and reputation of a single uberfeminist mentor. Instead, we argue for "networked mentoring," which may prove to be the feminist mentoring model with the greatest benefit for everyone involved as well as the best response to the question that motivates this essay: how can we remake our mentoring systems to respond to the new economy?

FROM MENTORING TO FEMINIST MENTORING

Rhetoric has always been a mentoring tradition, the pedagogical pursuit of artful and ethical speaking, writing, and being, a practice of teaching and mentoring that addresses the holistic development of the orator. In Plato's *Phaedrus*, Socrates teaches and mentors Phaedrus within the long-accepted tradition of master-apprentice, one reflecting the glories of the mentor-teacher's accomplishments vis-à-vis the struggles of the apprentice to master the art. The mentor is older, wiser, stronger. In the Homeric tradition, Mentor was the trusted friend whom Odysseus left in charge of his household and son for ten years. Athena, goddess of wisdom, sometimes assumed the form of Mentor, who guided Telemachus, Odysseus's son, on his quest for his long-missing father. This mythology suggests that the mentor is also a protector. The term *protégé* descends from the Latin verb *protegere*, meaning "to protect," and the common metaphor associated with mentoring a protégé—"taking him / her under my wing"—reflects the protective relationship of the mentor to his apprentice.

The age-old master-apprentice model worked successfully for millennia—as long as the master and apprentice were aristocratic males. As Cheryl Dahle writes, "The way mentoring used to work, a senior male . . . would anoint a younger version of himself as his protégé. . . . The mentor, who was several rungs higher up the ladder, could steer the lower man toward career-enhancing projects or plum assignments." Given that the mentor and his protégé were to have a great deal in common (gender, race, and social class, for example), any others (disfranchised in a number of different ways) remained outsiders, hoping "against all evidence that they, an exception, might join the blessed circle" (Heilbrun 1).

Until their numbers grew, women did pattern themselves after men. "When men were the only models we had," writes feminist cultural and literary critic Carolyn Heilbrun, only [white] men could exemplify the ideal life of a thinker, a writer, a public figure (1)—the life Heilbrun wanted so much for herself during the 1940s and on through the 1960s. It was not until the 1980s, when we were in graduate school, that women faculty entered the academy in sizable enough numbers to begin to change the system. Then, sparks from the women's movement finally lit fires in academia, changing the system to accommodate the lived and professional experiences different from those that had long circulated in the hallways and offices. Parental leave policies, pay equity, sexual harassment policies, and robust diversity hiring programs changed the way it felt to be a faculty member in higher education. To be sure, there were—and still are—the queen bees who try to hold on to their singularity, identifying with white masculine hierarchies and competing with—and thwarting the careers of—other women. The queen bee's presence in rhetoric and composition was one of the sad revelations in *Women's Ways*. But on the whole, the feminist incursion of the late twentieth century brought with it a rethinking of every feature of traditional academia, from curricular and research agendas to mentoring and teaching.

Unlike the traditional top-down mentoring model between like-minded males of different ages that Heilbrun limns so well, feminist mentoring strives to flatten hierarchies and to encourage greater flexibility in mentoring relationships. When we consider models in rhetoric and composition, the alternative perspectives and practices of Lunsford and Lisa Ede come to mind. For over thirty years, these two scholars have been nudging us toward establishing new ways to learn from one another; to cooperate without domination or submission; to respect and work with our mutual strengths, perceptions, and vulnerabilities; and, therefore, to stimulate the formulation of new ways of working together in the fields of rhetoric and writing. Such feminist engagements have stimulated the formulation of new ways of being rhetorical, teaching and practicing rhetoric, and, of course, mentoring.

Feminist mentoring has been compelled to move in this new direction. After all, "barriers still stand in the way of women's access to mentoring" (Rheineck and Roland 82). In addition, a good number of women would rather be mentored by women (or men) who demonstrate an authentic balance between work and family. Finally, many women hold values different from those regularly employed in traditional top-down mentoring: rather than waiting to be chosen by a mentor, striving to perform like the mentor, looking only upward toward the mentor, many women want a mutually nourishing relationship with their mentor, one that helps them both develop professionally and personally. Jenn Fishman and Lunsford urge us to move away from the term "mentor" because it obscures the reciprocal relationship that mentors and their apprentices can develop. Fishman and Lunsford would replace the word "mentor" with "colleague," which is a way of feminizing the master-apprentice relationship.

Nevertheless, the idea of mentoring is rooted in the Telemachus story. Fishman and Lunsford note in their essay on mentoring that this story, retold in a number of languages, is used throughout Western history to underscore the triumph of the individual over the collective (21). But there is a place for more traditional modes of mentoring. After all, as Audre Lorde admonishes, "It is the work of feminism to make connections, to heal unnecessary divisions," and to "pay attention to the voices we have been taught to distrust, [to] articulate what they teach us, and [to] act upon what we know" (qtd. in Bereano 8, 11). At the same time, Fishman and Lunsford underscore reasons for exploring other, more fruitful feminist mentoring practices that could prove to be more sustainable in the long run. Still, what all these feminist mentoring practices have in common is the reciprocity of the engagement and the shared responsibility for the success of the mentor-mentee partnership, and the overall flexibility that the three following models indicate.

THE FEMINIST-GURU MODEL OF MENTORING

Perhaps the most familiar model of feminist mentoring is that of feminist-guru mentoring, a regendered update of the traditional male-only, mentor-protégé relationship. Promoted within the last two or three decades, the feminist-guru model is intended to support younger female (or nonwhite) faculty and students as they ascend through the ranks. Thus, like the traditional model, the feminist-guru model presumes a hierarchical and nodal activity—but, this time, with an emphasis on female success. One experienced woman guides a younger, less-experienced woman into a successful career, helping her avoid obstacles. Like the traditional model, most of the lines of connection point upward toward the established guru herself as well as toward the firmament, the only place achievement could possibly lie.

In *Women's Ways*, Ballif, Davis, and Mountford profile nine individual women who have "made it" in the field, offering up their career paths and insights as models of scholar-teacher-mentors. In many ways, this book promotes the idea of the feminist-guru and is intended to stand in for or supplement the work of a rather traditional mentor. To be sure, the nine women featured in the book lead rich and complex lives and are self-reflexive about their mentoring of others. In particular, Andrea has lived and continues to lead a deliberate life that keeps her attuned to the needs and contributions of others—particularly her students. Keeping strict hierarchy at bay, Andrea models how to feminize and transform the mentoring relationships she forms, creating lifelong friendships with her protégés.[1]

When Andrea joined the faculty at Ohio State, she immediately regendered the professional landscape. Roxanne took several courses from her, learning in the process how important it is to network and collaborate with others (Andrea taught many books still in galleys and connected us with other scholars in the field). We both learned more about being in the profession from her than any of the men on the faculty. Maybe we learned so much because we paid such careful attention to (maybe even studied) the ways she negotiated her rhetoric-and-writing presence in a department dominated by literature and theory and performed her professionalism on a daily basis. Whether she was planning new courses, preparing for class, meeting with students, mapping out a workshop, discussing departmental politics with colleagues, or handling sticky departmental, personal, and professional matters, she did so with determination, generosity, and, most often, success. She also modeled how to live in a department, how to treat people, how to play well with others, and the harder-to-learn lessons of how to negotiate, hold one's tongue, strategize, and work hard (nearly) every day.

Andrea tells us that she was never our mentor (that she always felt more like a big sister or a friend to us), but most folks who know us would say that she has and continues to mentor us in many ways. In fact, a few years back, Roxanne told Cheryl about a rumor that had long been in circulation, that Andrea had given Cheryl "the keys to the queendom long ago." Roxanne wanted to know what they were, to which Cheryl could only reply that it was a fabulous urban legend.

But the incident sparked a phone call to Andrea, who laughed at the rumor and scoffed at the label of "mentor," "I somehow always feel that grad students are my colleagues and just act accordingly: i.e., I try to be helpful in any way I can think of. This probably turns out to be mentoring but that seems like a fancy name for it." We were not surprised that Andrea would shy away from the "mentor" label, simply given her personality and her commitment to a collaborative model. When we reminded her of the specific ways she had advised us (especially when we needed it the most but wanted it the least), she conceded that maybe she had mentored, but she felt more like a big sister.

We were—and still are—mentored by Andrea, just as we continue to mentor each other as well as others (more about that later). But we were never her only protégés, nor her first influences—not by a long shot. Nan Johnson writes of meeting Andrea for the first time back in 1978, describing her as "well, you know, Andrea: smart, caring, interested, funny—making a green kid feel comfortable in the presence of someone who seemed . . . to be the coolest of the cool" ("Andrea"). Johnson goes on to write about having had "many more mentoring lessons over the years from Andrea about the importance of 'making time' and treating everyone like colleagues" and about the foundation of Ohio State's Rhetoric and Writing Program being "first and foremost a community of scholars and teachers working together for a common goal" ("Andrea"). Such is the real Andrea, the authentic mentor behind the scholarly profile in *Women's Ways,* the woman Nan goes on to describe as "The Smile." She describes "The Smile" as the "welcome that Andrea has for each and every person, the way she attends, remembers, recognizes, listens, the way she offers to sit down and talk, read work, email, the many, many ways Andrea values Everyone as a colleague, the ways she makes time as if nothing [were] more important" ("Andrea").

Were we not privy to the living and breathing Andrea and the other eight women behind their profiles, we might believe that the nine women profiled in *Women's Ways* are traditional role models; but in fact, their feminist perspectives transform their work. As Andrea's example makes clear, feminists do not reserve the center; everyone takes turns at being the focus of attention; and, most important, protégés are not replicas of the mentor (nor are they "protégés," at least not to Andrea). So even though the feminist-guru model of mentoring appears to be a mere update of the traditional master-apprentice model, it certainly is not. Rarely is reciprocal, mutually respectful, place-changing (feminist) mentoring practice supported and replicated anywhere else, let alone within our traditional institutions.

Still, the feminist-guru model has its limitations. After all, institutional mentoring practices consist mostly of variations on traditional, hierarchical mentoring. Consider, for instance, entrance into graduate school. When students do so, they are often assigned a peer mentor (a more senior grad student); occasionally they are assigned a faculty mentor as well, but more often the burden of establishing a relationship with a faculty member falls upon the student (unless, of course, the student has been "chosen" by a mentor). When new lecturers or assistant professors enter the field, they, too, are almost always assigned a mentor until they pass over the next threshold of appointment, to senior lecturer or associate professor with tenure, for example. Furthermore, books like *Women's Ways,* based on literature reviews and interviews, admonish all newcomers to find a mentor (preferably a well-established, successful one, a guru) as soon as possible and to stick with that mentor. After all, the book admonishes readers that career success depends on guru mentoring. Without such a guru, there is simply no success—or safety. A final problem with finding a guru is that s/he is, often, a workaholic with extraordinary aptitude for academic research and teaching. And often, women academics are childless—one of the ironies of the profiles in *Women's Ways* (the authors and several of the exemplars are childless by choice). That is not to say that having a child is the best way to show one's ability to have a rich home life while also succeeding as an academic. But the point remains: gurus can intimidate students and colleagues with their remarkable productivity.

For many reasons, then, relying on the feminist-guru system of mentoring has drawbacks. First, this system *requires* mentoring, yet successful mentoring is not rewarded. Jane E. Rheineck and Catherine B. Roland write that "mentoring can be an essential component in assisting the development of a professional identity" (80), and Shalonda Kelly and John H. Schweitzer call it "the heart of graduate education" (130). In fact, many graduate recipients report that "their relationship with faculty [was] the most important aspect in their completion and satisfaction with graduate school" (Kelly and Schweitzer 13). Good mentoring is crucial, often required, yet despite this significance, it is rarely credited to the mentor during annual reviews. True feminist-guru mentoring consists of professional development and capacity building as well as personal support and guidance; nonetheless, its cultural currency converts only into "service," the least-valued category in the holy trinity of academia: research, teaching, and service. "Research" (another word for scholarly publications), on the other hand, carries with it the most cultural capital in the university's reward structure of tenure and promotion, merit raises, awards, and distinctions. Coming in (usually as a distant second) is "teaching," a metric usually limited to students' end-of-term evaluations.

Ironically, those who earn commendations for their research and teaching often have very little time for mentoring their graduate students and colleagues. Hence, the work of mentoring too often falls to those who *do* make the time, too often to women, and often at the expense of the time they can give to their research and sometimes even their teaching. Given the fact that women constitute only 31 percent of the tenured positions and just 24 percent of full professorships, pressure is on those relatively few senior women to mentor the junior women. The expense of time and energy is particularly dear for the even fewer academic women of color, an issue we take up below.

A second problem with the feminist-guru mentoring model is that not every feminist is good at mentoring, despite the best of intentions. Judging by our experience mentoring graduate students at six different universities, we know that some feminist faculty (male and female alike) simply lack the social skills, psychological wherewithal, or self-awareness to be an effective mentor. Perhaps these professors are mentoring the way they were mentored (expecting their mentees to arrive as replicas-in-waiting, as the mentors themselves had been earlier in their career); perhaps they are drawing on familiar nonacademic experiences such as church, social clubs, athletics, family (imagining that a missionary, competitive, emotionally dramatic, or even sexual relationship is acceptable); perhaps they are unaware of their effect on mentees (assuming unearned trust, friendship, or reverence; controlling and demeaning rather than advising them; carelessly stalling a student's progress); perhaps they gloss over the literature available on good mentoring (not knowing of its existence or not thinking they could benefit from it)—we do not know. What we do know is there are ineffective feminist-guru mentors.

If they are not careful, effective feminist-guru mentors can earn themselves an ever-growing cohort of mentees at the same time that they are spending their own limited supplies of time and energy. Therefore, the dependability and effectiveness of a feminist-guru mentor can lead to a third problem with this model: flat-out exhaustion. After all, only a small number of senior faculty (of any gender identity) are sought out as mentors in the first place. And popular feminist-gurus lose their ability to attend to others as well as take care of themselves when they are overcommitted. The problem of increased demand for mentorship is exacerbated when the feminist-guru embodies an underrepresented group (in terms of cultural ethnicity, race, physical ability, age, or sexual orientation). Not only will the university place demands on the mentor (wanting such representation on committees and task forces), but students and junior faculty will seek out the mentor as well. The latest available figures indicate that among tenured female faculty, "88.2 percent were white, 6.6 percent were black, 2.7 percent were Asian, 2.3 percent were Hispanic, and 0.3 percent were American Indian" (U.S. Equal Employment). With so few cultural-ethnic minorities available for mentoring, the demand on them remains intense.[2] Hence, the feminist-guru model holds great potential, but its weaknesses merit careful examination and urgent resolution.

THE FEMINIST GENERATIONAL MODEL OF MENTORING

The second model of mentoring we want to discuss is the generational model. A variation on the feminist-guru model, this model maps the tree of influence, much as does Sondra Perl's fabulous "Writing Studies Tree" project, which addresses the question, "What are the lines of descent or inheritance in [our] scholarly family?" (2011 CCCC Program, 82; see writingstudiestree.org). The generational model recognizes gurus, their ancestor-gurus, their generation, and their progeny. In other words, the generational model recognizes that every guru had his or her own guru (probably shared that guru with academic siblings), who had a guru, and so on, and that current protégés who are willing, able, and well rested will continue the tradition. The importance of such familial relationships is the focus of Janet Atwill's contribution to the recent Octalog retrospective.[3] Atwill invokes "the need to protect spaces where . . . colloquies and relationships can flourish" (249). She goes on to write, "By relationships, I mean something that includes—but is not restricted to—friendships. The Octalogs bear witness to the extent to which disciplines are embodied—handed off from mentors and shared among students and colleagues" (249). One has only to think of the Corbett and then the Corbett-Lunsford years at Ohio State, the James Sledd–James Kinneavy–Maxine Hairston years at the University of Texas, the Ross Winterowd years at the University of Southern California, the Janice Lauer–James Berlin years at Purdue, and the Winifred Horner–Richard Leo Enos years at Texas Christian (just to name a few) to evoke the generations in any one program. For example, we are part of the Corbett and then Corbett-Lunsford years, sharing this lineage with Lunsford herself, as well as with Robert Connors, Lisa Ede, Elizabeth Flynn, Suellynn Duffy, Krista Ratcliffe, Jaime Meija, Bob Yaglesky, Jerry Nelms, Becky Rickly, Sarah Sloane, Roger and Heather Graves, and many others.

There are good reasons to talk about academic mentoring in a familial-genealogical way, given that habits of thought, behavior, writing, and personal style are often modeled and passed down from one academic to another. In addition, successful mentoring entails "entrustment," a conscious decision to entrust oneself with another, who becomes a guide or point of reference, and the trustworthy so often appear within families (De Lauretis 22). After all, many established academics call upon their feminist-guru ancestry in order to talk through workplace issues, collegial interaction, and personal dilemmas. Despite the richness of a broader familial style of mentoring that has connections with all three models of mentoring we discuss, the feminist-generational-lineage model continues to hold more sway than the familial model in academia. Advisors such as Horner and Lunsford often invoke the genealogy of mentorship when their PhD students go on to mentor their own PhD students. At that point in the genealogy, Horner and Lunsford refer to themselves as the grandmothers of all those second- and even third-generation advisees. These kinds of references are often received with enthusiasm and pride. For everyone in the lineage—top to bottom, older to younger—such patronage helps ensure standards, quality, and a measure of protection.

The feminist-generational model of mentoring features a number of important qualities: it acknowledges that academics "embody" the discipline for the next generation of scholars, passing along a legacy of values, theories, habits, and assumptions that keep the discipline rolling. In real terms, a "discipline" is made up of relationships among individuals who dwell together for a time and then go forth to do work inspired, in part, by their mentors and friends. A graduate program that provides such an environment for students creates foundations courses and cutting-edge seminars that bring students into dialogue with what is going on in the field. This seems a simple formula—obvious, perhaps—but we both have witnessed far too many graduate programs in which faculty focused seminars so closely on their latest interest that it was impossible for students to do anything but reproduce that professor's work. Andrea has always taught seminars in new areas (for example, "How and Why We Remember: The Rhetoric of Mediated Memory"; "The Rhetoric of Difference: Race, Class, and Gender"; "The Rhetoric of Intellectual Property") as well as foundations courses that tap both established and groundbreaking research ("Studies in Composition," "Theories of Reading," and "Research Methods in Composition"), always encouraging her students to link their passions with the research questions in the field. At the point each of her mentees have coupled their passion with abiding disciplinary questions, the field always seemed to be ready for their work, just as we were ready for the field. Needless to say, students who receive this kind of mentoring who are not utterly selfish in their aspirations pass it on, mentoring and aspirations alike. This ethic of encouraging a student to link her own passions with the field's questions is something passed down Andrea's generational line.

Feminist-generational mentoring is functional in many ways, yet it involves two major problems. First of all, despite its appellation, the generational mentoring model does not highlight familial or aunting mentoring as a valid option. Emerging scholars often benefit from a number of mentoring relationships. Just as Cheryl must include Ed Corbett (a perfectionist with high expectations), Morris Beja (an energetic, visionary department chair), Dan Barnes (a brilliantly gifted teacher), and Jamie Barlowe (a fearless fellow graduate student) as her graduate-school mentors, Roxanne must include (then assistant professor) Beverly Moss. Although Beverly arrived at Ohio State after Roxanne had already finished coursework (including research methods) and exams, she agreed to serve on Roxanne's dissertation committee. Beverly's own dissertation had been a study of ministers and literacy practices, so she was well prepared to advise Roxanne as she investigated how gender affected the rhetorical practices of women ministers. Well versed in the unique issues involved in church-based studies, Beverly accompanied Roxanne to church where Roxanne met Reverend Barb, an African American minister. Ironically, Reverend Barb had been mentored by one of the ministers in Beverly's study. For Roxanne to gain entrance into an African

American church, let alone write about that fieldwork, was a challenge, but Beverly's mentoring supported her throughout—as did the mentoring of Nan Johnson. Nan taught Roxanne how to write a dissertation-long argument, critiquing every section of her work. There was also Kris Ratcliffe, who taught Roxanne how to enter the job market. There was Cheryl, who badgered Roxanne to submit her manuscript to the book series Cheryl and Shirley Wilson Logan coedit.

This broader network of mentoring is concealed as academic ancestors or other relations, even though these academic family members provide opportunities (however brief or intermittent) for spacious and responsible interactions. Blogger Alexis Pauline Gumbs calls them the "wonderful people who have raised me, fed me, affirmed and inspired me." Third-wave feminist Rebecca Walker (daughter of Alice Walker) calls them the "aunts, keepers, and teachers" who helped "raise [her] up" (Walker xxix–xl).

This translation of the feminist-guru model of mentoring into an ancestral model is referred to as "aunting" by Walker and others, Laura L. Ellingson and Patty Sotirin, in particular. These so-called aunts not only nurture the mentee's academic development but also provide what John Stewart calls "reflected appraisal," allowing mentees to see themselves as significant others (in this case, as academic relatives) see them. Various aunts, then, are diversely configured within the mentee's circumstances, offering mentoring, facilitating growth, and guarding well-being in ways that are less charged than those of most major gurus. Ellingson and Sotirin explain, "While some academic aunting relationships may be characterized by nurturing qualities and / or apprentice roles, other aunting relationships may be based on intermittent, even fleeting, connections that nonetheless hold considerable significance for both parties" ("Academic Aunting" 38).

These authors celebrate aunting for its reciprocity: the mentoring is not "self-interested and instrumental," so much as it is "mutually supportive and respectful, set in terms of what is done together—the practices of academic civility, the creation and preservation of academic wisdom" (Ellingson and Sotirin, "Academic Aunting" 38). Such a mentoring model is much more complex and robust than one indicating a clear descendant or strict lineage. After all, a number of academic relatives might be necessary for enabling every student's passage. If any of Roxanne's mentors or Cheryl's, for that matter, had retired or moved to another institution, such a network of mentors could still sustain them. And indeed, they still do. Yet only the official mentor, the dissertation advisor, gets the credit in the generational model. The genealogical chart resembles a patriarchal map, in which only the ancestors whose patronyms we inherit are actually visible, despite the fact that we inherit DNA from them all. In our view, then, it makes much more sense to talk about mentoring in terms of larger networks, which we discuss below.

The second major problem with the feminist-generational model is the presumption that mentoring flows in only one direction—from a mentor to her acolytes. Ruth Fassinger's progressive model of feminist modeling disrupts this unidirectional flow by placing "substantial emphasis on the relational component of mentoring as well as issues related to power and empowerment" (Benishek, Bieschke, Park, and Slattery 433). She describes her broadly adaptable mentoring model as the creation of a relationship "built on the sharing of power, mutuality, equality, and respect" (8). Such a relationship is also built on the reciprocity of information sharing, with the mentor rerouting some of her own power in order to empower the mentee. For Andrea, teaching and mentoring are a gift exchange: "When I think of my own experiences as a receiver of such gifts, I think most often of students who have been my teachers. . . . [So many of my students] have been and continue to be exemplars for me ("Metaphors" 7–8). Lunsford's mentoring stance empowers her students to be teachers of *her,* a perspective that emphasizes mentoring as a dialogical, reciprocal, two-way relationship rather than a hierarchical one. As Lunsford's practice suggests, the act of mentoring can sustain both the mentee and the mentor. Mentor benefits include increased "personal satisfaction via helping another's career" as well as "enthusiasm for research, teaching, and . . . practice" (Atkinson, Casas, Neville 42).

The generational model of mentoring has been heavily critiqued in professional settings, but not for the reasons we mention above. Instead, organizations are beginning to realize that the prior generation of leaders may not know best where or how to move the organization forward. As John Stuart Mill once put it, "That which seems the height of absurdity in one generation often becomes the height of wisdom in the next." In the business of making knowledge (as we academics do) or communicating knowledge (as the tech industry does), a one-way model of mentoring no longer makes sense. The new model emerging in business settings is "reverse mentoring," a term millennial Alexa Scordato coined to describe how she found herself mentoring her boomer boss. The two met weekly so that she could teach him how best to leverage various social media—including Facebook and Twitter—and collaborate on the fifty-three blog entries they eventually published.

Although many academics are rightfully wary of importing enterprise models into higher education, reverse mentoring appears to be a brilliant solution to the troubles with both feminist-guru and feminist-generational models that emphasize top-down mentoring. Reverse mentoring could be a way to credit graduate students for the mentoring they give their own mentors as well as other senior faculty, whether the mentoring focuses on course development, team teaching, shared administrative duties, convention planning, community outreach, and / or technological advancements. If our field is amenable to top-down mentoring and down-up mentoring, recognizing the advantages of both systems, surely it can benefit from a broader network of mentoring. We believe that the feminist-network model holds the most promise of all the feminist mentoring frameworks.

THE FEMINIST NETWORK MODEL OF MENTORING

Rhetoric and writing studies faculty often use the metaphor of networking. After all, we advise graduate students to attend professional meetings (particularly the Conference on College Composition and Communication, Rhetoric Society of America, Computers and Writing, and Writing Program Administrators), where they are to introduce themselves to scholars they admire, attend publishers' parties, participate in special-interest groups and workshops, and connect with graduate students from other programs. We always nudge our graduate students to make connections, to network. But the network itself—the constellations of connections among individuals, generations of individuals, scholarship, and information that comprise the field of rhetoric and writing studies—is vast. The use of various social media continues to accelerate, accentuating and creating connections in ways that were unthinkable even ten years ago. For example, many scholars now conduct a good part of their academic work through Facebook, establishing personal links, associating information and ideas and people in ever-expanding ways. A major feature of mentoring is revealing the grids of associated people and information that comprise any discipline or field. So how might we reimagine mentoring itself as a network?

In "Off-the-Hook Black Feminist Mentorship," Gumbs gives tribute to her nonacademic mentors, and then challenges the entire top-down mentoring system in higher education. Addressing her fellow aspiring black feminist scholars, she writes,

> I want you to know that there is no bourgeois scarcity when it comes to Black feminist mentorship. It is no use fighting each other or feeling like we have to compete for one of five tokenized mentors at the top who may be so stressed out by interim chairing two programs and half of a department that they should not be holding the whole task of mentoring you anyway.
>
> The more mentors we have, in more places, the better off we are, lest capitalism trick us into believing that only the well-funded, institutionally connected, socially secure Black feminist intellectuals have gifts for our sharp, critical anti-capitalist lifetimes.

That may be obvious to some. No one in her right mind thinks that one superstar feminist guru can be your only mentor, even if she is superwoman, an academic goddess, with god-like ancestors. But Gumbs is making a larger point here—higher education can make us so insular that too many of us tend to see the university as our "only source of support." She writes that "through practice and through the lives of my many mentors I know the academy is not the only nor the primary source of support for my brilliance and that the tenure track is only one of infinite paths that a Black feminist can choose to take." Gumbs's words serve to remind academics that our work is meant to serve people both inside and outside the academy. So if we want off-campus people to consider us part of their extended knowledge network, should we not consider them part of ours? Shouldn't we consider establishing mentoring relationships or partnerships off-campus as well as on? To that end, Gumbs would have us tap the full range of mentors—whether gurus, generations, or on- and off-campus networks, seeking mentors laterally as well as vertically.

> I have the deep luxury of not measuring my impact, success, and purposefulness on funding, tenure, bills paid on time—and I want that freedom for you. Build a base of badass mentors that take different risks, make different sacrifices from each other, work in different conditions and with different styles.

Gumbs challenges feminists to rethink the concept of mentoring altogether, perhaps considering it as a critical site for merging theories and practices, a site where we influence at the same time that we are being influenced within a dynamic system that is constantly shifting.

Despite the academic compulsion to stabilize knowledge through requirements, canons, exams, and departments, our work is promiscuous by nature.

The task of every scholar, then, is to jack into the network and begin finding the connections, sometimes by being taught they are there through coursework and other academic requirements, but also by proceeding directly to the conversations themselves, which are increasingly taking place online. Many academics spend time in social networking sites, where, amid the emoticons, inspirational posters, and happy birthday wishes, are clues, small and large, about how people and information are connected and where such connections lead. Younger and established scholars alike (mentees and mentors) log onto these grids and learn from one another. After all, as Paula Moya reminds us, "Unless we have access to alternative perspectives . . . we risk being arrested in the process of our intellectual and moral growth" (131).

Our networked reality has some problems, to be sure. In *Alone Together,* Sherry Turkle juxtaposes our new increased intimacies with others via social media with our isolation. Our gadgets, she argues, have enchanted us, replacing human contact. Our campuses are full of zombies—those students and faculty looking down at their phones, reading and texting, not looking up for oncoming human or vehicular traffic. Perhaps we are networked professionally yet isolated personally. Or vice versa. We remember when the only way to know what other scholars were working on was to hear them give papers at conferences—or to learn about their work when a visiting scholar returned with news. What made Andrea an especially valuable mentor in the years before the Internet was that she was constantly traveling to campuses across the nation and around the globe, returning home with the news of what others were researching, writing, and struggling with. We used to depend on such travels (others' or our own), but now we can all go to any scholar's website to read about their research or simply friend them on Facebook and read their status updates. Scholars and activists also keep blogs, where we can read and learn. Indeed, while there are certain tradeoffs to working in this social media-saturated world, we can be sure that it isn't going away. "In the network society," Shaviro argues, "experience will be digital or not at all" (248).

Higher education remains incredibly conservative, with its urge to stabilize and quantify. Despite the lightning-fast changes in knowledge exchange and publication venues, the academy, for the most part, remains fixed on the scholarly monograph (what digital humanities specialist Kathleen Fitzpatrick regularly calls "the walking undead") as the best means to circulate knowledge. Such print habits of sharing information have, in many ways, outlived their usefulness—just like our traditional, top-down mentoring systems. Identifying one human as the official guru, or one human as the site of lineage, is an outdated way of understanding the needs of new and established scholars alike—and not because of any lack in the feminist-guru or lineage.

Rather, given the academy's ease of networking, why not locate every student and advisor in a broader mentoring network, an interdisciplinary group of scholars addressing similar problems? Rather than working with or as a guru, scholars would work within an ashram, with each participant receiving credit for the progress of the protégés, the research, the collaboration. Such a network would provide, according to Gumbs, "an abundant ecology of living, ancestral mentors" and "badass mentors" alike. Our colleges and universities, we academics, have the ability to set up such networks, physically and socially as well as electronically.

In terms of stimulating an effective feminist-network-mentoring system, we in rhetoric and writing studies should continue to produce more conference presentations, online sites, articles, and (yes!) monographs like *Women's Ways*. After all, *Women's Ways* was written in response to an obvious professional need. Michelle Eble and Lynée Gaillet's *Stories of Mentoring* is another case in point. Given how quickly information can now be accessed and updated, both books have time-sensitive limitations and should be revised. Perhaps they should both go online so that others can expand upon the information within them, adding their own stories of mentoring.

BUT MOST IMPORTANT . . .

But most important, we believe that all scholars, teachers, and students in rhetoric and writing should be encouraged to see themselves as part of the network that is our discipline and to tune in. If we faculty can work to make ourselves more accessible, more approachable to other faculty and students alike, nationally and globally, we transform ourselves into the network. Many of us are already purposefully doing just that, leveraging social media to reach and be reached by others on the network. More of us should blog about the research and teaching we are doing, the scholarly problems we are engaging, and the fruitful collaborations we are participating in, demonstrating through a practice of speaking respectfully of others that the network we are part of includes students as well as members of the public. As more of us rhetoric and writing teachers and students consciously link ourselves and our work to the community, we can bring their needs and interests into our world and reciprocate by carrying any measure of expertise we have back into theirs. Feminist rhetoricians Sonja Foss and Cindy Griffin provide us a way for implementing such in-reach and out-reach work. By tapping their theory of "invitational rhetoric," we can extend an invitation for people within and outside our academic community (our larger network) to become part of our work, thereby creating a relationship rooted in equality, immanent value, and self-determination" ("Beyond" 5).

After all, the field of rhetoric and writing studies is about making knowledge that our communities can use now—today. We believe that rhetorical practices should *do* something, that rhetorical inquiry should make a difference in the world, that our teaching and mentoring should improve people's lives. And although agency is a contested term, our discipline does indeed have agency, the power to take efficacious action in our own community and beyond, to influence and be receptive to the influence of our colleagues, senior and junior alike. And even if that agency is always contingent, it can be adopted strategically (echoing Spivak), rigorously, and yet humanely to rewrite our practices, theories, and relationships, and to transform our older rhetorical selves as well as to prepare the next generation of rhetorically empowered scholars, teachers, and citizens.

As Adrienne Rich reminds us, it's folks like us—intellectuals, writers, teachers, *and mentors*—who must make and write such a mentoring future through the "sheer power of a collective imagining of change and a sense of collective hope" ("Arts" 167). Our hope for the future of rhetoric and writing studies is that we create a network of feminist mentoring that plays forward, backwards, sideways, and diagonally at the same time that it frames a scholarly and humane model of high expectations, rigorous preparation and execution, and (always) open communication. To be long-lasting, however, such networked mentoring relationships must be tempered by the honesty and hope that results from mutual respect, flexibility, receptivity, sensitivity, open dialogue—and hope. Paula Mathieu tells that to hope is "to look critically at one's present condition, assess what is missing, and then long for and work for a not-yet reality, a future anticipated" (19). To envision such a future requires imagination, to be sure, but also action, action put in the service of sustaining friendships, scholarly responsibility, ethical action, and the reciprocal shaping of the generations. Such is the work that we feminists do so well.

In closing, we want to circle back to Alexa Scordato, the millennial who mentored her boomer boss. One of the most energizing reasons to update our assumptions about mentoring is that doing so allows us to see that every generation, millennial or boomer, has its own networks of knowledge that we can join, different ways of mentoring that we can model. As a field, we in rhetoric and writing studies are enriched each time the circle of expertise expands to include our newest members. For these reasons, we want to close by challenging our readers to think differently of our knowledge-making / knowledge-sharing enterprise, not only in how we mentor and who mentors whom, but also in how we work, write, research, both alone and in collaboration. It's a challenging time to be in higher education, given budget cuts, endless assessments, public scrutiny, political derision, and the problems that race and income have long exacerbated. Therefore, there has never been a more crucial time to apply our feminist imagination to the enrichment of rhetoric and writing studies and the development of all practitioners.

Notes

1. Of course, we both benefited from talented male mentors from graduate school, including the intimidating and inspiring Mr. Corbett, who was, in his own way, a model for us all, writing beautiful, readable prose and serving the profession at every level. He took us seriously, preparing us both for a life in the profession.

2. Especially on relatively homogeneous campuses, white female faculty and male and female faculty of color feel pressured to "provide counseling and advising" for students who identify with them (Chandler 87).

3. Between 1988 and 2012, the annual convention of the Conference on College Composition and Communication has featured three Octalogs, colloquia featuring eight scholars who speak to the current state of rhetorical studies. *Rhetoric Review* has published each of the Octalogs, along with a 2011 retrospective on historiography and the three Octalogs, featuring fourteen of the previous participants.

Works Cited

Atkinson, Donald R., Antonio Casas, and Helen Neville. "Ethnic Minority Psychologists: Women They Mentor and Benefits They Derive from the Process." *Journal of Multicultural Counseling and Development*, vol. 22, no. 1, 1994, pp. 37–48.

Atwill, Janet. "The Octalogic Imagination." *Rhetoric Review*, no. 30, vol. 3, 2011, pp. 249–50.

Ballif, Michelle, Diane Davis, and Roxanne Mountford. *Women's Ways of Making It in Rhetoric and Composition*. Routledge, 2008.

Benishek, Lois A., Kathleen J. Bieschke, Jeeseon Park, and Suzanne M. Slattery. "A Multicultural Feminist Model of Mentoring." *Journal of Multicultural Counseling and Development*, vol. 32, 2004, pp. 428–42.

Dahle, Cheryl. "Women's Ways of Mentoring." FastCompany.com. 19 Dec. 2007. Accessed 10 April 2012.

De Lauretis, Teresa. "The Essence of the Triangle or, Taking the Risk of Essentialism Seriously: Feminist Theory in Italy, the U.S., and Britain. *Differences*, vol. 1, no. 3, 1989, pp. 3–37.

Eble, Michelle F., and Lynée Lewis Gaillet, eds. *Stories of Mentoring: Theory and Praxis*. Parlor, 2008.

Ellingson, Laura L., and Patty [Patricia J.] Sotirin. "Academic Aunting: Reimaging Feminist (Wo)Mentoring, Teaching, and Relationships. *Women and Language*, vol. 31, no. 1, 2008, pp. 35–43.

———. *Aunting: Cultural Practices That Sustain Family and Community Life*. Baylor UP, 2010.

Fassinger, Ruth E. "Dangerous Liaisons: Reflections on Feminist Mentoring." Woman of the Year. American Psychological Association Annual Meeting. Chicago. Aug. 2007.

Fishman, Jenn, and Andrea A. Lunsford. "Educating Jane." *Stories of Mentoring: Theory and Praxis*, edited by Michele F. Eble and Carrie Leverenz, Parlor, 2008, pp. 18–32.

Foss, Sonja, and Cindy L. Griffin. "Beyond Persuasion: A Proposal for Invitational Rhetoric." *Communication Monographs*, vol. 62, 1995, pp. 1–18.

Gumbs, Alexis Pauline. "Off-the-Hook Black Feminist Mentorship: An Anti-Capitalist Re-evaluation." *Thefeministwire* 21 Dec. 2011. Accessed 15 April 2012.

Heilbrun, Carolyn. *When Men Were the Only Models We Had*. U of Pennsylvania P, 2002.

Johnson, Nan. "Andrea as Mentor." Conference on College Composition and Communication. Atlanta, Georgia. April 2011.

Kelly, Shalonda, and John H. Schweitzer. "Mentoring within a Graduate School Setting." *College Student Journal*, vol. 33, no. 1, 1999, pp. 130–48.

Moya, Paula. *Learning from Experience*. U of California P, 2002.

Plato. *Gorgias*. *The Rhetorical Tradition*, edited by Patricia Bizzell and Bruce Herzberg, 2nd ed., Bedford / St. Martin's, 2001, pp. 138–68.

Rheineck, Jane E., and Catherine B. Roland. "The Developmental Mentoring Relationship between Academic Women." *Adultspan Journal*, vol. 7, no. 2, 2008, pp. 80–93.

Rich, Adrienne. "Arts of the Possible." *Arts of the Possible: Essays and Conversations*, Norton, 2001, pp. 146–68.

———. *Fox*. Norton, 2001.

Scordato, Alexa. "Reverse-Mentorship: Bridging the Digital Divide." Ted X Boston. 28 July 2009. http://tedxboston.org/speaker/scordato. Accessed 17 Feb. 2016.

Shaviro, Steven. *Connected, Or, What It Means to Live in the Network Society.* U of Minnesota P, 2003.

Stewart, John, ed. *Bridges Not Walls: A Book about Interpersonal Communication.* McGraw-Hill, 2002.

Turkle, Sherry. *Alone Together: Why We Expect More from Technology and Less from Each Other.* Basic, 2012.

U.S. Equal Employment Opportunity Commission. *Black Issues in Higher Education*, no. 10, vol. 17, 1991, p. 42.

Walker, Rebecca, ed. *To Be Real: Telling the Truth and Changing the Face of Feminism.* Anchor, 1995.

Wilson, Robin. "AAUP Report Blames Colleges for Gender Inequity among Professors." *Chronicle of Higher Education.* 3 November 2006. http://chronicle.com/article/AAUP-Report-Blames-Colleges/8774. Accessed 12 April 2012.

PART 4
THE IMPERMANENCE OF A CANON

THE EMPRESS AND THE SOPHIST
POWER AND ARTISTRY IN THIRD-CENTURY GREEK RHETORIC

SUSAN C. JARRATT

Historians of ancient rhetoric have barely begun to unfold its abundance. The richness of the pedagogical and theoretical tradition has, understandably, preoccupied many scholars, bringing forth more, and more interestingly varied, readings of Plato, Aristotle, Cicero, and Quintilian (e.g., Yunis, Atwill, Kinnerly, and Fleming, respectively). As the field gains depth and complexity in its reading of canonical figures, so has it also begun to stretch, expand, and extend its interest in less frequently studied periods, geographical sites, and figures.[1] What is required for bringing to life and to light more fully the *poikilos* nature of rhetoric in antiquity—its variety, manifold beauty, and intricate artistry—are not only languages, access to new archives and material culture, but also methods of reading. [2] The default texts of rhetoric from classical Athens and the Rome of the Republic are orations of the Aristotelian genres and the metarhetoric of treatises. We have spent the most time with these texts and have highly developed methods of reading them. When we move off these centers, rhetoric is fragmented into a jumble of genres; the aims of its authors, scenes of performance, and modes of circulation and reception become less certain—a phenomenon George A. Kennedy famously referred to as *letteraturizzazione*.[3] Where is the feminist scholar to go in search of reading strategies for such texts? As Susan Romano proposes, with reference to the contradictory accounts of a sixteenth-century woman religious teacher in New

Spain whose own writing is lost, the feminist historian with "no clear set of instructions for how to proceed" turns to the framing force of rhetoric itself.

Andrea A. Lunsford anticipates Romano's insight in the former's introductory essay for the 1995 collection, *Reclaiming Rhetorica,* noting with elegant simplicity that claims of newness usually fall short, and in fact, the diversity of rhetoric—and, by implication, the methods for interpreting such diversity—inhere within its very long tradition (6–7). Reading rhetorically, Lunsford argues, historians may use tropes of metonymy, metaphor, and consubstantiality just as well as those of division and definition (6). Echoing these themes, Suzanne Clark at the end of the volume in her essay on Julia Kristeva recommends changing rhetoric from within, unsettling the familiar by recognizing a strangeness that should not be associated with the alien or foreign (305). Bringing the woman intellectual / teacher / rhetor into focus can be a matter of shifting the *topoi* under which she has been placed, as Romano so eloquently argues, or it may require bringing to bear other rhetorical tactics characteristic of the age in which she lives.

I found myself in need of these resources when I came to a crossing—a surprising intersection—while following along the path of Greek rhetoric's fortunes under the Roman Empire. Arguably, the most significant text for such a project is the collection of intellectual biographies titled *Lives of the Sophists,* written in the 230s of the Common Era. Both coiner of the title "Second Sophistic" and himself a member of that group, Flavius Philostratus was a Greek whose rhetorical practice brought him into direct contact with Roman imperial power around the turn of the third century (some years before *Lives*). [4] In an earlier work, his massive and intriguing *The Life of Apollonius of Tyana,* a "hybrid of which biography is the dominant parent" (Bowie 28), Philostratus reports that the project was sponsored by Julia Domna, wife of Septimius Severus, empress of Rome from 193 to 211. Domna[5] survived her husband and became co-emperor with her son Caracalla until his death in 217, the year of her own death as well. This provocative reference linking the Syrian empress with the Greek second sophist challenges feminist historiographical methods, as we confront a woman for whom we have no authored texts but some tantalizing indications of her involvement in rhetoric. What can we know about Julia Domna—her intellectual accomplishments and rhetorical investments—given the scanty evidence? Further, how do we weigh the significance of her various ascriptions: gender, imperial power, intellectual formation, and Syrian ethnicity? And what does this inquiry matter for our understanding of rhetorical practice in the period?

FROM FEMINIST *TOPOI* TO SOPHISTIC READING

Much of what we know about Domna's life comes from historian Cassius Dio (163/64–229), a native of Nicaea in the province of Bithynia (modern Turkey), and thus a provincial elite: one with a rhetorical education and a strong identification as "Greek," but at the same time the son of a Roman senator and himself appointed Roman senator under Commodus. He rose to the position of consul (ca. 205 and again later) and also served as governor of Smyrna. In this dual position in the empire (insider and outsider), he was a personal observer of many of the events he narrates in an eighty-book history composed in Attic Greek, encompassing the years of Julia Domna's public life.

Unfortunately, nothing in Cassius Dio or elsewhere is recorded about Domna's education, but her birth into the household of the chief priest in Emesa (a city founded by Arabs, but also associated with the Phoenician cities of the Syrian coast) and the fact that she attracted the interest of another colonial subject with intellectual aspirations, Septimius Severus, a native of Northern Africa, suggest that she did receive some significant pedagogical experience. Birley speculates that she and her husband may have communicated in Greek, as well as in a combination of their native languages: Punic and Aramaic. This background may have predicted the linguistic competence and diplomatic skill Cassius Dio later reports. After her marriage in 187, she quickly bore two sons and became empress when Severus declared himself emperor in the field in 193. Age twenty-three in that year, Domna accompanied her husband on many campaigns, was designated "Mater Castrorum" (mother of the camp), and upon the family's return to Rome around the turn of the third century, she reportedly began keeping company with sophists, philosophers, medical scholars, religious sages, and astrologers. On campaign again in Africa and Britain, Domna was left as advisor to the co-rule of her sons when Severus died in 211.

Predictably, joint rule didn't go smoothly, and only a year later the older son, who came to be called Caracalla, murdered his younger brother, Geta, as Domna held him in her arms, wounding her in the process. To make matters worse, Dio writes,

> she was not permitted to mourn or weep for her son, though he had met so miserable an end before his time (he was only twenty-two years and nine months old), but, on the contrary, she was compelled to rejoice and laugh as though at some great good fortune; so closely were all her words,

> gestures, and changes of colour observed. Thus she alone, the Augusta, wife of the emperor and mother of the emperors, was not permitted to shed tears even in private over so great a sorrow. (Cassius Dio, *Roman History*, Book 78.2.5–6)

At this point in a narrative that I've been recounting rather neutrally, we may recognize that Dio is offering a certain *topos* or construction of Domna: a deep pathos surrounds the figure of the grieving mother who is not even allowed her grief. In her extremely learned and thorough biography, Levick highlights the process of constructing narrative frames for Domna, finding in her story "three dependent plots": a family romance, a story of dynastic women, and an account of the orientalizing of the Roman Empire (1).[6] Elaborating these narratives or *topoi* based on what we've learned so far, we might lay out a continuum, placing on one end the Eastern child-bride whose numerous representations in sculpture and painting show her to have a childlike, simple beauty of face and figure. The child-bride then becomes the devoted mother of the camp and then suffering widow, counselor of emperor-sons, and ultimately, the grieving victim of her violent son's assassination and oppressive control. At the other end of this continuum of powerlessness and pathos, we might place the Julia Domna who conspires with her powerful Emesene family to join forces with the future emperor, relishes her position of power over Caracalla, and shares this role with her sister and niece, who find themselves in similar circumstances over the subsequent decades. Also lingering around this end of the continuum would fall the impression of Domna as worshiper of an Eastern religion, an impression that would have grown in the face of a later Severan emperor, Elagabalus, one of the most bizarre and outlandish in his religious and sexual practices.

These stories or narrative frames—at both ends of this imaginary continuum—have powerful emotional charges conventionally associated with the feminine in many cultural times and places: excessive vulnerability and innocence on the one hand, and grasping power of the orientalized woman / empress on the other. A process of clearing out and holding at bay these powerfully charged impressions will allow us to bring forward the *topos* that links Domna with sophistic rhetoric. The historian Cassius Dio again comes to our assistance, describing Domna's intellectual and leadership abilities in service to the emperor Caracalla even after his fratricide. After that time,

> [Caracalla] was staining himself with blood, doing lawless deeds, and squandering money. Neither in these matters nor in any others did he

> heed his mother, who gave him much excellent advice. And yet he had appointed her to receive petitions and to have charge of his correspondence in both languages, except in very important cases, and used to include her name, in terms of high praise, together with his own and that of the legions, in his letters to the senate, stating that she was well. Need I add that she held public receptions for all the most prominent men, precisely as did the emperor? But, while she devoted herself more and more to the study of philosophy with these men, he kept declaring that he needed nothing beyond the necessaries of life and plumed himself over his pretended ability to live on the cheapest kind of fare; yet there was nothing on land or sea or in the air that we did not regularly supply to him both by private gifts and by public grants. (*History,* Book 78 18.1–3)

Here we see Domna as a woman of strength, intelligence, will, discretion, and tenacity. She is a diplomat and translator: an intellectual with an interest in the movements of language, cultural practices, and power. As such, she seems to be a strong candidate for the role Philostratus assigns her as sponsor of his biography. But the sophistic text serves as more than another piece of evidence.

In what follows, I will use the text of the sophist, as well as sophistic rhetorical tactics as interpretive levers, to gain several new angles of vision on this allusive ancient woman rhetor. First, we will examine the historical claim made by author Philostratus in the introductory frame for his biography as a way of adjudicating the question of Julia Domna's "circle." We will then turn to a method of reading the biography—copious, novelistic, episodic, full of movement and ideas—as a figured discourse, exploring Philostratus's strategies for coding within a complex sophistic text his own and his sponsor's precarious circumstances as subjects of empire. Of the many directions such a reading could take in this massive work, we will follow two, each suggested by the situation of Julia Domna: the *topos* of law and lawlessness and the issue of an Eastern / Syrian identity. These readings will be more like inroads into a labyrinth—partial mappings—than the decisive clearing away of all mysteries. There will be no unveiling of the real and true sophistic empress at the end, and a brief essay cannot pretend to offer a comprehensive reading of the *Life of Apollonius of Tyana*. But it will be established decisively that any easy dismissal of ancient rhetoric as "Western" and "male" is a mischaracterization. At the very least, the story of the empress and the sophist must begin to take apart any "seamless" story (Lunsford) of rhetoric's history.

READING PHILOSTRATUS LITERALLY: JULIA DOMNA'S *KUKLOS*

The Philostratus under consideration here is the most prominent of the Greek intellectuals bearing that name and the author also of *Lives of the Sophists* and *Imagines*.[7] His *Life of Apollonius of Tyana* is the story of a holy man (*theios anêr*) with miraculous powers who travels the world, compares customs (much like Herodotus), matches his philosophical wisdom with others, and also acts as an advisor to kings. The reference to Domna, contributing to her picture as an intellectual woman bringing together prominent men for study, comes early on, as the author is providing the rationale for his work. About Pythagoras, Philostratus writes, there are many stories preserved, but the practices of Apollonius, a historical figure from the first century of the Common Era, though much like the earlier philosopher, are not well known, despite his living much later. The itinerant Pythagorean philosopher traveled to India, Ethiopia, and elsewhere in the East; stayed in temples, taught, advised cities; and counseled some highly placed Romans, perhaps including the emperors Vespasian and Titus.

The sophist lists his sources: shrines, reports, and Apollonius's own letters. And it is here we find the empress: "But my more detailed information I have gathered as follows. There was a certain Damis, not devoid of wisdom, who once lived in Old Ninos. This man became a disciple of Apollonius and wrote up not only his journeys, on which he claims to have been his companion, but also his sayings, speeches, and predictions. The notebooks containing the memoirs of Damis were unknown until a member of his family brought them to the attention of the empress Julia." He goes on,

> Since I was a member of her circle (*kuklou*) (for she admired and encouraged all rhetorical discourse), she set me to transcribe these works of Damis and to take care over their style (*tês apaggelias),* since the style of the man from Ninos [Damis] was clear but rather unskillful. (1.3; trans. adapted from Jones)

We see here a woman associated with an emperor, who draws together a group engaged in the discussion, preservation, and circulation of important texts. Some adjustments to Jones's translation bring out the term "circle" (replacing his choice, *salon,* and thus helping us to avoid the anachronistic leap to seventeenth-century French aristocracy). We also see a concern for style, but the lexicon's assistance with the Greek *apaggelia*, giving "report, as of an ambassador," and, as a verb, "to bring tidings, to carry a report home, to narrate," would suggest an interest not in style more generally but in a kind of narration or storytelling necessary for crossing borders, a skill (shrewdness or cleverness) this character Damis, another Syrian, apparently lacks.

Classical scholars are of several minds on the question of Domna's *kuklos*. William Cave Wright, 1921 translator of *Lives of the Sophists,* takes it as fact that, sometime after 202, through the influence of Aelius Antipater, teacher of both Severus and Philostratus, "[the latter] entered the circle of the philosophic Syrian Empress, Julia Domna" and traveled with her and the emperor to Britain in 208, Gaul in 212, Pergamon, Nicomedia, and Antioch" (x). Later scholars are more circumspect. In her review of the question, Levick finds extreme views of Domna's circle: "at first romantic and exalted . . . and more recently severely reductionist" (107). But she takes the sponsorship of Philostratus's work seriously, speculating that the commission to a sophist to write a biography of a wise man suggests "a woman who was attracted to guides to life, especially guides for rulers. She had come to power suddenly from the outer reaches of imperial society and needed guidance" (123).

In the category of reductionism, Tim Whitmarsh catalogues Philosotratus's various uses of the term *kuklos,* finding that the sophist uses it more often as an evaluative measure than as an indicator of a physical space or actual social gathering: the *kuklos* "invokes the metaphorical idea of a boundary between insiders and outsiders" ("Prose Literature" 33). Both Levick and Whitmarsh call attention to the nature of the text, emphasizing the generic similarity of Philostratus's *Life* to the Greek novels of the era—complexly layered, highly crafted narratives, blending historical account with supernatural events. Given this parallel, and the fact that the purported source of the material, Damis, is attested nowhere else in the existing records, we might be inclined to treat a literal reading of this commission skeptically.

By reading the sophist's text rhetorically rather than historically, it is possible to construe something more in "the case of the woman and the sophist" than presence or absence. We would undertake such a rhetorical reading by considering the circumstances of the Greek rhetor in the imperial setting, with an attunement to the possibility for figured discourse at work in this novelistic text: a "lurking meaning" shielded by the writer for the dual purposes of showing off his cleverness and keeping himself safe (Ahl). In what follows, a first pass at interpretation suggests that the potential for violence in relations with the emperor are coded within discussions of law and lawlessness. The second reading, focusing on the character of Damis, a Syrian, suggests that he may figure as a stand-in for Domna, enabling reflections on tutelage and ethnic identity.

FIGURING LAW AND LAWLESSNESS

If Philostratus's biography were sponsored directly by Domna, his relationship to imperial power would have been also necessarily attuned to the "lawlessness" of her older son, whose assassination of Geta was only one of the occasions on which he "stained himself with blood." According to Bowie, Philostratus may have been connected with the imperial family from around 203 until 215, accompanying them from Rome to Gaul, Britain, Tyana, and Antioch. The sponsorship, and the work itself then, took shape during a particularly violent period in the history of the empire. Septimius Severus came to power through conspiracy and military conquest over his competitors, not in the sophist-friendly world of Hadrian or Marcus Aurelius. In the course of establishing his dominance, Severus marched into Rome with an army, entered the Senate under armed guard, ultimately put a number of senators to death, and eventually proclaimed his son Caracalla emperor-designate. Having accompanied his father on the path to rule by brutal force, Caracalla seems to have learned his lessons well. After Severus's death and the eventual return of Philostratus to Athens, imperial power through the subsequent decades continues in this pattern. The scandalous Elagabalus (218–22), grandson of Domna's sister, Julia Maesa, and Alexander Severus (222–35) were both assassinated.

Why this story, a biography of a first-century Pythagorean philosopher, for this time? Why would a sophist spend so much effort writing about a philosopher, when the two social types—philosopher and sophist—compete for cultural capital, students, and influence in his world? If we see the sophist as interested primarily in performative competition, we could observe that, in selecting Apollonius, Philostratus has given himself the pleasurable task of appropriating his competitors' discourse and manners, outdoing the philosopher at his own game, so to speak. In Philostratus's treatment, Apollonius certainly exhibits the features of a *theios anêr* in his adoption of modest dress and abstemious lifestyle, of a life of teaching, wandering, and poverty, in his devotion to virtue and the pursuit of truth. But rather than practicing within a single temple, Philostratus's Apollonius becomes a sophistic Socrates, carrying his questions about virtuous behavior and wisdom to India, Egypt, Ethiopia, and at two points, to Rome for encounters with two emperors. As Jones notes, "Apollonius is made to act very much like the public speakers whom Philostratus was later to describe in his *Lives of the Sophists*. . . . travel[ing] far and wide, curing cities of their tendency to faction . . . and counseling emperors" (9). This would be an answer focused on professional identity.

Taken another way, we could look to the preoccupations of the two imperial figures under whom Philostratus works at the time the composition was begun. On the one hand, we have the virtuous intellectual empress, admirer of religious and philosophical teachings, and also in an extremely precarious position *vis-à-vis* her violent and unpredictable son. Apollonius as a type stands in for those brought together by Domna in her circle to provide intellectual stimulation, balance, and good judgment in a precarious time. On the other hand, we have in Caracalla not only a "lawless" and violent tyrant, but also one, so Dio reports later in the same passage, with enthusiasm for companions and amusements of a lower order—*magoi* and *gonês*—magicians and sorcerers—so much so that he had a shrine erected to the historical Apollonius, reinterpreted as a master of the dark arts and the spirit world.

In choosing Apollonius as his subject, Philostratus could "speak"—indirectly—to both imperial figures. Not only do both Domna and Caracalla have a direct interest in the philosopher, though in very different qualities, but they, as well as other readers, would recognize the strong parallels between historical periods—their own and Apollonius's of 150 years earlier. Of the series of conspiracies and struggle for power following Commodus's murder, Colin Wells remarks, it is the year 69 all over again. The first phase of the empire came to a crisis in that year with the reign of Nero, whose ineptitude, violence, and insanity led to civil war—the chaotic year of four emperors. The crisis was overcome when the Flavian Vespasian took over and was succeeded by his sons Titus and then Domitian. While Vespasian famously founded the first chair in rhetoric, he also had a vexed relationship with philosophers. Domitian was much worse, exiling philosophers, including Dio Chrysostom, and generally restricting freedom of expression, especially criticism of himself. His death was much celebrated. Tacitus, for example, in his biography of Agricola and his *Dialogue on Rhetoric*, celebrates the release from constraints on thought and speech following Domitian's death.

The crisis of the late second century follows a similar pattern. Decades of enlightened and relatively peaceful rule under the Antonines (or so-called "adoptive" emperors) from 96 through Marcus Aurelius's death in 180 gave sophists and philosophers alike more freedom and intellectuals more relative safety. When Aurelius broke the pattern of adoption and turned the empire over to his incompetent son Commodus, things began to fall apart again. The parallel between the two periods enabled Philostratus to comment indirectly on contemporary affairs under the protection of historical distance and the documentary pretense of the genre of biography. Evoking through his narrative an earlier time of imperial violence and crisis, Philostratus followed the life of the philosopher through the reigns of Nero, the four emperors, and Vespasian, bringing the narrative to a dramatic climax through Apollonius's (most probably fictional) encounter with Domitian, enemy of philosophers. By Philostratus's era a century later, the "good" emperors are finished. No longer could a sophist imagine the rich intellectual climate and potential for influence enjoyed under a Hadrian or a Marcus Aurelius. With Christians still at risk of persecution, a repetition of Domitian's exile of philosophers does not seem totally improbable, a net in which a sophist could easily be caught, as was Dio Chrysostom in the first century. The recourse of the sophist is indirection, and the choice of Apollonius provides a wealth of opportunities for figuring discourse—embedding risky truths by calling into play the abundant resources of sophistic creativity: historical analogy, references to the classical repertoire, a revoicing of the holy man / philosopher, and a fictional recasting of structures of Greek forensic rhetoric.

What was "law" for Philostratus? Although Greek sophists could have practiced law in the period in question (Bowie suggests that Philostratus may have done so), like most of the prominent sophists, he was more interested in law as a regulatory or normative discourse than as lowly practice. Though the emperor, according to second-century jurist Ulpian, is above the law, Caracalla, like all but the most ruthless or crazed emperors, sought to legitimate his rule, cultivating *auctoritas* by periodically declaring his intention to live—and at times actually living—in accordance with the laws (Wells 263). In matters of life and death, the emperors act without check but not without being judged. To adapt the language of Giorgio Agamben, we could say that the genres of sophistic rhetoric create "constitutive fictions," bridging the distance between the arbitrary and unpredictable power of a tyrant and a vision of social order imagined through systems of law (991). For just this reason, Roman law and imperial lawlessness are *topoi* directly and indirectly addressed within second sophistic Greek rhetoric through a number of rhetorical subgenres: advice to kings, narratives of crime and punishment, and trial scenes. Wedged between Caracalla and Julia Domna, Philostratus found himself in a position, and gifted with the rhetorical ability, to fill in that space between imperial lawlessness and the normative expectations and hopes for human survival to which law gives rise in any state. I propose that the scenes of confrontation between Apollonius and two emperors (Nero and

Domitian), but particularly the apologia at the culmination of the philosopher's trial before Domitian at the end of the *Life,* offer a "figured" recognition of Domna's dilemma: an address to imperial violence and lawlessness—and at the same time, in a typical sophistic fashion, a self-conscious comment on the necessity for figuring discourse in dangerous times.

At the end of the narrative, Apollonius finds himself in Rome—at his peril. The emperor Domitian has trusted the accusation of an informant from Arcadia who claims that Apollonius is a sorcerer guilty of human sacrifice. The Socratic character of Apollonius is fully realized in the fifty-paragraph speech of defense that Philostratus "quotes" in Book 8. A preface provides readers with a caveat about the style of a passage in which the sophist disavows the "vulgar" style of the rhetor but at the same time endorses the "concealed craftiness" of the wise man who, despite his "craft," is nonetheless to be differentiated from "those trained in law."

> I am aware that admirers of a vulgar (*bômolochos*) style will criticize it as lacking the finish which they consider necessary and as overdone in its vocabulary and ideas. . . . I do not think a wise man would truthfully represent his own character by cultivating balanced phrases or antitheses, and making his tongue clack like a rattle, for these things are characteristic of practiced speakers (*rhêtorikois*). . . . For obvious craftiness (*deinotês*) in court will give a bad impression, as if the speaker were plotting against the jurors, while concealed (*aphanês*) craftiness will emerge the victor, since not letting your judges see that you are crafty is a craft (*deinotês / deinos*) of the truer kind. (8.6.1–2)

Philostratus's choice of a vivid descriptor of "vulgar" style cleverly implies a critique of the version of Apollonius Caracalla finds entertaining: *bômolochos* refers to a low jester or buffoon, one who lurked about the altars for scraps, a half-starved beggar (Lucian). We see next the familiar *topoi* of division: a wise man (*sophos*) does not need artifice, making a contrast between the philosopher and the rhetor / sophist. But the sophist emerges victorious in his advocacy of "concealed craftiness," a craft of a truer kind. [8] The narrator "Philostratus" goes on to contrast the desirable style of a *sophos* with that of the lawyer: "When a wise man defends himself, . . . he needs a manner different from those of men trained in law—a style that is practiced (*kateskeuasmenou*) without appearing to be" (8.6.1–2). Here Philostratus uses the term for the "confirmation" phase of argument in the advanced stages of the progymnasmata, again drawing a distinction between his philosophic-sophistic rhetoric and the rhetoric of the schools.

As the speech begins, Apollonius introduces the terms of what Foucault calls the *parresiastic* game or pact (*Fearless Speech* 17; *Government* 62–66) at the outset:

> You and I, Majesty, are playing for high stakes. You are running a risk that no emperor ever did before,—the emperor, opposing philosophy; the philosopher, being accused of *being* a spirit (not, like Socrates, merely *having* a *daimon*). Since both of us are exposed to so great a risk, I will not hesitate to give you advice in a matter about which I am certain. People presumed that you were going to let your anger determine how you listened to me, and that you might kill me in your anger. . . . Hearing this, I was not led to be prejudiced against you, or to condemn your judgment as other than upright. I submitted to the laws, and am standing trial. This is also what I want to advise you. (8.7.2, emphasis added)

Killing in anger is, in fact, what Caracalla did when he killed Geta. Apollonius says he will not prejudge the emperor (Domitian in the story) but will submit himself to the laws and advises the emperor to do likewise. With strong echoes of Plato's *Apology*, the "defendant" goes on the offensive against the emperor aggressively at the outset, calling him to account for his prejudice against the class of philosophers and the bad judgment of listening to an informant. Philostratus calls on his character Apollonius to contain and regulate the behavior of the emperor, perhaps especially in the interest of the safety of his sponsor, the empress.

The speech itself ends with simple eloquence. Apollonius has completed his own defense: he could not, would not, and did not take a life. Nor should the emperor imperil the lives of his subjects. To the emperor he remarks, "Human prosperity is cyclical, and pomp, Majesty, has only a brief span. . . . Think of that, my Majesty, put an end to exile and an end to bloodshed, treat philosophy as you please . . . but wipe away the tears of humankind" (8.7.49). We don't know whether Caracalla or any of his successors read or heard Philostratus's work, though the general practices of public performance in court and the circulation of written texts thereafter could have made such contact possible (Bowie 20–21). It was completed long after Domna's death. Could the text of the sophist temper the anger and violence of an emperor? We may only speculate that Philostratus constructed the narrative with such a scenario in mind.

JULIA DOMNA, THE SYRIAN: READING "THE EAST" IN A TEXT OF THE "WEST"

Rereading with attention to character and geography, we can see the threads Philostratus pulls from this historical knot of unfettered imperial power, family, gender, and cultural difference rewoven into a tapestry in which the emphasis is placed on religious / philosophical wisdom in a multicultural empire. In Apollonius, Philostratus has created a character somewhat like Julia Domna: virtuous, pious, philosophical. Despite his neo-Pythagoreanism, Apollonius respects the religion of the sun and its expression in the diverse cultures he visits (in Babylonia, India, Egypt, Ethiopia).[9] But notably he does not visit Syria, the homeland of Domna, where her father was a priest. [10] In a kind of indirection that shields both the sophist and the reputation of the late empress from the orientalizing demonization of "the Syrian," ever more rampant under Elagabalus, Philostratus novelistically splits Domna into two through a kind of dream-logic where the dreamer plays all the parts, through the creation of Damis, the Syrian amanuensis—an interlocutor very much like those of Socrates in Platonic dialogues. A bit like a Dr. Watson in relation to Sherlock Holmes, Damis constantly asks naïve questions that set up the wisdom of the sage.

Why would Philostratus insert a Syrian character into this project, a character decidedly subordinated to the Greek philosopher, Apollonius? One answer is that the two characters allow for debate about prudent conduct. In Book 7, for example, Apollonius is brought up on charges by Domitian (the paradigmatic bad emperor) for speaking in private and in public against him. In a conversation among Demetrius, Apollonius, and Damis about what to do in the case of death penalty,[11] Damis is loyal to the person of Apollonius but disinclined to die for philosophy, or for any cause. Apollonius takes the Socratic position that it is noble to die for principle, saying of Damis, "We must be forgiving of [him] for speaking timidly about our situation, for he is an Assyrian and has lived on the borders of Media, where they kowtow to tyrants, and he has no lofty ideas of freedom'" (7.14, 237–38). Here the character of Damis, the transcriber or translator, the cautious Syrian who wishes to live, could be read as a coded recognition of Julia Domna in her situation as Eastern empress of Rome, at risk of death, and at the same time, devotee of philosophy in its various forms (astrology, mathematics, medicine) and of religion. Apollonius gives parodic voice to the arrogance of the Greek with his ethnic slurs on Syrians from the pompous and protected position of detached philosopher who can magically escape the leg irons of the tyrant (which he does later in the chapter), but a reader may see in Damis, the Syrian, an admirable wish to live, to record history and philosophy, to be loyal to the philosopher, to follow him around the world, and to learn from him. This relationship marks the difference in life possibilities for the empress and the sophist. Philostratus can escape to Athens; Domna is trapped. Remembering Dio's chilling account of Caracalla's murder of Geta and Domna's situation thereafter, we may find it very difficult to imagine a life of such fear and surveillance, one in which "all her words, gestures, and changes of colour" were observed (Book 78.2) What enabled Domna's survival—not only survival but her exercise of political diplomacy at the highest level and the fostering of intellectual life under such conditions? I would suggest that the resources of sophistic rhetoric could have come to her aid: the ability to strategize, to shapeshift, to create the persona necessary for the occasion.

A final glimpse into the biography will give another angle on rhetoric as a survival strategy in the age of empire. The night before Apollonius's interrogation by Domitian, Damis advises Apollonius not to sleep but to stay awake and prepare. The philosopher asks how he can prepare before he knows what he will be asked, and Damis queries, "'Will you improvise, then (*autoschediaseis*) . . . when your life is at stake?' Apollonius replies, 'Yes indeed, Damis, . . . for my life is an improvisation [*autoschediadzô*]'" (Book 7.30). Repeating forms of a verb meaning "to act or speak off-hand, to devise off-hand, extemporize; in a bad sense to act, speak, or think unadvisedly, try rash experiments" (LSJ), Philostratus links through language the imperiled philosopher, sophist, empress, and imperial subject. This subject cannot count on a stable or safe future, so improvisation is essential. Preparation in the form of rhetorical education—one informed by the tactics of figured speech, the control of word, gesture, and even body—can be lifesaving.

CONCLUSION

As we move through the materials, Julia Domna shifts in and out of focus; the figure of the empress dims as the concerns, texts, and figure of the second sophist come out more strongly. The relationship faintly sketched through these texts brings to life the subtle power of sophistic rhetoric as an intellectual acquisition but more importantly as a stance and resource that served both empress and sophist in a violent and precarious world. A feminist rhetorical historiography will lead us to ask not which of Julia Domna's identities is most important or influential—which "trumps" the others—but rather how Domna claimed and inhabited each of them strategically, how she produced and cultivated them for survival: literal, spiritual, and intellectual. Sophist and empress are both bound, textually and materially, by the same chain of gold—complicity and artistry, artistry forged within and against their complicity in the Roman imperial regime.

Notes

1. A list of recent notable efforts toward expanding the canon of ancient rhetoric would include Carol Lipson's and David Hutto's work on Egypt; Philip Halldén on Arab Islamic rhetoric; studies by Mary M. Garrett and LuMing Mao among others on rhetoric in premodern China; and, Margaret D. Zulick on persuasion in ancient Hebrew. Fortunately, such research has developed sufficiently that it cannot be comprehended in a single footnote.

2. See Walker on rhetorical uses of *poikilos* in archaic and Hellenistic rhetoric.

3. Kennedy discusses *letteraturizzazione*—the movement from "primary" to "secondary" rhetoric—at length in *Classical Rhetoric and Its Christian and Secular Tradition*. See especially chapter 1 (4–5) and chapter 6 (108–19). Walker's *Rhetoric and Poetics in Antiquity* launches a convincing counterhistory of "literary" rhetoric and informs my project.

4. Jones dates the *Life of Apollonius of Tyana*, the longest surviving biography from antiquity, after Domna's death in 217 but before the publication of *Lives of the Sophists* in the 230s. Bowie puts it somewhat later (29).

5. It is thought that the Latin "Julia" was probably added after she became empress, so she is referred to as Domna in the scholarship (Levick).

6. Levick's evaluation of previous histories, both those written in Domna's era and nineteenth-century imperializing ones, calls attention to gender and ethnic biases.

7. The complexities of identifying the several ancient authors named "Philostratus" are discussed in Elsner. I follow the attributions of authorship posited there.

8. Jones translates *deinos* as "craft": what Demetrius in the first century identified as forceful style. See also Ahl on *deinos* as a feature of "free speech."

9. Scholars are divided on the question of Syrian religion as a sun worship, though some scholars view this association as mistaken. Philostratus may include it in the biography because of the resonances with Neo-Platonic philosophy; both imagine a harmonious universe ordered by a virtuous force.

10. This is disputed in some sources.

11. It is worth mentioning that the character Demetrius bears the name of the author of the Hellenistic text *On Style* that introduces *eschêmatismenos logos*: figured speech.

Works Cited

Agamben, Giorgio. *State of Exception.* Translated by Kevin Attell. U of Chicago P, 2005.

Ahl, Frederick. "The Art of Safe Criticism in Greece and Rome." *American Journal of Philology*, vol. 105, 1984, pp. 174–208.

Atwill, Janet M. *Rhetoric Reclaimed. Aristotle and the Liberal Arts Tradition.* Cornell UP, 1998.

Birley, Anthony R. *Septimius Severus: The African Emperor.* B. T. Batsford, 1988.

Bowie, Ewen. "Philostratus: The Life of a Sophist." *Philostratus.* Edited by Ewen Bowie and Jaś Elsner, Cambridge UP, 2009, pp. 19–32.

Cassius Dio. *Dio's Roman History.* Translated by Earnest Cary. Loeb Classical Library 9. Harvard UP, 1954. 9 vols.

Clark, Suzanne. "Julia Kristeva: Rhetorica and the Woman as Stranger." Lunsford, pp. 305–18.

Elsner, Jaś. "A Protean Corpus." *Philostratus*, edited by Ewen Bowie and Jaś Elsner. Cambridge, UP, 2009, pp. 3–18.

Fleming, David. "Rhetoric as a Course of Study." *College English*, vol. 61, no. 2, 1998, pp. 169–91.

Foucault, Michel. *Fearless Speech*, edited by Joseph Pearson. Semiotext(e), 2001.

———. *The Government of Self and Others.* Lectures at the Collège de France. 1982–83. Translated by Graham Burchell. Picador, 2011.

Garnsey, Peter. "Roman Citizenship and Roman Law in the Late Empire." *Approaching Late Antiquity: The Transformation from Early to Late Empire*, edited by Simon Swain and Mark Edwards, Oxford UP, 2004, pp. 133–55.

Garrett, Mary M. "Chinese Rhetoric." *Encyclopedia of Rhetoric*, edited by Thomas Sloane, Oxford UP, 2001, pp. 89–92.

Goldsworthy, Adrian Keith. *How Rome Fell: Death of a Superpower.* Yale UP, 2009.

Halldén, Philip. "What is Arab Islamic Rhetoric? Rethinking the History of Muslim Oratory Art and Homiletics." *International Journal of Middle East Studies*, vol. 37, 2005, pp. 19–38.

Herodian. *History of the Roman Empire from the Death of Aurelius to the Accession of Gordian III.* Translated by Edward C. Echols. U of California P, 1961.

Hutto, David. "Ancient Egyptian Rhetoric in the Old and Middle Kingdoms." *Rhetorica*, vol. 20, no. 3, 2002, pp. 213–33.

Jones, Christopher P. "Apollonius of Tyana in Late Antiquity." *Greek Literature in Late Antiquity. Dynamism, Didacticism, Classicism*, edited by Scott Fitzgerald Johnson, Ashgate, 2006, pp. 49–64.

Kennedy, George A. *Classical Rhetoric and Its Christian and Secular Tradition from Ancient to Modern Times.* U of North Carolina P, 1980.

Kinnerly, Michelle. "*Sermo* and Stoic Sociality in Cicero's *De Officiis.*" *Rhetorica*, vol. 28, no. 2, 2010, pp. 119–37.

Levick, Barbara. *Julia Domna: Syrian Empress.* Routledge, 2007.

Lipson, Carol, and Roberta A. Binkley, eds. *Ancient Non-Greek Rhetorics.* Parlor, 2009.

Lunsford, Andrea A. "On Reclaiming Rhetorica." *Reclaiming Rhetorica: Women in the Rhetorical Tradition*, edited by Lunsford, U of Pittsburgh P, 1995, pp. 3–8.

Mao, Lu Ming. "Searching for the Way: Between the Whats and Wheres of Chinese Rhetoric." *College English*, vol. 72, no. 4, 2010, pp. 329–49.

Philostratus. *The Life of Apollonius of Tyana.* Translated by Christopher P. Jones. Loeb Classical Library. Harvard UP, 2005. 2 vols.

Romano, Susan. "The Historical Catalina Hernández: Inhabiting the *Topoi* of Feminist Historiography." *Rhetoric Society Quarterly*, vol. 37, 2007, pp. 453–80.

Swain, Simon, Stephen Harrison, and Jaś Elsner, eds. *Severan Culture.* Cambridge UP, 2007.

Walker, Jeffrey. *Rhetoric and Poetics in Antiquity.* Oxford UP, 2000.

Wells, Colin. *The Roman Empire.* 2nd ed., Harvard UP, 1992.

Whitmarsh, Tim. "Prose Literature and the Severan Dynasty." *Severan Culture*, edited by Simon Swain et al., Cambridge UP, 2007, pp. 29–51.

Wright, Wilmer Cave, trans. *Philostratus, Lives of Sophists. Eunapius, Lives of Philosophers.* Loeb Classical Library. Harvard UP, 1921, pp. 2–315.

Yunis, Harvey. "Eros in Plato's *Phaedrus* and the Shape of Greek Rhetoric." *Arion*, vol. 13, no. 1, 2005, pp. 101–25.

Zulick, Margaret D. "The Active Force of Hearing the Ancient Hebrew Language of Persuasion." *Rhetorica*, vol. 10, no. 4, 1992, pp. 367–80.

RHETORICAL EDUCATION AT CATHOLIC COLLEGES FOR WOMEN IN OHIO
1925–1940

NAN JOHNSON

> To prepare for life and a chosen work . . . to enable her to take her place in the home, in the classroom, in the field of social service, and in such professional careers as are open to women.
>
> —St. Mary of the Springs College, Columbus, Ohio, 1937

My original interest in exploring the history of rhetorical education at Catholic women's colleges like St. Mary of the Springs was based on my curiosity about how the theological mandate of Catholic education might reveal itself in rhetoric, writing, and public speaking classes. It seemed a reasonable hunch that a theological dimension to the commitment to educating the Catholic woman might affect what courses were taught and how. I plotted a small study that would look at the rhetoric-related curriculum at three catholic women's colleges in Ohio. Instead of finding evidence of the ideological framing of rhetoric classes at St. Mary, Mount St. Joseph (Cincinnati), and Ursuline College (Cleveland), I had that "a-funny-thing-happened-on-the way-to-the-archive" experience. I discovered another story entirely.

While studying institutional histories, college catalogues, yearbooks, school newspapers, textbooks, and student papers for information about what rhetoric courses were taught at this trio of Catholic women's colleges, I found substantial evidence at all three institutions of a clear increase in number and range of rhetoric, writing, and public speaking courses between 1925 and 1940. During this same era, St. Mary of the Springs, Ursuline College, and Mount St. Joseph steadily revised their educational goals for Catholic women to include a more explicit focus on professional preparation. Fascinated by what struck me as a probable dynamic of reciprocity between professionalization mandates and rhetorical education, my research goal became to explore how this dynamic played out. My *new* hunch was that following this lead could reveal another layer to our understanding of the motives and results of rhetorical education for women in the still-understudied decades of change between the world wars.

BACKGROUND ON ST. MARY OF THE SPRINGS, URSULINE COLLEGE, AND MOUNT ST. JOSEPH

St. Mary of the Springs (Ohio Dominican University) formally opened as a Catholic liberal arts college for women in 1924. The original St. Mary was founded in 1911 as an academy by Dominican sisters. The "Ladies Literary Institute of St. Mary of the Springs" initially offered a course of study including languages, English, and philosophy. In 1925, the College of St. Mary of the Springs announced its new reorganization and mission: "providing for students a liberal education in Arts, Philosophy and Science, the College aims to develop their powers to high standards of moral, intellectual, and social efficiency. The ideal of its graduate is a woman capable of upholding in her life the noblest ideals of the home, the Church and the State" (*Catalogue* 1925–26, 9). Accredited by the Association of American Colleges and the National Catholic Educational Association by the 1930s, St. Mary of the Springs created a general course of study that educated Dominican sisters and lay women who would become teachers and prepared lay women for civic roles as community leaders. The catalogues from the 1930s stress objectives that refine the educational goal of preparing young women to take their place in professional and public life: "To be a woman living in the Catholic life, inspired by her faith and strengthened by Catholic philosophy to accomplish her chosen work. To prepare for life and a chosen work . . . to enable her to take her place in the home, in the classroom, in the field of social service, and in such professional careers as are open to women. . . ." (398). By 1936, St. Mary is even more specific about a professionalization mission in describing the goal of the college: "to prepare students for life and a work in life through a careful integration of studies based on faith . . . and by giving them . . . training that will enable them to take their places in the home, the classroom, the field of social service and other professional careers open to women" (1936, 11).

Rhetoric, writing, and public speaking courses at St. Mary expanded during the key decade of the 1930s and played a curricular role in how the college was preparing the St. Mary's woman to "take her place" and find "her chosen work." In the middle 1920s, the department of English lists Theme Writing and an Advanced Composition course. When the mission statement is revised in 1929 to stress preparing the student for "the responsibilities of our complex modern life," English offerings expand to include two required courses in theme writing, a public speaking course, and a course in feature writing (31). An interesting aspect of the feature writing course description is the highlighting of a professional approach to this genre of writing practice: "A study of the special articles, appearing in newspaper supplements, and of other newspaper features with practice of a varied character in preparing contributions covering the miscellaneous interests of the press. Students in this course are encouraged to submit their articles for publication" (31). By 1932, rhetoric-related courses have once again expanded to include two more courses in public speaking and another course in advanced composition (31).

An expanded course of study in rhetoric and writing at St. Mary was complemented by an "impressive annual public lecture series that brought to campus speakers of national and international reputations" including well-known women writers and lecturers (*Catalogue* 1939, 367). For example, in 1939, the St. Mary lecture program brought to campus Anne O'Hare McCormick, famed editorial writer for the *New York Times* and Pulitzer Prize winner. When McCormick visited St. Mary in 1936, she held the distinction of being the second woman to win the Pulitzer Prize. Also lecturing at St. Mary that same year was Edna Lee Booker, whose address to the women of St. Mary was titled "News Is My Job" (13). Booker was a well-known foreign correspondent who authored several books about China during the 1930s and 1940s. Campus programming persistently brought professional role models like McCormick and Brooker to lecture to packed auditoriums. Student life at St. Mary also reflected campus interest in encouraging opportunities to develop writing and speaking expertise. The student newspaper, *The Tower,* reports in 1936 that a debate club was being formed at St. Mary to give "students an opportunity to engage in the field of formal debate but also to acquaint them with the technique and methods of panel discussions" (22). In 1937, *The Tower* reports that the Debating Club attended the Ohio Intercollegiate Conference on Public Affairs at Denison University, Granville, Ohio, at which a range of public problems was debated, including "collective bargaining, a unicameral legislature, the sales tax, flood control, the power of the Supreme Court" (55–56). The student staff of *The Tower* urged students to see the campus newspaper as a medium of practical experience for students interested in journalistic writing and describe the goal of the paper to "express our opinions and ideas more thoroughly and satisfactorily on current thought and problems; on religion, literature, history, politics, arts, and science, besides recounting the local news here at St. Mary" (*The Tower*, 1936, 22).

Students at Ursuline College, 1927. *Used with permission.*

Ursuline College for Women was founded in 1871 in Cleveland as the first chartered college for women in Ohio. As an order dedicated to teaching, Ursuline sisters realized the need to offer higher education to women and defined the mission of Ursuline College as conferring the BA for Catholic women who would become teachers in all levels of schools. Many of the early students at Ursuline joined the order, and Ursuline's effort by the early 1900s was primarily that of preparing sisters to teach in Cleveland's far-flung Catholic school system. By the 1920s, Ursuline reinvigorated its BA curriculum in response to growing interest among Catholic lay women for an advanced education. At that time, a revised curriculum led to the Bachelor of Arts and Bachelor of Science degrees. By 1930, Ursuline College was approved by the Ohio Department of Education for the training of high school teachers, and the curriculum expanded to include English, languages, history, religion, mathematics, the sciences, the arts, music, and painting.

A close look at Ursuline's mission statements during the crucial decades of the 1920s and 1930s shows a persistently updated vision of the importance of professional preparation for women. The 1925 *Catalogue* states: "Ursuline College is an institution for the higher education of women under the direction of the Ursuline Nuns. It devotes its energies to the maintenance of a high standard of scholarship and offers such cultural advantages as will promote the physical, intellectual and moral development of our Catholic young women and fit them to enter the manifold avenues of thought and activity which today are open to them." By 1935, Ursuline specifically outlines areas of professionalization listing "Teaching, Social Service, Home Economics, and Business Training" as areas of study that can prepare a young woman "to marshal her energies in the furtherance of that kind of life which is profitable to herself and beneficial to society" (1935, 16). Expansions in course offerings in rhetoric, writing, and public speaking during the 1920s and the 1930s supported this increasingly more determined goal of professionalizing women by allowing them to "study of the beauties of English speech and literature . . . and acquire a knowledge and ability to use language both spoken and written" (1935, 15). In the 1920s, Ursuline offered a course called Principles of Composition (using Charles Sears Baldwin's *College Composition* as a textbook) and required a course in elocution called Dramatic Art. By 1925, the dramatic arts course had been retitled Oral English and the composition course had become Composition and Rhetoric. At the 1930 mark, the curriculum in rhetoric and writing expanded with the addition of a journalism course, a course titled Speech, and two required courses in composition and rhetoric.

By the end of the 1930s, journalism offerings increased to include courses in newspaper and magazine writing. A course called Principles of Discussion and Debate was added, which stressed the "working principles of discussion, debate, and parliamentary procedures." Course descriptions like this one highlight the goal of preparing women for roles beyond campus life as does the inclusion of letter writing in the second level Composition and Rhetoric course. (1945, 27; 1939, 27).

Excitement for the expanded rhetoric curriculum at Ursuline in the late 1920s and 1930s is reflected in numerous articles in the student newspaper, the *Ursuline Quill,* that profile courses and campus events. Enthusiasm about training in journalism and the promise of professional writing as a career is clear in the stance of articles as early as the mid-1920s. The original editors of the *Quill* stress the importance of being a writer: "A place for self-expression is what we desire our paper to be. A place where the student can bring the best that is in her . . . whether her ability lies in the lines of the literary, or the artistic, or the executive" (1924, 1). The 1925 edition of the *Quill* reviews the lecture of Miss Mary Lenore Linegan, a journalist at the city newspaper, the *Press and Plain Dealer,* on "the newspaper from the inside. . . . Her talk covered many interesting features of the inner workings of the modern newspaper . . . and the particular style of writing required on a newspaper . . . its chief characteristics being brevity, accuracy and strength" (1925, 20). By 1936, the profile of journalism on campus and the exposure of women role models in the profession prompts *Quill* staff writer, Mary McGraw (class of 1939) to claim a first page column on the topic "Magazine Writing as Character Builder." Mary is expansive in her advocacy of journalism training as she explains to her student readership how training in magazine writing develops a sense of "far-reaching values," thoughtfulness about public interests, and the expressive ability of "conscientious news writing" (1).

Coverage of oratory and debate are also featured in the *Quill,* which takes as its mission the coverage of all important aspects of student life. In 1925, the *Quill* announces the organization of "The Debating Society": "Membership is open to the entire student body. Class teams will be formed and much practice will result from inter-class relations" (1). In April 1930, the *Quill* announces in a banner headline, "Interclass Oratorical Contest Will Be Sponsored under the Supervision of the English Department." The article stresses that all students are eligible and encouraged to participate in this context, which will feature students speaking on subjects of their "own choosing" and on subjects "of campus interest" (1).

The College of Mount St. Joseph was founded by the Sisters of Charity in Cincinnati as an institution of higher education for women in 1920. Mount St. Joseph has been co-ed since the 1970s and, like Ursuline College, grants both BA and MA degrees. Originally growing out of an academy course of study, the college-level curriculum at Mount St. Joseph in the 1920s offered courses in "education, English, French, Latin, mathematics, philosophy, religion, social service, sociology, languages, and English." At this time, Mount St. Joseph also opened a normal school for the preparation of teachers. Reflecting a growing commitment to the professionalization of women, "Mt. St. Jo" added a baccalaureate in nursing in 1926. Mission statements from the 1920s and 1930s stress a commitment to educating women of "character" in the qualities of hard work, "humility, simplicity, and charity" (291). "In carrying out the idea of higher education, the College aims to inform the mind, to train the heart, to stimulate the will so the result will be a true woman ready to take her rightful place in the social, business, and the religious world" (*Catalog*, 1926–27). The college experienced rapid growth in the 1930s and was consistently involved in revising courses of study to strike an appropriate balance between training for women's vocations and educating women of "conscience" through "intellectual principles of the first order" (*Catalog*, 1931).

In the 1920s, Mount St. Joseph offered courses in elocution, public speaking, and writing. This course of study in the rhetorical arts was expanded in the important decade of growth of the 1930s to include two courses in composition and rhetoric (with John Franklin's Genung's *Working Principles of Rhetoric* as a required text), a public speaking course, and a range of journalism courses including the history and principles of journalism, feature writing, editorial writing, newspaper editing, and writing for magazines. By 1936, Mount St. Joseph also offered Principles of Composition, Description and Narrative Prose, Argumentation, and Public Address, which covered the public lecture, informal discussion at public meetings, and the after-dinner speech among other forms. George Pierce Baker's textbook *The Forms of Public Address* is required. In 1936, Mount St. Joseph offered a series of journalism courses and public speaking courses. By 1938, the public speaking courses were offered under the curricular heading Speech and Dramatic Art. Over the course of a single decade, rhetorical education at Mount St. Joseph expanded from a single course in rhetoric to a curriculum offering twelve courses in the rhetoric-related arts.

The expanded course of study in rhetoric, writing, and public address at Mount St. Joseph was complemented by a college lecture series described in the 1931 catalogue as having a special mission: "These lectures have the special end in view of developing a strong interest in the Art of Public Speaking and of affording opportunity of seeing and hearing the most distinguished authors and public figures of the day." Student publications also record the energetic presence of English, public speaking, and journalism in student life and the growing theme of professionalism that contextualized studies at Mount St. Joseph in general. The 1931 college yearbook *Mountings* proudly reports on popular college clubs such as the Stylus Club for students with "the creative urge" who want to become intellectual critics capable of discerning the "wheat from the chaff" and the Secretarial Club for those who are "enthusiastic" and "steadfast" in their interest in learning more about business professions (155–157). The Press Club is described as a major supporter of the popularity of the journalism and advertising classes and the description of the club's activities place Mount St. Joseph students squarely in a professional context: "During the year the club made several trips through newspaper plants and publishing houses in order that the members might become better acquainted with the actual making of a newspaper. Last year it sponsored a series of lectures by men and women prominent in newspaper work in Cincinnati" (156). The college newspaper, *The Mother Seaton Journal,* confirms the interests of Mount St. Joseph students in journalism in 1931 with several interviews with women newspaper writers and essayists and weekly coverage of the activities of the Press Club and the *Journal* staff, which included visits to city newspapers and attendance at the Ohio Newspaper Women's Association. In 1933, the *Journal* reports on the professional interest of the Commerce and Finance Club, and campus meetings to discuss Business Administration as a major and Secretarial Science as a major (1). An enthusiastic *Journal* staff writer grabs a front-page place in the November 5, 1935, edition with the leading story, "Women Have Future in Journalism Says Mayer Wilson in Interview," in which the mayor of Cincinnati is quoted proclaiming, "I think the future for women in journalism is very great. They certainly write as well as men" (1).

The triple focus of composition and rhetoric, public speaking, and journalism at Mount St. Joseph, Ursuline, and St. Mary coincided with the aims of Catholic educators to link their mission more deeply to preparing women for professional and public lives. This professionalizing mission mirrors the trajectory of the overall national trend at women-centered colleges of increasing the number of rhetoric, writing, and speaking courses as professionalization becomes more and more the focus of the BA degree. As Katherine Adams

Mother Seton Journal staff at College of Mount St. Joseph, 1933. *Used with permission.*

and David Gold have observed, the 1920s and 1930s were the decades of the greatest influx thus far of women into higher education, and that influx occurred when progressive ideals encouraged an ever-increasing goal of professionalization and an active citizenry.

We can learn more about the relationship between professional preparation and rhetoric, writing, and public speaking courses by looking more closely at the course materials and descriptions at Ursuline, Mount St. Joseph, and St. Mary. I was interested to discover an overt pedagogical emphasis in these courses on students producing public and professional discourse. Baldwin's *College Composition*, a revision of *A College Manual of Rhetoric*, (published in 1922 and used widely across the country into the 1930s) outlines a comprehensive course in composition and public speaking for the Ursuline curriculum in the 1930s. Baldwin's *College Composition* is a good example of the popular mode of textbooks in this era, which typically included instruction in public speaking as well as informative writing, persuasion, narrative and description, and often, letter writing for both business and social contexts. Ursuline women likely would have heard these kinds of characterizations of the study of writing and speaking through their study of Baldwin's *College Composition*:

> The study of writing and speaking is not primarily a study of words. . . . For vocabulary . . . merely reflects . . . experience . . . actual experience in [one's] own affairs and . . . vicarious experience thorough reading. . . . The study of writing and speaking . . . is a study of life, and . . . our first concern must always be what we have to say. . . . As all our studies and experiences should make us better, so this direct study (of writing and speaking) helps us express ourselves better." (1)

Like his contemporaries A. S. Hill, John Franklin Genung, and John Hart, Baldwin positions students as potential writers and readers of real world discourse. His textbook directs students to see practicing informative or expository writing as developing writing expertise in the kinds of discourses they would commonly read and could imagine producing, such as newspapers, columns, magazines, books, textbooks, histories or biographies (4). The practical and professional focus implied by a pedagogical stress on these kinds of "real world" genres is reiterated throughout Baldwin's text as illustrated by the section on writing informatively.

> Information is a boast of modern times. Every one, as we are wont to say, may know. What with public schools, public libraries, and above all newspapers, the whole world is informed. . . . Nevertheless, to make people really know is still as important as it is interesting. . . . Even as to the commonest topics of current discussion, such as the workings of a gas engine, for instance or the meaning of the Monroe Doctrine, or the organization of the National Guard . . . many of us have little exact knowledge. No improvement in ease of communication can ever preclude the necessity of study for finding facts or conveying them. These are the tasks of the educated: and it is especially a task of college education to discern the facts and convey them. (9)

The stance of Baldwin's discussion takes for granted that college students, the women of Ursuline included, are going to produce writing in professional and public contexts. Baldwin demonstrates this curricular point of view in his discussion of the importance of "concreteness" in the section on "News Reports" under "Current Forms of Presentation" (33–36).

> Descriptive concreteness is accepted as a merit in news reports, and even gives newspapers a recognized distinction of style. . . . Room for composition is given abundantly in supplement articles, interviews, and reviews of recent progress in commerce, finance, war, etc. For in any of these the

> form of the whole may be at the choice of the writer and is likely to be a main element of . . . success. (35)

It is the performative implication of Baldwin's pedagogical stance for the Ursuline student that is significant. Baldwin reiterates this assumption in his discussion of "Oral Address," which outlines the organization of a speech, the conduct of debate, and public speaking at a range of "occasions" (133–149). Here again, is Baldwin's assumption that the instruction he offers will prepare students to participate in public and professional contexts.

> Nothing takes more life out of debate than unreality. To fence with words over a matter that no one cares about, or without any audience to care, is uphill work. . . . What questions are alive depends on the community. Every large group of people, every town, every college, every society of more than a few members, buzzes with discussions. Whether these are on political questions suggested by the newspapers, or on questions of history suggested by books, or on town questions about a hospital or as to the number of saloons, or on the college question, they are live if people care to talk and hear about them. . . . The constant aim of the occasional speech is to rekindle interest in the subject by adapting it to the audience and the time. Its originality consists in a message felt by the speaker and brought home to the hearers. It is a perennial means of leadership. (140–41; 149)

Baldwin also invites students to project themselves into "occasions" for public speaking, including public holidays, the unveiling of tablets and monuments, the presentation of colors or a loving cup, commencements, public dinners, and sermons (148). In the context of courses relying on Baldwin's *College Composition,* Ursuline women were taught composition and public speaking from the pedagogical point of view that students would use the rhetorical arts in meaningful ways in their future professional and public lives.

At Mount St. Joseph during the late 1920 and 1930s, John Franklin Genung's *Working Principles of Rhetoric* is the required text in the two-level composition and rhetoric course. Like Baldwin's book, Genung's textbook covers both writing and oratory. Genung's key definition of rhetoric as an art of "the adapting of discourse to the requirements of reader and hearer, under the various conditions that call for such work" encourages students to see the study of rhetoric as a general expertise "cultivated for practical ends" (4–5). Genung's stress on rhetoric as a practical and adaptive art presumes that the real life occasions and contexts in which writing and speaking are required are too numerous and varied to mention. Genung's consistent use of the term "practical" is a consistent reminder of the assumed performative results he associates with rhetorical studies. Baker's textbook *The Forms of Public Address* is also required at Mount St. Joseph in the 1930s. The rationale for the study of persuasive public address is framed for students in these terms: "The very conditions of American life require that our educated youth shall be able to expound with clearness their business, financial, political, or even moral ideas or ideals. In nine cases out of ten, too, they will not merely print what they have to say but first say it" (ix). Baker insists that the study of "public discussion through the study of exemplary models included in the *The Forms of Public Address* will teach students how to choose topics, draft a plan of treatment, and shape it successfully to address the public about issues of permanent value" (xix). Here is the standard of performance that Baker sets as a goal for college students, including the women of Mount St. Joseph: "The secret of public address to-day is then: Have something to say; something you wish to say; something you wish to say so that those who hear you shall understand, and act as you desire" (xxiii). Baker's text is organized around types of public address: letters, editorials, the eulogy, commemorative addresses, dedications, speech of welcome, inaugural speeches of farewell, addresses for academic occasions, addresses on social questions, legislative addresses, political addresses, and after-dinner speeches. Approaching the "public address" as both written and oral, Baker clearly intends the study of this range of common genres to prepare students to step into these and similar contexts successfully when "years have given ample opportunity to apply the principles which they have learned" (xxii).

In addition to rhetoric and public speaking courses that had professional and outward-looking focus, the introduction of journalism courses at St. Mary, Mount St. Joseph, and Ursuline in the 1930s made professional writing an explicit curricular issue. The inclusion and gradual increase of the curricular profile of journalism courses is remarkably in step with the national rise in the progressive period of journalism as an advanced writing course—as Katherine H. Adams has documented in *A Group of Their Own: College Writing Courses and American Women Writers, 1880–1940*. Adams argues that advanced instruction in a widening arc of writing courses during the 1920s and 30s enacted the progressive goal of having "an active citizenry informed by well-trained writers" (54). The journalism courses put in place at Ursuline, Mount St. Joseph, and St. Mary in the mid-1920s and 1930s reflected the national trend in professional writing of offering courses in general newspaper writing, magazine writing, and community and church journalism (Adams 56, also Adams, *AHOPW* 116). By 1930 at Ursuline, journalism was taught in two sections and covered "news factors and analysis; news and feature stories; story structure and newspaper English; copy reading, headline writing; authority in the news; libel; the camera as a reporter" and writing about particular kinds of news events: "conventions; legislative proceedings; speeches; interviews . . . disasters; crime; . . . politics; business and finance; science and invention; social news; foreign correspondence; and editorials; etc." (1945, 27). Mount St. Joseph had a separate journalism department by 1933 that listed seven courses: Elements of Journalism, History and Principles of Journalism, Feature Writing, Editorial Writing, Newspaper Critical Writing, Journalistic Practice (31). This advanced track in journalistic writing courses mirrored the similar development of professional writing courses at nonsecular women's colleges at the same time, such as Mt. Holyoke and Barnard College (Adams 57).

As Adams has pointed out, advanced track writing courses also included business or professional writing by the 1930s. At Mount St. Joseph, Secretarial English, cross-listed as Commerce Writing, was offered by 1939 as a regular course. This business or professional writing course would expand by the 1940s to a set of courses covering writing for business administration. Although not showing up as a separate course at St. Mary and Ursuline in the 1920s, a careful reading of the college catalogue from the 1930s reveals that a secretarial course or business writing course was available between terms. By the late 1930s, Business Writing starts to appear as a separate course under English.

Women at Ursuline, Mount St. Joseph, and St. Mary were receiving instruction in rhetoric, various modes of writing, public speaking, journalism, and advanced composition that paralleled national trends at similar liberal arts colleges and public universities. For example, St. Mary women were being prepared quite similarly to their peers across town at both Capital University, a Lutheran co-ed liberal arts college, and at Ohio State University. Journalism courses had been added to the English course of study at Capital University by 1925 with Introduction to Journalism, a course that stressed professional preparation in ways that closely parallels how journalism is positioned at the St. Mary campus: "Introduction to Journalism: A study of the art of news gathering and writing. Practice in various types of journalism. Visits are made to newspaper offices and publishing houses" (*Capital University Bulletin* 1925, 73). Capital also offered public speaking courses from the mid-1920s on and offered three composition courses through the 1930s. An important expansion in Capital's writing curriculum in 1935 was the addition of a summer Business

Course. Echoing the explicit goal of professional preparation that called so many to business writing and commerce clubs at Ursuline and Mount St. Joseph, Capital promotes its business course with a focus that includes business writing as preparation for the field of business: "Since college students preparing themselves for the professions have found a good background in certain commercial subjects very useful . . . this course is highly desirable on the part of students who wish to specialize in the business fields by becoming efficient stenographers and secretaries' (*Bulletin,* 1935, 73).

During the 1930s, Ohio State offered two undergraduate courses in public speaking including Principles and Practice of Public Speaking and Argumentation under English, along with three courses in composition (OSU, 1935 and 1936–1937, 30–31; 75–76). Like composition and rhetoric courses at St. Mary, St. Joseph, and Ursuline, these courses outlined a course of study covering description, narration, exposition, and argument. Paralleling the addition and expansion of journalism courses at St. Mary, Ohio State had a Department of Journalism in place by 1935 that offered similar courses, such as News-Collecting and News-Writing, Feature Writing, and Editorial Writing. These courses were designed to prepare students to enter journalism by working on college publications to gain practical experience.

The professional stamp of Ohio State's journalism program shares with the rhetoric and writing curriculum at St. Mary, Ursuline, and Mount St. Joseph the goals of practical experience linked to professional opportunities. Reports from alumni about professional placement in the 1930s confirm that graduates were successful in securing jobs in teaching, nursing, journalism, Catholic community service, missionary service, business, government administration, library work, and social service. St. Mary's *The Tower* routinely reports on alumnae jobs and activities as this update from June 1937 illustrates.

> Mary Crowe, '34 of the Equitable Life Insurance Co., had the distinction of being the only one in her office group to exceed the annual sales goal set by the company during this last year. During her spare time Mary is taking a special law course and directing a class in dramatics at the Y.M.C.A. Many of the alumnae are at present employed in Columbus. Aileen Duffy, '32 is now working at the Carnegie Library on Grant Ave. Helen Foreman, '35 is bookkeeper at the Moores and Ross Co. on Washington Avenue. Mary Martha Sliter, '35 has had a position in the Federal Conservation Department on East State St. since last August. Mary Jane Corbett, '35 is doing research work for the National Youth Administration. (47)

A strong curriculum in the writing and speaking arts put in place throughout the 1930s at St. Mary, Ursuline, and Mount St. Joseph helped to prepare graduates like Mary, Aileen, Helen, Mary Martha, and Mary Jane and their peers for professional success. The voice of *The Tower* puts a personal face on the outcomes that St. Mary educators and their colleagues across Ohio hoped for: young Catholic women would find their voices and their way in the world of work and community and public service. The small story this study tells has led us to examine rhetorical education in three quiet corners of Ohio in the era between the world wars. As a historical scholar, I have come to believe more and more in the power of "small stories" to point us to significantly larger insights. Feminist scholarship on women's rhetorical practices has spent nearly two decades untangling the reality of women's lives from grand narratives that either obscure or erase their experience. When we see the faces of the St. Mary, Ursuline, and Mount St. Joseph women smiling with conviction from the pages of yearbooks and campus newspapers, I feel that we are seeing through the complexity of time and getting a glimpse into these young women's real lives. The adventure of exploring how rhetorical studies have played a part in those lives is the kind of research I hope we can all keep doing.

Works Cited

Adams, Katherine H. *A History of Professional Writing Instruction in American Colleges: Years of Acceptance, Growth, and Doubt.* Southern Methodist UP, 1993.

———. *A Group of Their Own: College Writing Courses and American Women Writers, 1880–1940.* State U of New York P, 2001.

Baker, George Pierce. *The Forms of Public Address.* Henry Holt and Company, 1904.

Baldwin, Charles Sears. *Composition: Oral and Written.* New York: Longmans, 1909.

———. *College Composition.* New York: Longmans, 1917.

———. *A College Manual of Rhetoric.* New York: Longmans, 1907.

Capital University Bulletin: Annual Catalog of Capital University, 1924–25; 1935–36; 1940–41.

Catalogue of College of Mount St. Joseph, 1925–26; 1926–27; 1927–27; 1927–28; 1930–31; 1931–32; 1932–33; 1933–34; 1936–37; 1937–38; 1938–39; 1939–40; 1950–51.

Catalogue of College of St. Mary of the Springs, 1890; 1925–25; 1928–30; 1930–31; 1931–32; 1932–33; 1934–35; 1936–37; 1941–42.

Catalogue of Ursuline College, 1922–1923; 1925–27; 1928–29; 1929–30; 1935–36; 1939–1940; 1945–46; 1949–51; 1954–56.

College of Mount St. Joseph. *Mountings of Nineteen Hundred and Thirty.* "Lectures," n.p; "June," p. 151.

———. *Mountings of Nineteen Hundred and Thirty-One.* n.d., pp. 155–57.

———. *The Seaton Journal*, vol. 9, no. 3, Dec. 1931; vol. 10, April 1933; vol. 12, March 1935; vol. 12, Nov. 1935.

Gaertner, Angela Marie. "Compulsory Public Unemployment Insurance: A Thesis Submitted to the Social Science Department of Ursuline College . . . in Partial Fulfillment of the Requirements of Bachelor of Arts." Ursuline College Archives.

Genung, John Franklin. *The Working Principles of Rhetoric.* Ginn, 1900.

Gold, David. *Rhetoric at the Margins: Revising the History of Writing Instruction in American Colleges, 1873–1947.* Southern Illinois UP, 2008.

Gold, David, and Catherine Hobbs, eds. *Rhetoric, History, and Women's Oratorical Education: American Women Learn to Speak.* Routledge, 2013.

Oliver, John William, Jr., et al. *Cradles of Conscience: Ohio's Independent Colleges and Universities.* Kent State UP, 2003.

Scott, Fred Newton, and Joseph Villiers Denney. *The New Composition-Rhetoric.* Allyn and Bacon, 1911.

St. Mary of the Springs College. *The Tower.* Columbus, Ohio, November, 1936; June 1937; November 1937.

University Calendar, The Ohio State University: 1919–20, 1920–21, 1935–36, 1936–37, 1940–41.

Ursuline College. *Cedar Glen Echo*, vol. 1, 1936, p. 2.

———. *Ursuline Quill*, vol. 1, 1924; vol. 5, no. 3, 1925; vol. 5, no. 6, 1930; vol. 10, no. 6, 1936.

Ursuline College Archives. Ursuline Students Photograph, Merici Hall, 1927. Used with permission.

Wright, Elizabethada A. "'God Sees Me': Surveillance and Oratorical Training at Nineteenth-Century St. Mary-of-the-Woods in Indiana." *Rhetoric, History, and Women's Oratorical Education*, ed. David Gold and Catherine L. Hobbs, Routledge, 2013.

FEMINIST PERSPECTIVES ON POSTCOLONIAL RHETORICAL PRACTICES

SPIVAK'S COSMOPOLITAN ERUDITION AND NAZER'S SURVEILLED SILENCE

ELIZABETH A. FLYNN

Wendy Hesford and Eileen Schell begin their introduction to the special issue of *College English,* titled "Configurations of Transnationality: Locating Feminist Rhetorics," by suggesting that Gloria Anzaldúa has become "a transnational figure, an iconic border crosser, and a champion of mestiza rhetoric (code-switching, multilingual, mixed genre)" (461). Very quickly, however, it becomes clear that this is not a good thing. They continue, "Anzaldúa's canonical location is emblematic of the field's modernist tendencies, namely how we continue to privilege the individual author / critic, in this case the postcolonial writer, over the study of transnational and postcolonial rhetorical practices" (461–2). The danger in embracing the work of prominent postcolonial and transnational figures, they suggest, is that doing so risks "institutionalizing certain forms of resistance, romanticizing mobility and hybrid identities, and tokenizing individual writers over and above a contextual and geopolitical analysis of alternative rhetorical practices" (462). They are not suggesting, of course, that we cease examining the work of individual rhetoricians. How would that be possible? In the issue they have coedited, for instance, Theresa Kulbaga examines Azar Nafisi's *Reading Lolita in Tehran.* Rather, they are concerned that individual rhetoricians not become iconized, privileged, romanticized.

Following is an overview of postcolonial feminist theory and practice within the context of the field of rhetoric and composition followed by a critical examination of the rhetorical practices of two very different women—Gayatri Spivak, prominent literary theorist and activist, and Mende Nazer, a Sudanese woman who was enslaved and then rescued in the late twentieth century and coauthor of the best-selling testimonial *Slave*, cowritten with Damian Lewis. The juxtaposition provides a contrast between the postcolonial metropolitan intellectual free to traverse geographical and intellectual domains and the silent, resistant, immobile, postcolonial subaltern slave. While it might be tempting to focus on Spivak as an iconic figure, juxtaposing her story with that of Nazer emphasizes Spivak's privilege. It also emphasizes the wide distances that often separate postcolonial women; Spivak and Nazer might be seen as two extremes. As I will demonstrate, however, Nazer is becoming an international figure of considerable stature as a result of her coauthored book as well as a play, a film, and numerous videos based on her experience. She is no doubt better known than Spivak outside the academy, at least in England.

As my title indicates, Spivak is a cosmopolitan intellectual whose erudition is extraordinary.[1] She was born into the Brahmin class in India, received her PhD from an elite U.S. university, Cornell, is best known for her translation of Jacques Derrida's *Of Grammatology*, and holds the position of University Professor at Columbia University, a considerable distinction since only a small number of professors in the country hold such a title. Telling her story as director of a literacy project in the poorest region of India provides yet another perspective on her life and work. I also make it clear that I do not consider her to be a rhetorician, and she does not consider herself to be one. My goal is to situate Spivak's work and Nazer and Lewis's testimonial within feminist, postcolonial, rhetorical, and what Wendy Hesford and Eileen Schell, after Inderpal Grewal, call "transnational connectivities" (470). First, though, I provide a brief overview of work on feminist approaches to postcolonialism within the field of rhetoric and composition.

FEMINIST POSTCOLONIAL RHETORIC

Feminist rhetoric is beginning to make important contributions to postcolonial studies, with sites of investigations beginning to shift east and south. This process will necessarily change the nature of the field in dramatic ways. New geographies will enable the study of new women's movements, new processes of resistance, new languages, and new urgencies. In this process of development, it will be important to continue examining feminist postcolonial work in other fields such as that of Spivak within literary studies as well as new testimonials such as that of Nazer and Lewis.

Feminist literary studies has attended to postcolonial issues for several decades and has influenced the development of feminist postcolonial rhetoric, especially in terms of defining where the postcolonial is located, what it is, and how power is dispersed in postcolonial sites. Spivak is among the most influential. Another U.S. intellectual born in India but educated in the United States who focuses on the problems of Third World women within the context of literary studies is Chandra Talpade Mohanty. In the introduction to her coedited book *Third World Women and the Politics of Feminism*, Mohanty emphasizes complexity and relationality and speaks of a world "traversed with intersecting lines of power and resistance" (2). In the essay she defines the Third World through geographical location as well as particular socio-historical conjunctures, thus including so-called minorities and peoples of color within the United States (2).[2]

Focus on postcolonial concerns within feminist rhetoric and composition followed developments within literary studies. If Mohanty's broad definition of postcolonial feminism, which includes attention to the problems of underrepresented groups within the United States, is used, such work begins to emerge in the late 1980s and early 1990s with essays and books by bell hooks, Jacqueline Jones Royster, Shirley Wilson Logan, and others.[3] An early collection focusing on feminist teaching of writing, *Teaching Writing: Pedagogy, Gender, and Equity* edited by Cynthia Caywood and Gillian Overing and published in 1987 does not attend to issues related to underrepresented groups, an indication that the field's embrace of what has sometimes been referred to as multiculturalism came later. The Caywood and Overing book, however, is one of the first to attend to feminist concerns and is therefore a useful marker within this context.[4]

Here, however, I am defining feminist postcolonialism in relation to women of color outside the United States and Europe, what Schell in her essay on Vandana Shiva calls women from the two-thirds world. This work is considerably less well developed within rhetoric and composition and is better spoken of as emergent rather than established. It is important because it expands the scope of the field's vision beyond the United States and Europe and introduces issues heretofore unexamined within the field such as human trafficking and twentieth- and twenty-first-century slavery.

Work on feminist postcolonial rhetoric developed from work on postcolonial rhetoric that emerged in the late 1990s and early 2000s and focused on representational strategies used by postcolonials and readers of postcolonial texts. Andrea Lunsford and Lahoucine Ouzgane in their edited collection *Crossing Borderlands: Composition and Postcolonial Studies*, published in 2004, traces postcolonial concerns within rhetoric and composition to a 1998 special issue of *JAC: A Journal of Composition Theory* guest edited by Lunsford and Ouzgane and devoted to the topic.[5] A version of Susan Jarratt's essay "Beside Ourselves: Rhetoric and Representation in Postcolonial Feminist Writing" in the Lunsford and Ouzgane collection was originally published in the *JAC* issue, as were several other essays in the collection.

Jarratt traces representational strategies in postcolonial rhetoric "by analyzing changes in concepts of *ethos* and audience under the historical conditions of postcoloniality; by describing complex processes of writing the self, and by attending to the ways teachers and students in U.S. universities 'read' (about) formerly colonized people" (111). She uses the rhetorical figures of metaphor and metonymy to analyze the ways postcolonial feminist writing calls attention to dual processes of representation, political and pictorial (113). In developing her argument, Jarratt turns to the writings of Spivak, Vietnamese filmmaker Trinh T. Minh-ha, and Guatemalan Quiché Indian Rigoberta Menchú. Jarratt sees Spivak as practicing a "reactive strategy," "adopting different identities at different times to create a consciousness of the hazards of fixity and substitution" (117). She sees Spivak's work as "textual traces of a strained encounter with multiple forms of dominance" (118). Jarratt sees both Trinh and Spivak as recasting images to "frustrate any simple process of representation" (121). In contrast, Menchú, according to Jarratt, does not hesitate to claim representative status. Here, Jarratt claims, there is "no hedging about subject positions or the problem of speaking for others" (123).[6] As I discuss below, however, Menchú's testimonio has been controversial, suggesting that representation is always already interpretive and subject to debate.

SPIVAK: COSMOPOLITAN ERUDITION

Jarratt emphasizes Spivak's use of rhetorical figures, and Spivak is familiar, of course, with rhetoric as a body of knowledge and as influential in the development of poststructuralism. Spivak, however, does not self-identify as a rhetorician. Phillip Sipiora and Janet Atwill begin their interview with Spivak, "Rhetorical and Cultural Explanation: A Discussion with Gayatri Chakravorty Spivak," by indicating that Spivak is somewhat unfamiliar with the field of rhetoric and composition (243). When asked about the discipline of rhetoric at the beginning of the interview, Spivak says, "As for the discipline, I cannot say very much because I don't know much about its performance. I've been involved in the teaching of comparative literature, English, and, of late, cultural studies. I can't really comment on what goes on *in* the discipline" (244). Influenced by Paul de Man's *Resistance to Theory,* she sees rhetoric as "the name for the residue of indeterminancy which escapes the system" (244). She also observes that Jacques Derrida does not use the term often, usually only when he is actually dealing with Greek material (244). Although Bizzell and Herzberg in *The Rhetorical Tradition* include the work of Michel Foucault, Derrida, and Anzaldúa, they do not include work by Spivak. Rather than claiming Spivak for the field of rhetoric and composition, I am interested in examining her rhetorical strategies as a feminist postcolonial writer, theorist, critic, and activist.

Spivak was born in India in 1942, five years before India gained independence from England. Her family, as I indicated earlier, belonged to the Brahmin caste. She has distinguished herself as a Western academic through her publication of numerous books, articles, book chapters, and interviews. She is fluent in both French and German and has read widely in and published widely on continental philosophy and literature. She is a transnational figure in multiple ways. An Indian woman who lives in the United States, she has traveled extensively. In the foreword to *Outside in the Teaching Machine* (1993), for instance, she mentions recent presentations in the United States, Britain, Canada, and France (ix). She also travels to India on a regular basis, often in her capacity as director of a literacy project in the poorest area of India. Her work on Derrida might indicate a primarily Western orientation, though Derrida is himself a postcolonial figure given that he was born into a Jewish family in Algeria. Indeed, much poststructuralist theory has been developed by individuals from non-Western cultures. Julia Kristeva was born in Bulgaria and became radicalized, in part at least, as a result of her visit to Mao's China. Hélène Cixous, like Derrida, was born in Algeria to Jewish parents.

Deconstruction is Spivak's primary rhetorical strategy, which she sees as critiquing tendencies to universalize and homogenize. When necessary, however, she employs what she calls "*strategic* use of positivist essentialism" ("Subaltern Studies: Deconstructing Historiography" 204, emphasis in original). In an interview with Sneja Gunew, she speaks of the dangers of tokenism, ghettoization, chromaticism (basing everything on skin color), genitalism (depending on what kind of genitals you have, you can or cannot speak in certain situations) (61). As part of her insistence on specificity, Spivak observes in thc Gunew interview that the Indian diaspora had different effects on different Western countries. Indian indentured laborers were first sent to the Afro-Caribbean. Indians then moved to Africa and then on to England. It wasn't until the early 1960s that educated Indians moved in large numbers to the United States—what Spivak calls a brain drain (61). Spivak herself was part of that movement.

Another rhetorical strategy, though inadvertent, is the difficulty for which she is famous. Spivak did not begin to explore postcolonial theory until several decades after doing work in British literature and continental philosophy and about a decade after beginning to do work in feminist theory. Her career is one of continued challenges and opportunities to expand her frames of reference, to venture into discourses with which she is not entirely comfortable or familiar. She says in a 1993 interview with the editors of *The Spivak Reader,* Donna Landry and Gerald MacLean, that she was not even thinking about feminist issues until she was asked by the editors of the *Yale French Studies* issue *Feminist Readings: French Texts / American Contexts*, published in 1981, to contribute a piece. In not turning her attention to feminist concerns until the late 1970s, Spivak was not a part of the numerous feminist conversations that occurred when feminist literary studies emerged in the early 1970s. In the same way, when she turned her attention to subaltern concerns at the invitation of the Subaltern Studies Group in the late 1980s, she had missed a decade of conversations on this topic. Her dissertation, written in the mid 1960s, was on the poetry of William Butler Yeats. She continued to publish on Yeats until the mid-1970s. Her next big project was translating *Of Grammatology,* which came out in 1976. Always exploring new terrain often resulted in difficult prose.

Especially difficult is "Can the Subaltern Speak?" the postcolonial work for which Spivak is best known. Originally published in 1988 in *Marxism and the Interpretation of Culture* edited by Cary Nelson and Lawrence Grossberg and revised several times, the essay focuses on the colonial subject as Other. Spivak uses the term *subaltern* to speak of colonized peoples, and especially women. In the version of the essay I will refer to here (her essay was excerpted from chapter 3 of *A Critique of Postcolonial Reason: Toward a History of the Vanishing Present,* reprinted in *Feminist Literary Theory and Criticism* and reprinted in Susan Gubar and Sandra Gilbert's *Feminist Literary Theory and Criticism*), she states, "If, in the context of colonial production, the subaltern has no history and cannot speak, the subaltern as female is even more deeply in shadow" (804).

Spivak tells us that she derived the term *subaltern* from the work of the Subaltern Studies Group, which Gilbert and Gubar see as a group of radical historians in India associated with the annual publication of *Subaltern Studies*, founded in 1982 (n. 5, 801).[7] This group, in turn, according to Gilbert and Gubar, derived the term from Antonio Gramsci who, in *The Southern Question,* speaks of the "subaltern classes," extending the class position / class-consciousness argument in Marx's *The Eighteenth Brumaire* (801). Spivak finds that the Subaltern Studies Group *must* ask, "Can the subaltern speak?" (801, emphasis in original). Influenced by Foucault, according to Spivak, the group's project is "to rethink Indian colonial historiography from the perspective of the discontinuous chain of peasant insurgencies during the colonial occupation" (801). She identifies Ranajit Guha as the founding editor of the collective (801) and quotes from Guha, making clear that the Group is anti-elitist, opposed to both colonial elitism and bourgeois-nationalist elitism (802). Spivak emphasizes, predictably, that "the colonized subaltern *subject* is irretrievably heterogeneous" (802, emphasis in original).

In "Can the Subaltern Speak?" Spivak is clearly not writing to a subaltern. She assumes an audience of intellectuals steeped in the work of Foucault, Deleuze, Lacan, Marx, Freud, and others as if the reader were thoroughly familiar with it and with the conversations and disputations those discourses have engendered. The first passage of the shortened version of "Can the Subaltern Speak?" in the Gilbert and Gubar collection reads as follows:

> In the face of the possibility that the intellectual is complicit in the persistent constitution of the Other as the Self's shadow, a possibility of political practice for the intellectual would be to put the economic "under erasure," to see the economic factor as irreducible as it reinscribes the social text, even as it is erased, however imperfectly, when it claims to be the final determinant of the transcendental signified. (799)

This passage is quite difficult for someone not steeped in French critical theory. What is behind the reference to the "Other as the Self's shadow," for example? What does it mean to put something "under erasure"? What is the "transcendental signified"? It is not so much that the syntax is garbled as that clarifications and explanations are not provided that would help the general reader through the text. Indeed, the general reader is not the audience for the text. This version of the essay was originally published in Spivak's 449-page tome *A Critique of Postcolonial Reason: Toward a History of the Vanishing Present,* published by Harvard University Press. Spivak speaks here as an extremely well-read intellectual, though she admits in the *Spivak Reader* interview to not knowing the work of Lacan as well as she knows that of Derrida and Foucault and to hardly knowing the work of Bakhtin at all (301).

Much of Spivak's work is difficult because she is often employing complex theoretical concepts and writing to a specialized audience familiar with this theory. Work on the subaltern is especially difficult because Spivak admits that in entering this conversation, she is grappling with material that is unfamiliar and challenging to her. In the Landry and MacLean interview she explains that Landry and MacLean wanted to reprint a version of "Can the Subaltern Speak?" in their collection, but she preferred an interview that focused on important concepts in the essay. She says that when she is working through a topic or an issue that is new to her, she does not and cannot fully control her writing. If ideas that she is just beginning to work with are not entirely clear to her, they will not be entirely clear to her readers. She says that she struggled with the concept of the subaltern, even with the word, and defends herself against critics who say that the subaltern does speak. She explains that *subaltern* is preferable to "Third World" because it doesn't need the apologetic qualifier, "the so-called Third World." She also wonders if "postcolonial" is okay anymore (290).

She explains in the interview with Landry and MacLean that by using the term *speaking* in "Can the Subaltern Speak?" she was talking about the transaction between speaker and listener. The woman who took her own life wanted to speak but did not, could not. Spivak says, "Even that incredible effort to speak did not fulfill itself in a speech act" (289). Her recounting this event resulted in what she calls "rhetorical anguish" (289). Another way in which the subaltern cannot speak is the discrediting of the work of the Subaltern Studies Group by traditional historians such as those at Cambridge. In the interview, Spivak provides a third example of a way in which the subaltern has been silenced. When the British colonized India, they allowed canals that had been built in feudal times to deteriorate, not recognizing that they were vital to irrigation and flood management. The canals were built painstakingly and slowly and could not be rebuilt with modern building methods (291). Not maintaining the canals effectively silenced the subaltern. Spivak says, "So, 'the subaltern cannot speak,' means that even when the subaltern makes an effort to the death to speak, she is not able to be heard, and speaking and hearing complete the speech act" (292).

In responding to critics of "Can the Subaltern Speak?" she explains in the interview she now thinks the essay is "too complicated" and "too uncontrolled"

(288). She expected that an editor would cut it, but this did not happen. She also explains that the essay reflects the struggle she was going through when she wrote the piece. She was blocked and couldn't write it for some time. A difficulty she had with the essay was discussing the suicide of a young Indian woman alongside the work of Foucault and Deleuze. The young Indian woman was supposed to represent the subaltern, but Spivak explains in a footnote that since the woman was middle class, she could not easily be romanticized. The woman's gender also complicates the issue of subalternity. In speaking of the essay, Spivak says it was "the beginning of something" (288) just as she was at the beginning of thinking about feminism in the early 1980s. Focusing on the subaltern was a "second step" after focusing on feminism, but she didn't know enough to take the step (288). Spivak's writing is sometimes more lucid when she takes on the role of translator and teacher as she does in the translator's preface to *Of Grammatology.*[8]

Spivak's discussion of Indian writer Mahasweta Devi's "Stanadayini" (Spivak translated and published in *In Other Worlds,* in her essay "A Literary Representation of the Subaltern: A Woman's Text from the Third World," also included in *In Other Worlds*) is also deconstructive and also difficult. Described as an essay that focuses on pedagogy, Spivak invokes the work of theorists such as Foucault, Ernesto Laclau and Chantal Mouffe, Louis Althusser, Lacan, and others. Here, Spivak describes her deconstructive position as recognizing that "truths" are constructions and that we cannot avoid producing them (247). Some of the constructions she outlines include *(1)* the historian and teacher, whom she sees as needing to critically "interrupt" each other (241); *(2)* Devi's account, which amounts to depicting a parable of India after decolonization (244), an interpretation that Spivak takes issue with; *(3)* an account that sees the subaltern as a class-subject, which Spivak disagrees with because she sees the subaltern as a gendered subject; *(4)* "elite" approaches such as Marxist feminism, which Spivak thinks does not fit because it provides too neat a narrative for the "bewildering cacophony" of "Stanadayini" (252); and *(5)* liberal feminism, which Spivak critiques because logical and legal-model demonstrations alone cannot bring about counterhegemony (256). Spivak sees the story as showing us some of the limits and limitations of elite arguments about subaltern literature (241). She also sees that the teacher of literature must "re-constellate" the text, wrench it out of its proper context, in order to interpret it (241).

Spivak's writing about teaching is sometimes clearer than her writing about difficult philosophical concepts, and the roots of her activism can be found in this writing. One of her books is entitled *Outside in the Teaching Machine*, and one of the essays in that book is entitled "Marginality in the Teaching Machine." Her essay, "Finding Feminist Readings: Dante-Yeats," published in *In Other Worlds: Essays in Cultural Politics*, describes a course she taught focusing on the work of Yeats. These essays are accessible. Spivak takes her teaching seriously. She also no doubt became an activist as a result of her experiences in India as a child, an adolescent, a young adult, and a successful professional. In her activism she has found a way to embody and operationalize the theory that she has worked so hard to comprehend and explain.

We get quite a different perspective on Spivak's commitment to the improvement of the subaltern, however, if we examine her literacy project in the poorest area of India. My source for understanding Spivak's project is a September 14, 2007, article in the *Chronicle of Higher Education* by Liz McMillen entitled "The Education of Gayatri Spivak." McMillen introduces Spivak as "leading postcolonial critic, translator of Derrida, high priestess of literary theory." She juxtaposes this identity, though, with a glimpse of Spivak's teaching—asking schoolchildren to write about themselves, on their own. Her work, McMillen explains, involved one-on-one encounters with children who live in abject poverty, one manifestation of which is their having no running water or electricity. They are members of indigenous nomadic tribes with their own languages and are sometimes thought to be primitive and ineducable. McMillen explains that Spivak had been visiting this part of India for years and knew of the region's problems—"the government's neglect of rural areas, the 80-percent illiteracy rate, the emphasis in the poorest schools on rote learning and memorization," according to McMillen. In asking the children to write about themselves, Spivak learned that they were unable to do so. She says, "I could not imagine heads that had been jammed shut." "It's a killing of the imagination." According to McMillen, Spivak speaks of "the ethical task of teaching" and wants the students "to learn from below." She also wants to learn from the process. McMillen quotes Spivak as saying, "If you know the answer as you go in, you won't be able to learn yourself."

McMillan describes Spivak's, by then, twenty-year-old project, a nonprofit organization that supports seven primary schools. Her aim, according to McMillen, is to instill "critical-intelligence skill in children cut off from mainstream Indian society." She is trying to develop "rituals of democratic habits." Her schools employ the national curriculum with the hope that the students will be prepared for India's secondary schools. Her Pares Chandra and Sivani

Chakravorty Memorial Literary Project has been generously funded (over half a million dollars so far), primarily through her salary and money from a translation project, and has a board consisting primarily of former graduate students, most of whom have academic positions in the United States. According to McMillen, she visits the schools several times a year, staying two nights at each of the seven "schools"—not buildings but gatherings of children, teachers, and blackboards. Spivak is involved in recruitment of teachers, paying their salaries, and providing meals.

McMillen, too, speaks of Spivak's "dense, difficult prose," especially in the context of "Can the Subaltern Speak?" and cites Terry Eagleton as saying her work is sometimes dismissed as "unreadable." According to McMillen, however, Spivak's colleagues speak positively about her managing "hands-on details of teacher recruitment and classroom instruction." Her activism, in other words, forces her to be organized and clear. It also forces her to confront the harsh realities of the least privileged groups in the two-thirds world and to attempt to improve their situations.

NAZER: SURVEILLED SILENCE

Mende Nazer and Damien Lewis's book *Slave: The True Story of a Girl's Lost Childhood and Her Fight for Survival* enables the subaltern to speak. First published in 2004 by Virago Press in Great Britain, it was subsequently published in the United States by PublicAffairs under the title *Slave: My True Story.* The title page lists Nazer as first author on the book, and her name is in larger print than Lewis's. In "A Note from Damian Lewis," a brief essay that follows the testimonial, Lewis, a white Englishman in his late thirties, explains that he heard from a Sudanese friend of Nazer's escape from slavery several days after it occurred in a North London suburb on September 11, 2000. The Sudanese friend wanted the assistance of a journalist to bear witness to the escape so that there would be a record of it. Lewis agreed to help. The note was written two years after the event. He explains that names were changed and locations altered for security reasons (340). He also says that the account has been fictionalized to an extent: "Some scenes and parts of the narrative have been deliberately fictionalized in order to protect identities and to aid the narrative flow of the story" (340). These explanations no doubt ensure protection against accusations of inaccuracy.

An award-winning writer and filmmaker, Lewis has directed and filmed documentaries on war, conflict, and disaster in Asia, South America, and

Africa that have appeared on the BBC, CNN, and ABC and has produced over a dozen films about war and slavery in the Sudan. He speaks in the afterword of the Nazer of 2002 as young, vivacious, and highly intelligent. He describes the process of the collaborative effort as beginning in July of 2001 when the two spent time at a friend's house in the west of England. Nazer only spoke basic English and Lewis spoke no Arabic. Lewis considered working with a translator but decided against it since Nazer's story was so deeply personal and the material so difficult to share. They worked together slowly, in English, using an English-Arabic dictionary when necessary. They also purchased any books they could find on the subject of the Sudan, the Nuba Mountains where Nazer was from, and slavery. They drafted together from July until September, sitting side by side at a desk, Lewis typing the story into his laptop. Sometimes Lewis asked Nazer to draw if they were having difficulty communicating, or Lewis would draw to see if his understanding matched hers. They also sometimes acted out scenes. It was during walks in the woods, however, that many of Nazer's childhood memories came back to her. Lewis speaks in the afterword of the depth of detail of Nazer's memories. After a draft was completed, Lewis and Nazer spent four months revising numerous times. Lewis read through the last of the revised drafts with Nazer, making sure that everything in the story was what she intended.

Nazer was born in the Nuba Mountains of South Kordofan in the Republic of Sudan, a region that borders the new country, the Republic of South Sudan, established in January 2011. The separation of the Sudan into two countries was a result of centuries of conflict between the Muslim North and the Christian South. Under colonial rule, sometimes a coalition between the British and the Egyptians, the South was separated from the North by geography and culture, and its people were often the victim of attacks by mujahedin who raided villages, often capturing young girls and selling them as slaves in the North.[9] *Slave* begins with a first-person description of Nazer's capture when her village in the Nuba Mountains was attacked by Arab raiders in 1994 when she was twelve. She was dragged away by one of the raiders, leaving the burning village behind. The book then shifts to the period prior to the raid and to the specifics of Nazer's happy childhood with her family, again using first-person narrative. Nazer tells us that she was the fifth and last child who lived in adjoining mud huts with her parents and siblings. Her father had a herd of fifty cattle and so was neither rich nor poor. Nazer describes her father getting her a kitten, the kitten's antics, the roasted sorghum and peanuts her mother would cook, or a curried stew of vegetables and meat. The eight chapters in part one of the book describe her success in school, including her learning Arabic and then moving on to English, her brother's prowess as a wrestler, and her very painful circumcision. She then describes, again in vivid detail, her capture, her molestation by her captor, and her sale to a Khartoum family who forced her to do domestic work including cleaning, caring for children, and cooking from early morning until late at night. She was unable to leave the house, had no time off, and received no compensation. Her only solace was the relationship she formed with the children. She was then sent to her owner's sister's residence in London where she had to care for children with whom she had formed no bond. Her situation became so desperate that she contemplated suicide. It was only when the London family returned to the Sudan for a visit, leaving her in London with a family who only suspected her status, that she was able to develop a plan to escape. Not wanting to implicate the family with whom she was staying temporarily, she waited until she returned to the home of her owners to flee by leaving the house on the pretense of emptying the garbage, running down the driveway, and jumping into the car of a fellow countryman who had arranged to assist her.

Drawing on the work of Frantz Fanon, Kelly Oliver in *Witnessing: Beyond Recognition* observes that oppression works by denying individuality to the oppressed and stereotyping them (35), denying them any internal life (24). In his preface to Fanon's *The Wretched of the Earth*, Jean Paul Sartre writes, "Violence in the colonies does not only have for its aim the keeping of these enslaved men at arm's length; it seeks to dehumanize them" (15). Invoking both Fanon and bell hooks, Oliver finds that "overcoming oppression does not require seeking recognition from the oppressors but being the source of one's own meaning" (29). Citing Fanon, Oliver sees reflection and self-reflection as antidotes to the logic of oppression (39).

After Nazer is enslaved, she is treated like an inert object, neither permitted to speak nor listened to. Describing her situation just after she was sold but before she was taken to the home of her owners, she says of three Arab women, "They just ignored me and carried on chatting" (135). A little later she says, "She ignored me and carried on chatting about the forthcoming Ramadan festival" (135). When she is told that she cannot say good-bye to her friends before she leaves, she says she was about to answer back but is warned against doing so. She says, "I kept silent" (136). Silence and invisibility are common themes in her slave narrative. Her owner refers to her repeatedly as "Yebit," an Arabic insult that means "girl worthy of no name" (139). For dinner, she is given the scraps left over from her owners' dinner. She observes, "In our village you would give a dog what you couldn't eat in a bowl in the corner of the room" (145). She says, "I craved human affection and warmth" (148). She makes repeated references to being treated like an animal. As punishment for breaking a vase, she is beaten. She observes, "This was the first time that I'd ever been beaten in my life. My parents had always been gentle and loving" (149). She concludes chapter 14, entitled "Master Rehab," "It was clear that I couldn't expect any fairness or kindness from these people" (150). In the next chapter, entitled "No Escape," she reflects on her invisibility: "Being a slave, nothing was ever explained to me. But as no one seemed to notice I was there most of the time, I could glean some information by eavesdropping on other people's conversations" (156).

Once she realizes that she must focus on survival, she tries to become invisible (156). She also prays, though she is told that "'Islam isn't for black people like you'" (172). She reflects that her masters had stolen her childhood and destroyed her dreams (173). Although she is living increasingly in her memories and daydreams, she learns never to speak her Nuba language, never to sing, and never to mention her past life (175). It is only when the children of her owners start to show affection toward her that she begins to feel human again (176). As she is never allowed to leave the house in which she resides, she speaks of it as her "prison" (176). She begins to fear that her master will kill her. She says, "She had beaten me, abused me and killed any sense I once had of my own worth" (187). In despair, she laments, "There was no one that I could turn to, no one with whom I could talk about the past, no one to help me remember the faces and the stories, the laughter and the love, to reaffirm my true identity" (190). Sometime later, she observes, "After all those years, Rehab had completely destroyed my sense of my own identity and my own self-worth" (200). After traveling to London to become the slave of her master's sister, Hanan, who initially treats her better than Rehab had done, she says, "I'd spent so many years being treated like a slave that that's what I'd become used to" (259). Here, however, because she does not have the affection or warmth of Hanan's children as she did with Rehab's, her situation is even worse than it was. She says, "I was completely isolated and alone" (277), and she becomes suicidal: "Killing myself seemed a much better alternative to staying alive" (279). When Hanan, her husband, and her children return to the Sudan for a visit, she is placed in the home of a family who is unaware that she is a slave, and she finally experiences a "happy atmosphere," and is given some freedom of movement beyond the home. It is on one of her walks that she seeks the help of a Sudanese man in a car repair shop with whom she plans her escape. In the final chapters, she describes the challenges of her newly found freedom—learning to use money, trying to learn English, learning how to make friends. She also describes her desperate attempt to gain asylum in London, her initial failures to do so, and her fear that if she has to return to the Sudan, she will be killed. She observes that her study of English is beginning to pay off. She is still disoriented, though. At the end of the final chapter, she asks, "Where are my roots now? My real identity? My tribe? Am I still a Nuba girl? Or am I a best-selling author? Am I an escaped slave, or an award-winning human rights activist? Am I Sudanese? British? Or just a citizen of the world? I am probably a hybrid of all these things" (334–35).

The collaboration between Nazer and Lewis in some ways resembles *testimonio* or witnessing as described by Mary Louise Pratt in her essay "*Me Llamo Rigoberta Menchú:* Autoethnography and the Recoding of Citizenship." Writing within the context of the collaboration between Rigoberta Menchú and Elizabeth Burgos-Debray that resulted in *I, Rigoberta Menchú: An Indian Woman in Guatemala,* Pratt says, "Testimonios are produced through voluntary collaboration between a metropolitan intellectual and a subaltern or grassroots individual" (65). She explains that the genre results from a need "to renegotiate relations between intellectuals and grassroots constituencies in the domain of print culture" (64). Such collaboration, however, is not always a happy one. In the case of the collaboration between Menchú and Burgos-Debray, the accuracy of some of the details in *I, Rigoberta Menchú* was challenged by anthropologist David Stoll in his book *Rigoberta Menchú and the Story of All Poor Guatemalans.* U.S. academics, including Pratt, came to Menchú's defense in *The Rigoberta Menchú Controversy.* Pratt argues in her essay "*I, Rigoberta Menchú* and the 'Culture Wars'" that Menchú, in speaking for all Guatemalans, is sometimes describing what happened to others as her own experiences (43). Pratt also questions the accuracy of some of Stoll's information (44). In an ironic twist, Elizabeth Burgos (by now divorced from radical Regis Debray) writes the foreword to an expanded edition of Stoll's book, explaining and defending him. She says of the collaborative testimonio with Menchú, "The project was intended to serve a political campaign, not anthropology or literature" (xi). The goal was to arouse international opinion regarding the devastating massacres in Guatemala (xi).

The collaboration between Nazer and Lewis is quite different. They would no doubt be considered by Kelly Oliver to be reliable witnesses even though some of the account is fictionalized. For Oliver, a true witness is a responsible witness. According to Oliver, true witnesses provide testimony, sometimes eyewitness, to the extreme trauma of victims of oppression in an ethical way. True witnessing is challenging, though, because the reality that victims have experienced is both visible and invisible, even to themselves, so witnesses often have to acknowledge the reality of experiences that are incomprehensible to them (106). Both Nazer and Lewis provide satisfying, responsible, and direct accounts of Nazer's enslavement, life as a slave, and escape. Their rhetorical purpose is to make readers aware that slavery still exists in late twentieth-century and early twenty-first-century Sudan and even London and to do what they can to end the practice. Their rhetorical strategy is to describe in vivid detail and as convincingly as they can what Nazer experienced as a slave. The human rights work they undertake is high risk since Nazer's life has been threatened since she escaped. They are also pointing toward the difficulties others in Nazer's position have in obtaining asylum in England. In telling one story, Nazer and Lewis are telling the stories of many and attempting to end the enslavement of young African women.

It is shocking to think that slavery existed in late twentieth-century London. It is also shocking to think that thousands of slaves still exist there— and elsewhere in the so-called developed world including the United States. Especially pernicious is sex slavery— all too common. When Spivak speaks of the subaltern, she speaks of the poor, of those whose families derive from the lowest caste in India. Surely, though, the subaltern who is relegated to the lowest position in a culture is the slave who has no opportunity for physical movement, psychological development, or intellectual growth, who is completely isolated—invisible and silenced. Slaves' transnationality occurs because of their transport as human cargo at the whim of their owners. It is sobering to think of those who haven't been able to escape, who can neither speak nor be listened to, for whom rhetoric is an effectively meaningless term. Nazer did escape, though, through her own ingenuity and courage, and she took the risk of telling her story. She is receiving the recognition she deserves in a play based on her experience and in a film that is loosely based on it. She has become both visible and audible.

As transnational and postcolonial feminist rhetorics develop, they need to focus on women from diverse backgrounds who have diverse stories to tell. Juxtaposing such stories mitigates the tendency to place any one woman at the center and thus the tendency to iconize individual women. For every Gayatri Spivak, there are thousands of women from two-thirds world countries who have been enslaved. By one estimate, there are about four thousand slaves in London alone. Mende Nazer is their synecdochic representative.

Notes

1. Wendy Hesford in "Cosmopolitanism and the Geopolitics of Feminist Rhetoric" uses the term "cosmopolitan" pejoratively, referring to "feminist formations of global citizenship particularly as these formations inform human rights advocacy, and the privileging of Western feminist cosmopolitans' encounter with the women and children of third world countries, namely those construed as non-Western or marginalized U.S. subjects" (55). Jacques Derrida, in contrast, provides an appreciative extended definition of the term in his essay "On Cosmopolitanism," tracing it to Greek Stoicism, Pauline Christianity, and Kant's Enlightenment (19).

2. Mohanty avoids essentializing: "Thus, it is not color or sex which constructs the ground for these struggles. Rather, it is the *way* we think about race, class, and gender—the political links we choose to make among and between struggles" (4). For Mohanty, Third World women do not constitute any automatic unitary group (7). Rather, what constitutes "third world women" is "a *common context of struggle*" (7, emphasis in original). Mohanty published a single-authored book on the same subject in 2003: *Feminism without Borders: Decolonizing Theory, Practicing Solidarity.*

3. Important early work within rhetoric and composition that attends to the situations of women of color includes the publication of Gloria Anzaldùa's mixed genre reflection on the physical, psychological, sexual, and spiritual borderland between the United States and Mexico, *Borderlands: La Frontera: The New Mestiza* in 1993; Jacqueline Jones Royster's essay on Ida B. Wells in Andrea Lunsford's edited collection *Reclaiming Rhetorica*, published in 1995; Royster's response essay in Louise Wetherbee Phelps and Janet Emig's *Feminine Principles and Women's Experience in American Composition and Rhetoric,* also published in 1995; Shirley Wilson Logan's essay on race, gender, and composition studies in Susan Jarratt and Lynn Worsham's collection *Feminism and Composition Studies: In Other Words,* published in 1998; and Min-Zhan Lu's exploration of the problematic of experience in the same volume. Subsequent work would continue the discussion of African American, Hispanic American, Native American, and Asian American issues as well as concerns related to gay, lesbian, and transgender sexual identity.

4. My essay "Composing as a Woman," published in 1988, is often mentioned as the first essay within rhetoric and composition to deal with feminist concerns. The 1987 Caywood and Overing book came earlier, however, as did Mary Hiatt's Braddock Award-winning essay (1979), "The Feminine Style: Theory and Fact," published in 1978.

5. In identifying previous work on postcolonial approaches to rhetoric, Lunsford and Ouzgane mention the collection of interviews *Race, Rhetoric and the Postcolonial,* edited by Gary Olson and Lynn Worsham and published in 1999. Although this collection includes Andrea Lunsford's interview with Anzaldúa and interviews with East Indian intellectual Homi Bhabha, African American intellectual Michael Eric Dyson, Argentinian intellectual Ernesto Laclau, French intellectual Chantal Mouffe, and Caribbean / British intellectual Stuart Hall, it does not focus specifically on two-thirds world peoples from a feminist perspective.

Subsequent work in feminist rhetoric that does have a transnational perspective includes my essay "Reading Global Feminisms" published in 2002 in my book *Feminism beyond Modernism;* essays in the collection *Just Advocacy? Women's Human Rights, Transnational Feminisms, and the Politics of Representation* edited by Wendy Hesford and Wendy Kozol published in 2005; and the guest-edited issue of *College English* on Transnational Feminist Rhetorics coedited by Hesford and Schell referred to above. My essay "Reading Global Feminisms" distinguishes among modern, antimodern, and postmodern feminist approaches to two-thirds world cultures, demonstrating, especially, the value of a hybrid approach suggested by global postmodern feminism. I also deal with postcolonial feminist concerns in my coauthored essay "Rhetorical Witnessing" published in the *Community Literacy Journal* in the spring of 2008.

Hesford and Kozol's edited collection *Just Advocacy?* attempts to work out a postmodern feminist rhetorical approach to the issue of human rights for women from two-thirds world cultures. Essayists focus on universal human rights for women but do so in a critical way. In her foreword to the collection, Inderpal Grewal observes that for the contributors to the volume, the concept of human rights for women becomes an object for analysis rather than a goal to endorse (vii). She explains that the concept of universality needs to be examined rather than accepted (vii). Hesford and Kozol explain that their goal is to examine "the gendered terrain of human rights as it has developed historically in a vexed relationship with national and international security agendas" (4). They examine the documents that are available in understanding the situation of oppressed women such as testimonials and visual evidence, but they do not presume that this evidence is transparent (9). Instead, they "foreground the ethical quagmires and urgent questions with which critical theorists and human rights activists continue to struggle in representing human rights abuses" (9). Essays in the collection focus on diverse issues including forced sexual servitude during World War II (Smith), global sex work and video advocacy (Hesford), and gender and sexuality at the UN General Assembly Special Session on HIV/AIDS (Raimondo).

6. In "Beside Ourselves," Susan Jarratt analyzes the work of Spivak, Trinh T. Minh-ha, and Rigoberta Menchú within a rhetorical context. Jarratt speaks of Spivak's rhetoric as follows:

> Sometimes tortured, almost always tortuous, her prose seems at times almost to parody classical philosophical argument. Deeply engaged with the most traditional philosophical issues, Spivak's prose is full of "lurches": unconventional word use (e.g., "to operate" as a conceptual process), abrupt transitions, unexpected juxtaposition of subjects. Whereas most academic readers are accustomed to the Aristotelian format—state your case and prove it—Spivak seems to work laterally, moving from case to case, point to point, rarely offering examples. (118)

7. I must confess that I've always been uncomfortable with the term *subaltern*, with its suggestion that colonized people are inferior, and wondered why Spivak chose it. I have since learned that *subaltern* is primarily a British word used extensively in Britain and its former colonies and is not necessarily pejorative. The first definition in *Webster's New World Dictionary* (2nd ed.) is "subordinate; of lower rank." The second, which is noted as specifically British, is "holding an army commission below that of captain." A subaltern in this context is not necessarily inferior, simply lower in rank. Webster's also tells us that subaltern in traditional logic means "particular," with reference to a universal proposition of which it is a part (1416). The *Oxford English Dictionary* says that subaltern is a joining of the prefix "sub," which they define as "next below," "near," or "close (to)," "subsequent (to)" (3117) with "altern," which they define as "every other one," or "one after the other" (65). Their first definition of *subaltern* is "succeeding in turn" (3117). A subaltern, then, is someone who is lower in rank but who can move up—an alternate. The dictionary also indicates that subaltern can mean of inferior status, quality, or importance, but that this usage of the term is now rare (3117). A synonym that Spivak sometimes uses is "aboriginal."

8. A paragraph from Spivak's preface is helpful in understanding the passage from "Can the Subaltern Speak?" quoted above. It reads as follows:

> Derrida's second point of disagreement with Lacan relates to the "transcendental signifier." . . . Derrida cautions us that, when we teach ourselves to reject the notion of the primacy of the signified—of meaning over word—we should not satisfy our longing for transcendence by giving

> primacy to the signifier—word over meaning. And, Derrida feels that Lacan might have perpetrated precisely this. (lxiv)

This explanation is more straightforward than the passage from "Can the Subaltern Speak?" and clearer than Derrida's clarification in an endnote in *Of Grammatology.* Here Derrida explains: "The signifier will never by rights precede the signified, in which case it would no longer be a signifier and the 'signifying' signifier would no longer have a possible signified." He suggests that privileging one over the other makes signification "impossible" (n 9, 324). In her translator's preface, Spivak has not only translated Derrida, she has made difficult concepts more accessible to readers new to Derrida's work.

9. A number of books have appeared recently documenting, in vivid detail, the sufferings endured by the Lost Boys of what is now South Sudan. As Judy Bernstein explains in her introduction to *They Poured Fire on Us from the Sky* by Benson Deng, Alephonsion Deng, Benjamin Ajak, and Bernstein, the boys, estimated to be more than twenty thousand, were forced from their homes after a fundamentalist jihad of the northern government of the Sudan. Those who survived, and more than half did not, walked barefoot without food and water, traveling thousands of miles until they at last found sanctuary in a refugee camp in Kenya. Bernstein says,

> Ignited in 1983, Africa's longest-running war is still going on. North against south. Muslims against animists and Christians, Arabs against blacks. Huge oil reserves in southern Sudan being held by the northern Muslin government fuel the war. Race, religion and riches. The same things people always kill each other over. With no solution in sight, 2 million blacks in the south have already died. More casualties than Angola, Bosnia, Chechnya, Kosovo, Liberia, the Persian Gulf, Sierra Leone, Somalia and Rwanda combined. Two million dead. Five million displaced and at risk. A holocaust happening today. (xvii)

Some of these accounts of the lost boys are first-person narratives by the lost boys themselves, sometimes in collaboration with an American writer such as Bernstein, while others have been written about the lost boys in the third person. Dave Eggers's *What Is the What* is a partially fictionalized account.

Works Cited

Althusser, Louis. *For Marx.* Translated by Ben Brewster, Verso, 1969.

Anzaldúa, Gloria. *Borderlands: La Frontera: The New Mestiza.* Aunt Lute Books, 1987.

Bakhtin, Mikhail. *The Dialogic Imagination: Four Essays*, edited by Michael Holquist. Translated by Caryl Emerson and Michael Holquist, U of Texas P, 1981.

Bernstein, Judy. "An Introduction to the Lost Boys." *They Poured Fire on Us from the Sky.* Benjamin Ajak, Alephonsion Deng, and Benson Deng with Judy Bernstein, PublicAffairs, 2005, pp. ix–xxi.

Bhabha, Homi K. *The Location of Culture.* Routledge, 1994.

Bizzell, Patricia, and Bruce Herzberg, eds. *The Rhetorical Tradition: Readings from Classical Times to the Present.* 2nd ed., Bedford/St. Martin's, 2001.

Burgos-Debray, Elizabeth. "Introduction." *I, Rigoberta Menchú: An Indian Woman in Guatemala.* Verso, 1984, pp. xi–xxi.

Caywood, Cynthia L. and Gillian R. Overing, eds. *Teaching Writing: Pedagogy, Gender, and Equity.* State U of New York P, 1987.

Cixous, Hélène. *"Coming to Writing" and Other Essays.* Translated by Sarah Cornell, Deborah Jenson, Ann Liddle, and Susan Sellers, Harvard UP, 1991.

Deleuze, Gilles. *What is Philosophy?* Columbia UP, 1994.

De Man, Paul. *Resistance to Theory.* U of Minnesota P, 1986.

Deng, Benson, Alephonsion Deng, and Benjamin Ajak. With Judy A. Bernstein. *They Poured Fire on Us from the Sky: The True Story of Three Lost Boys from Sudan.* PublicAffairs, 2005.

Derrida, Jacques. *Of Grammatology.* Translated by Gayatri Spivak, Johns Hopkins UP, 1976.

———. "On Cosmopolitanism." *On Cosmopolitanism and Forgiveness.* Translated by Mark Dooley and Michael Hughes, Routledge, 2001, pp. 3–23.

———. "Force of Law: The 'Mystical Foundation of Authority.'" Translated by Mary Quaintance. *Deconstruction and the Possibility of Justice. Cardozo Law Review,* vol. 11, no. 5–6, 1990, p. 1035.

Dyson, Michael Eric. "Race and the Public Intellectual: A Conversation with Michael Eric Dyson." Interview with Sidney I. Dobrin. Olson and Worsham, pp. 81–126.

Eggers, Dave. *What Is the What: The Autobiography of Valentino Achak Deng: A Novel.* McSweeney's, 2006.

Fanon, Frantz. *The Wretched of the Earth.* Grove, 1963.

Flynn, Elizabeth A. "Composing as a Woman." *College Composition and Communication,* vol. 39, no. 4, 1988, pp. 423–35.

———. *Feminism beyond Modernism.* Southern Illinois UP, 2002.

Flynn, Elizabeth A., and Rüdiger Escobar Wolf. "Rhetorical Witnessing: Recognizing Genocide in Guatemala." *Community Literacy Journal,* vol. 2, no. 2, 2008, pp. 23–43.

Foucault, Michel. *The Archaeology of Knowledge.* 1969. Translated by A. M. Sheridan Smith, Routledge, 1972.

Freud, Sigmund. *The Basic Writings of Sigmund Freud.* Modern Library, 1938.

Gramsci, Antonio. *Selections from Political Writings (1921–1926)*, edited and translated by Quinton Hoare, U of Minnesota P, 1978.

Grewal, Inderpal. Foreword. *Just Advocacy? Women's Human Rights, Transnational Feminisms, and the Politics of Representation*, edited by Wendy S. Hesford and Wendy Kozol. Rutgers UP, 2005, pp. vii–ix.

Grewal, Inderpal, and Caren Kaplan. "Global Identities: Theorizing Transnational Studies of Sexuality." *GLQ: A Journal of Lesbian and Gay Studies*, vol. 7, 2001, pp. 663–79.

Guha, Ranajit. *Dominance without Hegemony: History and Power in Colonial India.* Harvard UP, 1997.

Hall, Stuart. "Cultural Composition: Stuart Hall on Ethnicity and the Discursive Turn." Interview with Julie Drew. Olson and Worsham, pp. 205–39.

Hesford, Wendy S. "Cosmopolitanism and the Geopolitics of Feminist Rhetoric." *Rhetorica in Motion: Feminist Rhetorical Methods and Methodologies*, edited by Eileen E. Schell and K. J. Rawson, U of Pittsburgh P, 2010, pp. 53–70.

Hesford, Wendy S., and Wendy Kozol. *Just Advocacy? Women's Human Rights, Transnational Feminisms, and the Politics of Representation.* Rutgers UP, 2005.

———. Introduction. Hesford and Kozol, pp. 1–29.

———. "Kairos and the Geopolitical Rhetorics of Global Sex Work and Video Advocacy." Hesford and Kozol, pp. 146–72.

Hesford, Wendy S., and Eileen E. Schell. "Configurations of Transnationality: Locating Feminist Rhetorics." *College English*, vol. 70, no. 5, 2008, pp. 461–70.

Hiatt, Mary. "The Feminine Style: Theory and Fact." *College Composition and Communication*, vol. 29, no. 3, 1978, pp. 222–26.

hooks, bell. *Teaching to Transgress: Education as the Practice of Freedom.* Routledge, 1994.

Jarratt, Susan. "Beside Ourselves: Rhetoric and Representation in Postcolonial Feminist Writing." *Crossing Borderlands: Composition and Postcolonial Studies*, edited by Andrea A. Lunsford and Lahoucine Ouzgane, U of Pittsburgh P, 2004, pp. 110–28.

Jarratt, Susan, and Lynn Worsham, eds. *Feminism and Composition Studies: In Other Words.* Modern Language Association, 1998.

Kristeva, Julia. *The Kristeva Reader*, edited by Toril Moi. Columbia UP, 1986.

Kulbaga, Theresa A. "Pleasurable Pedagogies: *Reading Lolita in Tehran* and the Rhetoric of Empathy." *College English*, vol. 70, no. 5, 2008, pp. 506–21.

Lacan, Jacques. *The Language of the Self: The Function of Language in Psychoanalysis.* Johns Hopkins UP, 1968.

Laclau, Ernesto. "Hegemony and the Future of Democracy: Ernesto Laclau's Political Philosophy." Interview with Lynn Worsham and Gary A. Olson. Olson and Worsham, pp. 129–62.

Laclau, Ernesto, and Chantal Mouffe. *Hegemony and Socialist Strategy: Toward a Radical Democratic Politics.* Verso, 1985.

Lewis, Damian. "A Note from Damian Lewis." Nazer and Lewis, pp. 337–46.

Logan, Shirley Wilson. "'When and Where I Enter': Race, Gender, and Composition Studies." Jarratt and Worsham, pp. 45–57.

Lu, Minh-Zhan. "Reading and Writing Differences: The Problematic of Experience." Jarratt and Worsham, pp. 239–51.

Lunsford, Andrea. "Toward a Mestiza Rhetoric: Gloria Anzaldúa on Composition and Postcoloniality." *Race, Rhetoric, and the Postcolonial,* edited by Gary Olson and Lynn Worsham, State U of New York P, 1999, pp. 43–78.

Lunsford, Andrea and Lahoucine Ouzgane, "Composition and Postcolonial Studies: An Introduction." *Crossing Borderlands: Composition and Postcolonial Studies,* edited by Andrea Lunsford and Lahoucine Ouzgane, U of Pittsburgh P, 2004, pp. 1–8.

Marx, Karl. "The Eighteenth Brumaire of Louis Bonaparte." *Die Revolution.* New York, 1852.

McMillen, Liz. "The Education of Gayatri Spivak." *Chronicle of Higher Education* 14 Sept. 2007. http://chronicle.com/article/The Education-of-Gayatri/14782. Accessed 16 Mar. 2011.

Menchú, Rigoberta. *I, Rigoberta Menchú: An Indian Woman in Guatemala.* Verso, 1984.

Mohanty, Chandra Talpade. "Cartographies of Struggle: Third World Women and the Politics of Feminism." *Third World Women and the Politics of Feminism,* edited by Chandra Talpade Mohanty, Ann Russo, and Lourdes Torres, Indiana UP, 1991, pp. 1–50.

———. *Feminism without Borders: Decolonizing Theory, Practicing Solidarity.* Duke UP, 2003.

Mosaku, Wunmi. "Wunmi Mosaku on Being Mende Nazer in *I Am Slave.*" http://www.nigeriamovienetwork.com/articles/read-wunmi-mosaku-on-being-mende-nazer-in-i-am-slave-new-movie_112.html. Accessed 7 Dec. 2011.

Mouffe, Chantal. "Rethinking Political Community: Chantal Mouffe's Liberal Socialism." Interview with Lynn Worsham and Gary Olson. Olson and Worsham, pp. 165–204.

Nazer, Mende. Interview with Mende Nazer for Feelgood Theater Productions' play "Slave—A Question of Freedom." Youtube. http://www.youtube.com/watch?v=TWLBxvl_yss. Accessed 7 Dec. 2011.

Nazer, Mende, and Damian Lewis. *Slave: My True Story.* PublicAffairs, 2003.

Oliver, Kelly. *Witnessing: Beyond Recognition.* U of Minneapolis P, 2001.

Olson, Gary, and Lynn Worsham, eds. *Race, Rhetoric, and the Postcolonial.* State U of New York P, 1999.

Pratt, Mary Louise. "*I, Rigoberta Menchú* and the 'Culture Wars.'" *The Rigoberta Menchú Controversy*, edited by Arturo Arias, U of Minneapolis P, 2001, pp. 29–48.

———. "*Me Llamo Rigoberta Menchú:* Autoethnography and the Recoding of Citizenship." *Teaching and Testimony: Rigoberta Menchú and the North American Classroom*, edited by Allen Carey-Webb and Stephen Benz, State U of New York P, 1996, pp. 57–72.

Raimondo, Meredith. "Intensifications: Representing Gender and Sexuality at the UN General Assembly Special Session on HIV/AIDS." Hesford and Kozol, pp. 195–220.

Royster, Jacqueline Jones. "In Search of Ways In." *Feminine Principles and Women's Experience in American Composition and Rhetoric*, edited by Louise Wetherbee Phelps and Janet Emig, U of Pittsburgh P, 1995, pp. 385–93.

———. "To Call a Thing by Its True Name: The Rhetoric of Ida B. Wells." *Reclaiming Rhetorica: Women in the Rhetorical Tradition*, edited by Andrea Lunsford, U of Pittsburgh P, 1995, pp. 167–84.

———. *Traces of a Stream: Literacy and Social Change among African American Women.* U of Pittsburgh P, 2000.

Sartre, Jean Paul. Preface. *The Wretched of the Earth.* Frantz Fanon, Grove, 1963, pp. 7–31.

Schell, Eileen. "Vandana Shiva and the Rhetorics of Biodiversity: Engaging Difference and Transnational Feminist Solidarities in a Globalized World." *Feminist Rhetorical Resilience*, edited by Elizabeth A. Flynn, Patty Sotirin, and Ann Brady, Utah State UP, 2012, pp. 30–55.

Simons, Marlise. "After Rape, a Lifetime of Shame. It's Morocco." *New York Times* 1 Feb. 1999. http://www.nytimes.com/yr/mo/day/news/worl00d/morocco-singlemoms.html.

Smith, Sidonie. "Belated Narrating: 'Grandmothers' Telling Stories of Forced Sexual Servitude during World War II." Hesford and Kozol, pp. 120–45.

Spivak, Gayatri Chakravorty. "Can the Subaltern Speak?" *A Critique of Postcolonial Reason: Toward a History of the Vanishing Present*, Harvard UP, 1999, pp. 266–307.

———. "Can the Subaltern Speak?" *Marxism and the Interpretation of Culture*, edited by Larry Grossberg and Cary Nelson, U of Illinois P, 1988, pp. 271–313.

———. "French Feminism in an International Frame." *Yale French Studies*, vol. 62, 1981, pp. 154–84.

———. *In Other Worlds: Essays in Cultural Politics*. Routledge, 1987.

———. *Outside in the Teaching Machine*. Routledge, 1993.

———. "Translator's Preface." *Of Grammatology*, by Jacques Derrida, translated by Gayatri Chakravorty Spivak, Johns Hopkins UP, 1974, pp. ix–lxxxvii.

Spivak, Gayatri, with Sneja Gunew. "Questions of Multi-culturalism." *The Post-Colonial Critic: Interviews, Strategies, Dialogues: Gayatri Chakravorty Spivak*, edited by Sarah Harasym, Routledge, pp. 59–66.

Spivak, Gayatri, with Donna Landry and Gerald M. MacLean. "Subaltern Talk: Interview with the Editors." *The Spivak Reader*, edited by Landry and MacLean, Routledge, 1996, pp. 287–308.

Spivak, Gayatri, with Phillip Sipora and Janet Atwell. "Rhetoric and Cultural Explanation: A Discussion with Gayatri Chakravorty Spivak." *(Inter)Views: Cross-Disciplinary Perspectives on Rhetoric and Literacy*, edited by Gary A. Olson and Irene Gale, Southern Illinois UP, 1991, pp. 243–54.

Stoll, David. *Rigoberta Menchú and the Story of All Poor Guatemalans*. 1999. Westview P, 2008.

"Subaltern." *Oxford English Dictionary*. Vol. 2. Oxford UP, 1971, pp. 3117–18.

"Subaltern." *Webster's New World Dictionary*. 2nd ed., edited by David B. Guralnik, World Publishing, 1972, p. 1416.

Trinh, Minh-ha T. *Woman, Native, Other: Writing Postcoloniality and Feminism*. Indiana UP, 1989.

Yeats, William Butler. *The Collected Poems of W. B. Yeats*. Macmillan, 1956.

TRANSLATING NORA
CHINESE FEMINISM AND GLOBAL RHETORIC

BO WANG

I begin with moments of the translation and performance of *A Doll's House* (1879) in early-twentieth-century China.[1] In 1914, Chunliu she 春柳社 (the Chunliu Troupe)[2] performed *Wanou zhi jia* 玩偶之家 (*A Doll's House*)[3] in Shanghai, arousing the public's fascination as well as apprehension about Nora Helmer—perhaps the most famous female character in Henrik Ibsen's oeuvre. Despite a controversial reception, Nora would become an inspiration for thousands of Chinese women who pursued *nüquan* 女权 (women's rights, women's power) and sought independence and freedom in that era. Beginning in 1914 and continuing for the next thirty years, Chinese intellectuals and artists translated and performed *A Doll's House* in major cities across the country. In 1935, *Nala* 娜拉 (a Chinese transliteration of Nora) was performed in Shanghai, Nanjing, and other cities with great artistic success. As the playwright Tian Han 田汉 famously declared, the year of 1935 was "The Nora Year." In January 2014, over a century later, to celebrate the hundredth anniversary of the first Chinese performance of Ibsen's work and pay tribute to the Norwegian playwright, the National Grand Theater produced *A Doll's House* in Beijing. Interestingly, in this production, the director was reported to have downplayed the theme of *nüquanzhuyi* 女权主义 (women's rights-ism, feminism) and foregrounded marriage and family—a theme of greater concern for the contemporary Chinese audience. However, for my purpose,

Nora's many trips to China illuminate the discursive relationship between China and the West in the modern and contemporary period.

In this essay, I will argue that the translation and performance of *A Doll's House* in China constitute a "transrhetorical practice," wherein we can read the production and transmission of knowledge across cultural and geopolitical boundaries and discern the shaping of discursive and cultural relationships. Situating this project in conversations about the global turns of rhetoric and composition studies, I use the Chinese translation of Ibsen's play in the early twentieth century to explore what it means to globalize rhetoric in our own time. I trace the changing meanings given to Nora in a series of commentaries and responses following the initial staging of the play, as she ceases to resemble a late-nineteenth-century Norwegian middle-class woman in Ibsen's drama and becomes a symbol for women's emancipation in China. More than just changes in theatrical adaptations, the translation and reception of *A Doll's House* illustrate the evolving discursive formation of a Chinese feminist discourse, a transformation driven by social realities and political aspirations. Chinese intellectuals' reinvention of Nora to imagine the Chinese new woman enriches and complicates contemporary discussions of transnational feminist rhetorics and of globalizing rhetorical studies.

AFTER THE GLOBAL TURN

Since the publication of Andrea Lunsford and Lahoucine Ouzgane's 2004 coedited collection *Crossing Borderlands,* scholars in rhetoric and composition have further called for "globalizing" or "internationalizing" rhetorical studies in the face of postcolonial globalization. In her *PMLA* essay "Global Turns and Cautions in Rhetoric and Composition Studies," Wendy Hesford argues for "greater cross-reading, collaboration, and coalition building across the humanities" to meet the methodological challenges as we turn toward the global (788). For Hesford the global turn entails new critical literacies and frameworks that are linked to "global citizenship" and interrogates "the binary frames of subject / object, self / other, and Western / non-Western" (796–797). Genuine efforts have been made by scholars to integrate global and transnational studies into the discipline's critical operations. For example, the 2008 *College English* Special Issue on "Transnational Feminist Rhetorics" demonstrates what a transnational analytic can do to enrich our understanding of feminist rhetorics in a global context. As the coeditors Wendy Hesford and Eileen Schell and the contributors suggest, a transnational rhetorical perspective can help rhetorical studies to address how certain concepts are "shaped by cultural, social, and economic interconnectivities" and "cross-cultural mobilizations of power, language resources, and people" (465). In *Feminist Rhetorical Practices,* Jacqueline Jones Royster and Gesa Kirsch observe that "a dynamic expansion of local knowledge amid global knowledge . . . has . . . generated a clearer potential to magnify and amplify our understanding of women's participation within an integrative view of rhetorical processes" (111). These scholars' works have not only envisioned a more inclusive, globalized view that recognizes transnational constructions of rhetorical enterprises but have also articulated a set of larger goals and objectives for the future.

In the past few years, a substantial body of work has been produced in the intersecting fields of rhetoric and composition to reset scholarly visions and priorities from a globalized, transnational perspective. Scholars have used global and transnational studies to challenge the existing theoretical assumptions and rethink the parameters of analysis in feminist rhetoric, comparative and cultural rhetoric, human rights rhetoric, composition, literacy studies, and other areas in the discipline (e.g., Baca; Canagarajah; Dingo; Hesford, *Spectacular Rhetorics;* Lipson; Lyon; Mao, "Beyond Bias"; Olson; Queen; Romano; Schell; Swearingen; and Wang, "Comparative Rhetoric"). Notably, in a cluster of articles on "Transnational Feminisms" published in *JAC* in 2013, the coeditors Rebecca Dingo, Rachel Riedner, Jennifer Wingard and the contributors argue forcefully for "the centrality of transnational rhetorical analysis to different areas of rhetorical scholarship" (522). The transnational literacy practice of networking arguments and transnational feminist pedagogies developed by these and other scholars enable us to see how the circulation and exchange of texts and artifacts in transnational spaces can alter our assumptions about rhetorical argument, audience, and situation(s).

To be sure, the new transnational literacies and pedagogies crafted in recent scholarship have helped us rethink how we can connect localized, individual stories to global networks so as to expose, rearticulate, and transform the global power relations, yet further advancing global and transnational rhetorical studies requires more. Using the transnational as an active site of critical engagement with global power, asymmetries, and inequalities (Inderpal Grewal and Caren Kaplan), in my view, also means that we ought to think about how we can begin to move beyond analyses based on and articulated in euroamerican terms and concepts. That is, we need to consider local, native discourses and interventions as coeval contributions in the global making of rhetorical theory. This more inclusive approach entails careful recovery of the marginalized works by rhetors and writers outside of the metropolitan centers as well as reenvisioning global / transnational rhetoric from the other's perspective.

Here, I look briefly at the work of two scholars who model this approach well. In *Deliberative Acts: Democracy, Rhetoric, and Rights*, Arabella Lyon analyzes U.S. media representations of human rights in noneuroamerican countries and challenges us to rethink the assumptions operating in the euroamerican-centric rhetoric of human rights. Lyon notes that if the vernaculars of human rights should be more diverse than those in the Western conception, then interpreting what one sees as a human rights violation or protection should be more complex. She cogently points out: "To recognize human diversity—including a diversity of ethics and rights traditions—critical interpretations and representations of human rights should acknowledge views based in cultural difference, human capacity, and communitarian rights models as well" (104). By historicizing different views on human rights and situating these perspectives in their own cultural contexts, Lyon's analysis encourages us to eschew two dogmatic tendencies: uncritically applying a transhistorical / transdiscursive approach that uses euroamerican concepts as the norm and falling into a hopeless cultural relativism.

Eileen Schell's study of the Kenyan environmentalist activist Wangari Muta Maathai's ecological rhetorics provides an example of what a recovery of noneuroamerican rhetorics may look like. Schell examines Maathai's memoir, speeches, and documentaries—a body of work Maathai composed to disseminate her vision of ecological literacy in Kenyan and other African countries. As Schell observes, Maathai's invocation of the "woman of Yaounde" in the form of the African dilemma story—a rhetorical feature in the African oral tradition—helps audiences understand and identify with "her experience as an African woman and that of other rural African women" and allows her to create a compelling narrative for the Green Belt Movement (597). Through Schell's analysis, we can hear Maathai speak about environmental conservation in a uniquely Kenyan voice yet from a perspective that is both Kenyan and transnational.

Lyon's and Schell's studies as well as other scholars' work have opened up new ways of doing global and transnational rhetoric. Their work also prompts us to consider a new set of questions after the global turn: What does it mean to "globalize" or "internationalize" rhetorical studies? How do we develop a globalized view of rhetoric? In whose terms, in the name of what kinds of knowledge or intellectual authority are such scholarly practices performed?

What kinds of approaches and practices would constitute a new paradigm allowing for critical analyses of texts by rhetors / writers from various historical periods across cultural, national, geopolitical borders?

I explore some of these larger questions through a reading of the Chinese translation and reception of Ibsen's *A Doll's House* in the early twentieth century. Chinese intellectuals' responses to the play demonstrate what I call "transrhetorical practice"—the dialectical process by which new terms, concepts, statements, discourses, and genres are translated, recontextualized, reframed, and reiterated to invent new cultural narratives about woman, nation, and modernity in China as it contacts and clashes with euroamerican languages and cultures. The translations of the play show us how concepts such as "women's rights" and "feminism" were translated and reconceived as Chinese *nüquan* 女权 (women's rights) discourse emerged and how new cultural narratives were borne and subsequently circulated.

NORA 娜拉 TRAVELS TO CHINA

Ibsen's work was translated and introduced to China along with many other euroamerican political, philosophical, literary, and historical texts as part of a larger intellectual project to create a new culture and modernize the country in the late nineteenth and early twentieth century. To some extent, the translation of *A Doll's House* is synecdochal of the translation of feminist discourse in both a Chinese and transnational context.[4] The translations and performances of *A Doll's House* were launched not merely as theatrical events but rather as rhetorical transmissions—processes of interpreting and rearticulating Ibsen's work across different temporal-spatial spheres and cultural sites. Such transmissions enable the concept of Nora to move across time and space. One dimension of such movement involves a large measure of recontextualizing Ibsen from both a Chinese and transnational perspective for the Chinese audience. As LuMing Mao suggests, "the art of recontextualization" entails a dialectical process of moving between the native's point of view and a critical vantage point outside the native tradition ("Searching for the Way" 334). To do so, the translators must stand in a liminal space neither within nor outside of their own culture. It is from this position that Ibsen's work was recontextualized in order to help develop a new heuristic and vocabulary through which the "traditional" Chinese culture could be reevaluated. The translators and commentators (mostly male intellectuals) seemed more interested in using Nora to explore theoretically how to solve

China's social problems and reconstruct a new society. Though these male intellectuals' work contributed to the debate on the woman question, within this framework, women's emancipation was considered a means to revitalizing the nation rather than an end in itself. We see this type of recontextualizing in Hu Shi's famous essay "Yibusheng zhuyi" 易卜生主义 (Ibsenism) and in Lu Xun's polemic essay "Nala zou hou zenyang" 娜拉走后怎样 (What happens after Nora leaves home) that appeared in *Funü Zazhi* 妇女杂志 (The Ladies' Journal) in 1924. The writing of Hu Shi and Lu Xun brought more attention to the debate about Ibsen's play and its implications for Chinese society.

After the initial performance of the play (1914) by the Chunliu Troupe, in June 1918, *Xin Qing Nian* 新青年 (The New Youth) published a special issue on Ibsen, which included a biographical essay, a critical evaluation of his work by Hu Shi, a translation of *A Doll's House,* and partial translations of *An Enemy of the People* and *Little Eyolf.* The figure of Nora circulates in Hu Shi's essay as an embodiment of *gexing* 个性 (individuality) and *weiwo zhuyi* 为我主义 (individualism), as part of his synthesis of Ibsen's plays, letters, and European critics' analysis of Ibsen, as well as Confucianism and China's social reality.[5] Hu Shi considers *A Doll's House* a full-blown example of Ibsen's realism—which contains a devastating critique of the existing social order entwined with a trenchant analysis of theatricality of the everyday and a preoccupation with the conditions of the self and society in modernity. Though Ibsen only offers "a diagnosis of the social problems without prescribing specific solutions," Hu observes, his play calls for a radical transformation not just of laws, morality, institutions, and the relationship between the individual and society, but of human beings and their ideas of individuality and society (502). In Hu's view, this critical attitude is the essence of Ibsenism—a critical, problem-solving habit of mind that can be used to critique and transform Chinese society.

Hu Shi characterizes Nora's problem primarily as society's suppression of one's *gexing* 个性 (individuality) and Nora as a personification of *weiwo zhuyi* 为我主义 (individualism). Though Hu espouses Ibsen's individualism, he incorporates in it the Confucian concept of self-cultivation for the purpose of serving society. To a certain degree, Hu's individualism is a hybrid of Ibsen's individualism—where little concern is shown for the relationship between the individual and society—and Confucian self-cultivation—where the emphasis is always on social interdependence. For Hu, Nora left to find out how she should cultivate herself so as to be of use to society. When Hu described and discussed Nora he utilized terms such as *ziji* 自己 (self), *renge* 人格

(individual character/spirit), *geren* 个人 (individual), *gexing* 个性 (individuality), and *zeren* 责任 (duty, responsibility), bringing the Chinese concept of self in dialogue with Ibsen's notion of individualism. We can see some of these terms in Hu's translation of the famous dialogue between Nora and Torvald Helmer in Act 3:

> HELMER: What "duties" might you have in mind?
> 郝尔茂: . . . 你且说那些责任是什么?
> NORA: *My duties to myself.*
> 娜拉: 是我对于我自己的责任。
> HELMER: You are first and foremost a wife and a mother.
> (郝): 最要紧的, 你是一个妻子, 又是一个母亲。
> NORA: I no longer believe that. *I believe that I am first and foremost a human being, just as much as you*—or, at least, that I'll try to become one. (Moi 243)[6]
> (娜): 这种话我现在不相信了。我相信第一我是一个人正同你一样。—无论如何, 我务必努力做一个人。(Hu 503–4, emphasis in original)

Hu Shi sees a parallel between Nora's dilemma and the plight of Chinese women who were tied to their role as wives and mothers in the old family system. Helmer's biggest mistake is that he sees Nora as a plaything and doesn't allow her to have free will or take responsibility for the family; thus, Nora does not have any opportunity to develop her individual character and realize her potential as a human being (504). Hu points out that the demands for chastity, arranged marriage, and lack of education were the major forces that prevented Chinese women from cultivating an independent will and develop their own *renge* 人格 (character). Some vocabulary that Hu and his student Luo Jialun 罗家伦 used to translate *A Doll's House* became the basic terms to be adopted by others to discuss Chinese women's potential and prospect later.

These terms reframe Ibsen's work, reorienting the character of Nora and her action in terms familiar to the Chinese audience; at the same time, the Chinese terms acquire new meanings by naming that which is foreign and unfamiliar experientially to the audience. They help form a "collective action frame," to borrow David Snow's term, enabling Hu to focus on certain aspects of *A Doll's House,* tell a different story of Nora, and articulate a set of meanings that is more significant to Hu's readers (384). Consequently, the new frame alters the meaning of Ibsen's Nora and her relationship to Chinese readers / viewers. This frame is not necessarily constructed or negotiated *de novo,* but exists, instead, in the elements of the culture shared by Hu and his audience. In turn, Hu's interpretation of Nora was to be reinterpreted and transformed later; the transformations, fleeting or enduring, would shape the dynamic contour of Chinese *nüquan* discourse.

As the debate on women's emancipation continued, the focus of the discussion shifted from Nora's decision to claim her humanity to her fate after she leaves home. If the initial translation and staging of Ibsen's play are driven by desires for a new vocabulary outside of the Confucian paradigm during the early May Fourth period,[7] subsequent endeavors seem intended to circulate and solidify the new discourse. As neologisms and other linguistic and generic innovations explode in all areas of the cultural terrain, Nora as a new term to be integrated into Chinese *nüquan* discourse takes time to catch hold. As late as the early 1920s, commentaries and essays published in newspapers and periodicals focused on introducing Ibsen's work to the readers. From May 11 to May 18, 1923, following a performance of *A Doll's House* by the Peking Women's Normal School, *Chenbao Fukan* 晨报副刊 published a series of essays about the performance. One author commented on the audience's response, noting that many people in the audience left halfway through the play perhaps because Nora's act of leaving her husband and children was incomprehensible to them. The character of Nora in these essays prompts diverse responses, wins sympathy in some viewers, and causes misunderstanding in others. Nevertheless, Nora and her action form a part of the conversation between the authors and readers. A novel idea, the notion that a woman leaves her husband and children in order to develop her independent spirit can stir as much admiration as anxiety and apprehension.

Lu Xun's 1924 polemic essay, "What happens after Nora leaves home," poses an important question concerning Nora that engaged both progressive intellectuals and average readers who might remain doubtful of Nora's choice.[8] Introducing a Chinese translation of the title of the play (based on a German translation)—*Kuilei jiating* 傀儡家庭 (a puppet's house), Lu Xun elucidates the figure of the puppet / doll—the most important metaphor in Ibsen's play: "Puppet may refer to a puppet that moves, a doll in a child's arms, or a person who is manipulated by others" (1218). In his famous satirical style, Lu Xun goes on to extrapolate Ibsen's metaphor, speculating about Nora's fate:

> But if we look at the reality and make a guess, perhaps Nora would only have two paths: to come to a bad end or to come back. If she were a little bird, of course it would give her no freedom to stay in a cage; however, once the bird flew out of the cage, she might encounter an eagle or a cat

> or something else; if caging had numbed her wings and she forgot how to fly, then surely there would be no path. Still there might be another possibility: She would starve to death. Starving to death would cost her life and therefore that cannot be a path. (1219)[9]

The figure of the puppet / doll goes through a metamorphosis and becomes a caged little bird. If "the image of the doll-woman is often found in the borderlands between Gothic horror and romanticism" in European literature (Moi 235), the image of a caged little bird is almost always associated with a gentle, docile, dependent woman in Chinese literature. With striking affinities, both images evoke the uncanny and reduce a woman to a voiceless nonhuman, though the figure of the caged bird also alludes to physical and spiritual bondage and confinement. The subtle shade of difference between the two images discloses the author's metonymic selection of certain specific attributes of the translated text to construct authority through his representations of both Ibsen's and his own culture. Ibsen's Nora finally finds her voice and claims her own humanity: "I believe that I too am first and foremost a human being, just as much as you." But how can the Chinese new woman find her voice and claim her humanity? Lu Xun seems to suggest that the solution to women's problem is constrained by various social ills, which should be dealt with first. By invoking the image of the caged bird, Lu recontextualizes and reframes Nora for his audience and points to the social realities that he believes Chinese women must confront before they walk out of their home.

Theoretically, Lu Xun's essay departs from Hu Shi's argument and echoes many commentaries on women's economic independence in relation to women's emancipation. For example, a 1924 Special Issue of *Funü zazhi* 妇女杂志 (The Ladies' Journal) focused on women's professions and women's economic opportunities.[10] We can see that Lu Xun shares some of the contributors' concerns, particularly, the hostile social environment and lack of institutional support for professional women. Though seemingly pessimistic, Lu shows an acute awareness of the challenges many Chinese women were facing at that time. He writes, "If we put ourselves in Nora's shoes, we know that money, or economy, to say it elegantly, is the most important. . . . In the current society, women's rights to equal economic opportunities would be crucial" (1220). In his view, Nora can't be idealized and transplanted directly from late nineteenth-century Norwegian society to early twentieth-century Chinese society. Though Lu and Hu interpreted Ibsen's play differently, the dialectical doubleness of the translation process is noteworthy in both intellectuals' work.

Whereas Hu synthesizes Confucianism and Ibsen's writing to come up with his version of Ibsenism, Lu puts Ibsen's play in a conversation with the realities of Chinese women to ask a culturally and socially specific, thought-provoking question. Thus, their transrhetorical practices bring self and other together and subject both to transformation in a close cultural and linguistic encounter.

Rhetorically, "what happens after Nora leaves home" marks the moment of shift in Chinese translation and reception of *A Doll's House:* although Lu Xun recontextualizes Nora to explore the theoretical issue of women's liberation in China, he begins with a detailed introduction of the play, its title and plot, keeping the audience aware of the social and cultural context of Ibsen's heroine. In Lu Xun's essay, initially the character Nora not only comes from Norway, but she also dances her tarantella and speaks like a Norwegian middle-class woman. As later women's rights advocates increasingly attend to the specific solutions to the inequalities in Chinese society, Nora ceases being represented in the current fashion. Instead, she begins speaking like a Chinese new woman, and gradually becomes a symbol for women's emancipation in China.

NORA 娜拉 BECOMES A CULTURAL TROPE

In nineteenth- and early twentieth-century colonial and imperialist discourse, the travel of theories is often conceived as a one-way trip and evokes the notions of Enlightenment, expansion, progress, and teleological history. Postcolonial theorists have generally viewed "travel" in a different light, often with skepticism, seeing it as an activity that opens up possibilities for cultural interchange in an ambivalent environment. Edward Said takes travel as a trope for the activity of theory itself, creating a fluid sense of discursive practice (226–247). Complicating Said's notion of traveling theory, Lydia H. Liu argues that "meanings . . . are not so much 'transformed' when concepts pass from the guest language to the host language as 'created'" (26). Thus, translation is no longer a neutral event but rather the very site for political and ideological struggle where two or more languages encounter one another and irreducible differences between them are fought out, authorities invoked or challenged, until new concepts and meanings emerge. Chinese intellectuals translated concepts such as "human rights," "natural rights," "civil rights," "women's rights," and "feminism," which helped create a Chinese feminist discourse in the first three decades of the twentieth century.[11] Not until the May Fourth era did changing notions of women's rights provoke a women's movement that focused on women's individuality and women's human rights. The image of Nora gradually became established in China's cultural scene, symbolizing the idea of women's individuality and humanity in women's emancipation.

In the early phase of Chinese *nüquan* discourse, we can see a tremendous collective effort to recontextualize and reframe Western feminist texts so as to develop a new critical vocabulary. In the late 1920s and 1930s, the translated terms, concepts, and neologisms were gradually detached from the original contexts as they were reiterated in the flourishing printed media. Such circulations and reiterations allow many translated terms to take hold and become part of the new Chinese feminist lexicon. The figure of Nora, like many other new terms, enters and moves across the discursive field of *nüquan*. The translations, performances, and citations of *A Doll's House* reiterate and reinvent Nora, transforming Ibsen's heroine from a complex, married, middle-class woman from Norway having trouble with her marriage into a cultural trope for women's emancipation in China.

Two women intellectuals' writings during the 1930s perform just that work of reiteration and reinvention: "中国妇女将来如何" (What will happen to Chinese women in the future)—an essay by Huang Xinmian 黄心勉—first published in *Funü Zazhi* 妇女杂志 (The Ladies' Journal) in 1931 and then reprinted in her 1932 monograph 中国妇女的过去和将来 (The past and future of Chinese women) as well as in her coedited journal *Nüzi Yuekan* 女子月刊 (The Ladies' Monthly) in 1934,[12] which alludes to Ibsen's heroine; and Lu Yin's essay "今后妇女的出路" (Women's path in the future) originally published in the journal *Nü Sheng* 女声 (Women's Voice) on March 16, 1933,[13] and reprinted in Lu's 东京小品 (Glimpses of Tokyo—miscellaneous essays) in 1935, in which she directly uses *A Doll's House* both at the beginning and the end of the essay. Theoretically and rhetorically, these two essays build on the notion of *nüquan* as realizing women's "*duli renge*" 独立人格 (independent character) and "economic independence" articulated in the earlier works about Nora's choice and its implications for Chinese women's liberation, further moving Nora from the late nineteenth-century Norwegian society to 1930s China while expanding the conceptual domain of *nüquan* identified in Hu Shi's and Lu Xun's essays.

Huang Xinmian's essay "What Will Happen to Chinese Women in the Future" responds to the passage of the Family Act and Inheritance Act in Chinese civil law by the Kuomintang government on May 5, 1931. The new laws for the first time granted women the freedom and rights to choose a partner, marry, divorce, and remarry and to inherit family property equally with their male relatives. Huang muses, "Not only women but also the whole nation have gained a new life" because of these new laws. She continues to remind her readers of the historical significance of the new legislation: "We must celebrate this day as the birthday of the Chinese new woman and cultivate this newborn woman into a *ziyou ren* 自由人 (free human being)" (42). Thus, an allusion to Nora's claim that she is "first and foremost a human being" helps establish an identification with the audience (educated women and men), many of whom might have seen, read about, or heard of Ibsen's play. The allusion also frames the new laws in new terms. The attributive *ziyou* 自由, a "return graphic loan" (which was used to translate "freedom" as early as 1868 and became widespread in China via round-trip diffusion from Japan),[14] qualifies *ren* 人 (human being), articulating a new notion of womanhood. The Chinese new woman comes into sight, whereas the figure of Nora fades into the background, where her voice is blended with other women's voices until she becomes an idea. Having set the stage for the Chinese new woman, Huang proceeds to provide a detailed depiction of what she needs to do to claim her humanity by moving Nora into 1930s Chinese society.

And it is the very movement of such small concepts as "Nora" across cultural and geopolitical boundaries that enables feminist theory to be remixed and reinvented as it travels. Whereas Nora crosses the border in numerous trips through multiple languages such as Norwegian, German, English, and Japanese, reiterating "Nora" and other related terms across different temporal-spatial spheres and cultural sites sets the act of translation in *motion*—as a dialogic and dynamic process—wherein new meanings and new concepts are invented. Huang contemplates the past and prospect of Chinese women, envisioning a future path toward real, meaningful emancipation. She argues that women should use the new civil law as a starting point and actively pursue *nüquan* in three dimensions: the rights to a healthy body, to equal educational opportunities, and to economic independence. Women's rights to their own body, Huang notes, can prevent women from being bound and confined by men. Only until women have a strong, healthy body of their own, can they become a *ziyou ren* (45). Equal opportunities for education allow women to develop their intellectual ability so that they can live an independent life and use their talents to create knowledge and serve society. Further, equal economic rights enable women not only to inherit property but also have a profession and share economic responsibilities (46). One can easily see the conceptual connection, rupture, as well as expansion of *nüquan* discourse from Hu Shi to Lu Xun to Huang Xinmian as the figure of Nora moves from Ibsen's drama to the stage of the Chinese women's movement. Huang puts contemporary Chinese women as the subject front and center —a position different from Hu Shi and Lu Xun, suggesting that women's emancipation should be an end in itself in relation to nation building, not the other way round.

By the time Lu Yin 卢隐 published her essay "Women's Path in the Future" in *Nü Sheng* 女声 on March 16, 1933, Nora was a controversial household name in urban areas. From 1934 to 1936, *A Doll's House* was staged in major cities across the country. The year of 1935 was later called "The Nora Year" by many intellectuals including the playwright Tian Han, the novelist Mao Dun 茅盾, and the literary critic A Ying 阿英. The global and domestic antifeminist undercurrents during the pre-World War II period renewed a discussion of Ibsen's play.[15] The debates focused on such topics as the purpose of women's emancipation, the means by which women were to be emancipated, and the constraints women experienced in a patriarchal society. Clearly, the changed social and political situation abroad and at home led many intellectuals and writers to rethink the question posed by Lu Xun nearly a decade ago: "What happens after Nora leaves home?"

To respond to conservatives' call for women to return home, Lu Yin, who was already a well-known fiction writer, composed a provocative essay. She begins the piece with a reference to Nora: "Ibsen pointed out a path for women a long time ago—Nora's leaving is a legitimate choice and shouldn't be doubted. However, in reality, the Noras are only a small minority, and most women still play a leading role in *kuilei jiatin* 傀儡家庭 (the puppet's house)" (233). Then she explains in detail the consequences of the reactionary trend, warning her readers that the cult of "good wife and virtuous mother" would deprive women of their *duli renge* 独立人格 (independent character), their social position, and their *gexing* 个性 (individuality). Lu Yin declares her position on women's future at the end of the essay, alluding to Ibsen's play again: "In my view, women's path in the future entails breaking down the confinement of home to go to society and leaving *kuilei jiatin* to live a human life. My only slogan is: We should *not only live as a woman but as a human being*" (235). Though one can hear Nora's voice through Lu Yin's citation, Ibsen's Nora has become a Chinese Nora in the third sentence of the first paragraph in Lu's essay. Nora is used only to make a point about Chinese women's future.

During the same time period, a series of responses and commentaries by Lu Yin's contemporaries was published in various women's journals, with their authors citing or alluding to Nora and *A Doll's House*. *Nüzi Yuekan* (The Ladies' Monthly), for example, published several responses in different genres including an essay titled "娜拉何处去?" (Where does Nora go?) in October 1934, a poem "出走后的娜拉" (We are the Noras who left home) in September 1936, and then another essay "期望与中国娜拉者" (Our expectations for the Chinese Noras) in October 1936. Wang Ning may have perceived such commentaries on and references to *A Doll's House* as unpromising for "'a return to the real Ibsen as an artist' and 'an aesthetic turn' in China's Ibsen studies" (138). But "many of Ibsen's ideological insights" that are "communicated symbolically rather than literarily" consolidate the trend I have been describing, and cement Nora as an important symbol for Chinese women's liberation (138–39). In fact, the image of the Chinese Nora can also be seen in Lu Yin's own fiction and in the work of such artistically successful writers as Bai Wei 白薇, Guo Moruo 郭末若, Chen Hengzhe 陈衡哲, Bing Xin 冰心, Ding Ling 丁玲, and Mao Dun.

Social critiques / commentaries such as the essays by Huang Xinmian and Lu Yin demonstrate another dimension of the movement of the concept of Nora: through numerous reiterations, the proper name "Nora" becomes a conceptual-metaphor for "women's rights" and a new term in the Chinese feminist lexicon. When many a writer begins alluding and referring to Nora as a representative of new women in the Chinese context, the transformation happens. Cross-cultural synecdochal reference guarantees the figure of Nora (and other terms alike) as the transferable, reproducible, and hence mutable meme for Chinese *nüquan*. Further, Nora becomes identified with the Chinese new woman by moving *across* cultural and generic boundaries. The metatheatricalilty (in Lionel Abel's sense of the word) of Ibsen's play is reproduced and reinvented in Huang's and Lu's essays in the sense that both women essayists work to change the prescribed societal norms—they not only use Nora metaphorically to imagine a future for women in writing but also play the role of their imagined Nora in their own lives.

Nora's trips from Ibsen's late nineteenth-century Norwegian society to early twentieth-century Chinese theaters and to the worlds of Chinese writers' fictional, dramatic, poetic, and prosaic work reveal her rhetorical force and a cross-fertilization despite the supposed rigidity of genre and the artificial divide between the symbolic and the literary. In her study of the Chinese reception of Ibsen, Elisabeth Eide laments, "The Chinese Nora, abstracted from the actual context of Ibsen's play, is reduced to a one-dimensional figure" (90).[16] Her perception unfortunately resembles some scholars' arguments that *A*

Doll's House needs to be rescued from feminist "ideology" so that it can emerge as a classic and Ibsen can assume his place in the pantheon of true artists.[17] In their eyes, an ideological reception of Ibsen's work reduces his characters to idealized archetypes and the didactic transformation of Nora overlooks or misinterprets Ibsen's art. "Ideological" though the Chinese translations / interpretations of Ibsen may be, they do not preclude any representational function. A representation of self and other gets forged when perspectives are created, phenomena defined, mores constructed in cross-cultural discursive encounters. As Maria Tymoczko noted long ago, the *metonymic* process of translation entails the translator's participation in the dialectic of power and strategies of change that are inevitably associated with politics and ideology.

> The metonymies of translation are a key to the construction of the representations that translations project—whether they are representations of history, culture, values, or literary form. The metonymics of a translation are, thus, not simply of abstract interest. They cast an image of the source text and the source culture; they have political and ideological presuppositions and impact; they function in the world. For the receiving audience the translation metonymically constructs a source text, a literary tradition, a culture, and a people, by picking parts, aspects, and attributes that will stand for wholes. Such metonymies of translation play a part in establishing a symbolic order within which a people is construed or even construes itself. (57)

The metonymies of translation suggest that translation is "a locus of the formation of knowledge," hence a contested site for meaning making (Tymoczko 294). In the process, the translators rhetorically construct authority by responding to the political, social, aesthetic, and ideological context of the receiving culture and giving voice to the native experience. In response to their own political and social context, Chinese intellectuals recontextualize and reiterate Ibsen's work to articulate their experience and serve their purposes. Their recontextualization and reiteration—examples of transrhetorical practice—enable the figure of Nora to move across cultural and generic borders to finally transcend the stage of Ibsen's drama and acquire legitimacy as a cultural trope for *nüquan* on the political stage.

Establishing a symbolic order or a hybrid framework in the colonial context involves resistance, exchange, appropriation, negotiation, as well as co-authoring. Recontextualization and reiteration, however, do not mean merely mechanically repeating words, terms, and concepts from the guest language, nor do they imply that the discourse of the (semi-) colonized is homogeneous. On the contrary, the discourse created in the host language (which reveals itself to be heterogeneous) is open to multiple interpretations over time and each act of recontextualizing and reiterating is a rearticulation and reinvention. As Chinese intellectuals recontextualized and reiterated Nora for their audience, the conceptual domain of women's rights shifted to both reflect and respond to Chinese women's realities. Consequently, "women's rights"—a major concept in the discursive field of Chinese *nüquan* discourse—was reimagined and reconceived through each reiteration of the translated terms. Such catachrestical reclamations of "women's rights," as Gayatri Chakravorty Spivak might indicate, are not only *petits recits* but tamper with the authority of storylines in the "great narratives"(229). The local short tales, in turn, have global "reverberations" of their own, to use Joan Scott's term.[18]

The Chinese translations of *A Doll's House*, to a great degree, constitute a new locus of enunciating "women's rights" in transnational and transcultural spaces. Nora's trips to China gave her new meanings that rearticulate subaltern and hegemonic knowledges from the location of the subaltern produced by local modern / semicolonial histories. Thus, transrhetorical practice becomes a trope of epistemological crossing, a way of "border thinking" (Mignolo). Though laden with anxiety and vulnerability, this dialectical and dynamic *process* promises new meanings, new conceptual categories, new ways of naming, for in the imagining of other cultures and other rhetorics, there is unavoidably the imagining, or reenvisioning of the self—in its past traditions, in its current conditions, and, more importantly, in its future potentials. As the Chinese case has shown, through layered recontextualizations and reiterations of other cultural / rhetorical concepts *across time and space*, transrhetorical practice connects cultural specificities of language / symbolic practices in a local environment to the larger geopolitical forces / networks. In this paradigm the creation of new languages and concepts through linguistic and cultural encounters is no longer merely spontaneous and improvisational as implied in Pratt's notion of "contact zones," but rather it becomes the very condition of living, being, and knowing.

As our discipline moves to further globalize / internationalize rhetorical studies, performing transrhetorical practice means that we need to think about the question of "speaking from" and consider native, noneuroamerican rhetorics as coeval contributions to a globalized canon. Identifying specific terms and concepts in noneuroamerican rhetorics to develop plural local terms and hybrid analytical frameworks would help expand our analytical vocabulary and include the other in the domain of a cross-cultural dialogue. The point of departure in such a dialogue is no longer necessarily always anchored in the euroamerican terms and concepts with which we are familiar and comfortable. We may as well experiment with various local terms and use what we have learned from other cultures and rhetorics to engage with the critical issues that concern the people across cultural and geopolitical boundaries. Then we might be able to view these issues through perspectives created from a dialectical and dialogic engagement with the other. We might be able to see Nora Helmer through the eyes of the Chinese new woman. Let the dialogue begin.

Notes

1. *A Doll's House* was published on December 4, 1879, in Copenhagen. The first performance took place at the Royal Theatre in Copenhagen on December 21 in the same year, with Betty Hennings as Nora.

2. Chunliu she 春柳社, a Chinese modern theater troupe, was established in Tokyo in 1906 by Li Shutong 李叔同 and Zeng Xiaogu 曾孝谷. They created wenming xin xi 文明新戏 (enlightened new play)—the earliest theatrical form of Chinese modern spoken drama, bringing together elements of Western drama and traditional Chinese singing opera. See Chen Baichen and Dong Jian, 中国现代戏剧史稿 (1899–1949) (A History of Modern Chinese Drama), Zhongguo Xiju Chubanshe, 2008.

3. At that time there were several different Chinese translations of the title *Et dukkehjem* (A Doll's House). For example, *Wanou zhi jia* 玩偶之家, a literal translation of A Doll's House, might be translated from an English version of Ibsen's play. Another Chinese version *Kuilei jiating* 傀儡家庭—based on a German translation—means a puppet's house. Still another version is simply *Nala* 娜拉, which uses the Chinese transliteration of Nora as the title. Each version reflects a particular Chinese translator's emphasis and is conditioned by his or her knowledge of a specific European language.

4. I use "translation" in a broader sense here, which includes two interconnected discursive activities: translating and reframing Western concepts and discourses and rereading and redefining Chinese classical texts.

5. From Hu Shi's essay, it is clear that Hu had read European critics' works on Ibsen including George Bernard Shaw's *The Quintessence of Ibsenism* and Georg Brandes's *Henrik Ibsen and Bjornstierne Bjorn.*

6. The English translation of the dialogue between Nora and Torvald Helmer is by the Ibsen scholar Toril Moi, whose rendition is quite close to Hu Shi's and Luo Jialun's Chinese version.

7. The May Fourth Movement, initially spearheaded by students protesting the government's humiliating policy toward Japan, was turned into a series of demonstrations, amounting to a social and intellectual revolution, from 1919 to 1925.

8. Lu Xun's piece was originally delivered as a speech at Peking Women's Normal School on December 26, 1923, and then was revised and published in *Funü Zazhi* 妇女杂志 (The Ladies' Journal) in October 1924.

9. Unless otherwise indicated, all translations are mine.

10. *Funü Zazhi* 妇女杂志 published a special issue on women's economic independence and profession in August 1924, which included titles such as "The Primary Issue of Women's Profession," "Are Women Really Not Suitable for a Profession," "Women's Profession and Motherhood," "The Current Situation of Women in Business," and "Professional Women in the United States."

11. In "Concepts of Women's Rights in Modern China," Mizuyo Sudo examines the emergence of the concepts of "women's rights," "civil rights," and "natural rights" in China in the late nineteenth and early twentieth century. She compares the changing meanings given to these concepts in Japan and China. Sudo identifies four different interpretations / views of "women's rights" from the publications by four Chinese intellectuals during the pre-May Fourth period at the turn of the twentieth century: "mother to the nation," "equals in duty to men," "self-determination," and "disavowals of female citizenship." These prototypes of the Chinese version of "women's rights" influenced the later generations of Chinese feminist thinkers. The translations of Ibsen's work and other euroamerican feminist texts during the May Fourth era deepened the discussion and changed the Chinese discourse of women's rights in the sense that women's individuality and women's human rights became the predominant concern during the 1920s and 1930s. The discussions about women's rights during this period became more nuanced and thorough in the publications I examine in this study. Tani Barlow's *The Question of Women in Chinese Feminism* examines the permutations of feminist theories in modern China, but her claim about the centrality of eugenic theory in Chinese feminism seems to be based on a limited historical archive of theoretical works mainly written by male intellectuals. In *Tales of Translation,* Hu Ying analyzes the construction of the new woman through translation in Chinese popular media during the pre-May Fourth period, though her study also leaves women's works largely unexplored. For a discussion on Chinese feminism during the post-Mao period, see Hui Wu's translated collection *Once Iron Girls: Essays on Gender by Post-Mao Chinese Literary Women.*

12. Huang Xinmian 黄心勉 (1902–35) was a well-respected essayist and editor during the 1930s. With her husband Yao Mingda 姚名达, Huang cofounded and

coedited Nüzi Yuekan 女子月刊 (The Ladies' Monthly) and coestablished a small independent publishing house Nüzi shudian 女子书店 (Women's bookstore), which was well known for publishing Chinese feminist works and translated feminist texts. Despite her phenomenal work as a feminist theorist, writer, and editor in her time, Huang Xinmian's name, like many other women who wrote about women's rights in the early twentieth century, can rarely be found in contemporary scholarship on Chinese feminism.

13. For a detailed discussion of Lu Yin's work, see Wang, "Breaking the Age of Flower Vase."

14. According to Lydia H. Liu, the term "return graphic loan" refers to classical Chinese-character compounds that were used by the Japanese to translate modern European words and were reintroduced into modern Chinese (302).

15. In women's journals published during the pre-World War II period, many intellectuals responded to the antifeminist forces abroad and at home. They were particularly concerned with Adolf Hitler's call for women to return to the kitchen and Chinese conservatives' call for reviving the "good wife and virtuous mother" model. See Wang, "Engaging *Nüquanzhuyi*: The Making of a Chinese Feminist Rhetoric."

16. Elisabeth Eide conducts a close analysis of the Chinese reception of Ibsen in her monograph *China's Ibsen—From Ibsen to Ibsenism*. Her study has informed my work, though I do not fully agree with her view about Chinese interpretations of *A Doll's House*.

17. For further discussion of Ibsen and feminism, see Joan Templeton, "The Doll House Backlash, Criticism, Feminism, and Ibsen"; Gail Finney, "Ibsen and Feminism"; Toril Moi, *Henrik Ibsen and the Birth of Modernism—Art, Theater, Philosophy*.

18. In her recent book *The Fantasy of Feminist History*, the historian Joan Wallach Scott offers an insightful analysis of the global circulation of feminist strategies and feminism. She uses "echo" and "reverberation" to characterize the translations and transmissions of feminism around the world.

Works Cited

Abel, Lionel. *Tragedy and Metatheatre: Essays on Dramatic Form*. Holmes and Meier, 2003.

Baca, Damián. *Mestiz@ Scripts, Digital Migrations, and the Territories of Writing*. Palgrave, 2008.

Barlow, Tani E. *The Question of Women in Chinese Feminism*. Duke UP, 2004.

Canagarajah, Suresh. *Translingual Practice: Global Englishes and Cosmopolitan Relations*. Routledge, 2013.

Chen Baichen and Dong Jian. *Zhongguo xiandai xijiu shigao* 中国现代戏剧史稿 (1899–1949) [*A History of Modern Chinese Drama*]. Zhongguo Xiju Chubanshe, 2008.

Dingo, Rebecca. *Networking Arguments: Rhetoric, Transnational Feminism, and Public Policy Writing.* U of Pittsburgh P, 2012.

Dingo, Rebecca, Rachel Riedner, and Jennifer Wingard. "Toward a Cogent Analysis of Power: Transnational Rhetorical Studies." *JAC*, vol. 33, no. 3-4, 2013, pp. 517–28.

Eide, Elisabeth. *China's Ibsen—From Ibsen to Ibsenism.* Curzon, 1987.

Finney, Gail. "Ibsen and Feminism." *The Cambridge Companion to Ibsen*, edited by James McFarlane, Cambridge UP, 1994, pp. 89–105.

Grewal, Inderpal, and Caren Kaplan. "Global Identities: Theorizing Transnational Studies of Sexuality." *GLQ: A Journal of Lesbian and Gay Studies*, vol. 7, 2001, pp. 663–79.

Hesford, Wendy S. "Global Turns and Cautions in Rhetoric and Composition Studies." *PMLA*, vol. 121, no. 3, 2006, pp. 787–801.

———. *Spectacular Rhetorics: Human Rights Visions, Recognitions, Feminisms.* Duke UP, 2011.

Hesford, Wendy S., and Eileen E. Schell. "Introduction: Configurations of Transnationality: Locating Feminist Rhetorics." *College English*, vol. 70, no. 5, 2008, pp. 461–70.

Hu Shi. "Yibusheng zhuyi" 易卜生主义 ["Ibsenism"]. *Xin Qingxian* 新青年 [*New Youth*], vol. 4, no. 6, 1918, pp. 489–507.

Hu Ying. *Tales of Translation: Composing the New Woman in China, 1899–1918.* Stanford UP, 2000.

Huang Xinmian. *Zhongguo funü de guoqü he jianglai* 中国妇女的过去和将来 [*The Past and Future of Chinese Women*]. Nüzi Shudian, 1932.

Lipson, Carole S. Introduction. *Ancient Non-Greek Rhetorics*, edited by Carol S. Lipson and Roberta A. Binkley, Parlor, 2009, pp. 3–25.

Liu, Lydia H. *Translingual Practice: Literature, National Culture, and Translated Modernity—China, 1900–1937.* Stanford UP, 1995.

Lu Xun. "Nala zouhou zenyang" 娜拉走后怎样 ["What Happens After Nora Leaves Home"]. *Funü zazhi* 妇女杂志 [*The Ladies' Journal*], vol. 10, no. 8, 1924, pp. 1218–22.

Lu Yin. "Funü jinhou de chulu" 妇女今后的出路 ["Women's Path in the Future"]. *Dongjing xiaopin* 东京小品 Beixin shujü, 1936. Rpt., edited by Xiao Feng, *Lu Yin* 卢隐, Renmin chubanshe, 1984.

Lunsford, Andrea, and Lahoucine Ouzgane, eds. *Crossing Borderlands: Composition and Postcolonial Studies.* U of Pittsburgh P, 2004.

Lyon, Arabella. *Deliberative Acts: Democracy, Rhetoric, and Rights.* Pennsylvania State UP, 2013.

Mao, LuMing. "Searching for the Way: Between the Whats and Wheres of Chinese Rhetoric." *College English*, vol. 72, no. 4, 2010, pp. 329–49.

———. "Beyond Bias, Binary, and Border: Mapping out the Future of Comparative Rhetoric." *Rhetoric Society Quarterly*, vol. 43, no. 3, 2013, pp. 209–25.

Mignolo, Walter D. *Local Histories / Global Designs: Coloniality, Subaltern Knowledges, and Border Thinking.* Princeton UP, 2000.

Moi, Toril. *Henrik Ibsen and the Birth of Modernism—Art, Theater, Philosophy.* Oxford UP, 2006.

Olson, Christa J. *Constitutive Visions: Indigeneity and Commonplaces of National Identity in Republican Ecuador.* Pennsylvania State UP, 2014.

Queen, Mary. "Transnational Feminist Rhetorics in a Digital World." *College English*, vol. 70, no. 5, 2008, pp. 471–89.

Romano, Susan. "Orality and Presence: Relational Rhetorics in Latin American Contexts." *Rhetoric Society Quarterly*, vol. 45, no. 3, 2015, pp. 212–24.

Royster, Jacqueline Jones, and Gesa E. Kirsch. *Feminist Rhetorical Practices: New Horizons for Rhetoric, Composition, and Literacy Studies.* Southern Illinois UP, 2012.

Said, Edward. *The World, the Text, and the Critic.* Harvard UP, 1983.

Schell, Eileen E. "Transnational Environmental Justice Rhetorics and the Green Belt Movement: Wangari Muta Maathai's Ecological Rhetorics and Literacies." *JAC*, vol. 33, no. 3-4, 2013, pp. 585–613.

Scott, Joan Wallach. *The Fantasy of Feminist History.* Duke UP, 2011.

Snow, David. "Framing Processes, Ideology, and Discursive Fields." *The Blackwell Companion to Social Movements*, edited by David Snow, Sarah A. Soule, and Hanspeter Kriesi, Blackwell, 2004, pp. 380–412.

Spivak, Gayatri Chakravorty. "Poststructuralism, Marginality, Postcoloniality and Value." *Literary Theory Today*, edited by Peter Collier and Helga Geyer-Ryan, Cornell UP, 1990, pp. 219–44.

Sudo Mizuyo. "Jindai Zhongguo de nüquan gainian" ["Concepts of Women's Rights in Modern China"]. *Bainian zhongguo nüquan sichao yanjiu* 百年中国女权思潮研究 [*Feminist Thought in China over a Century*], edited by Wang Zheng and Chen Yan, Fudan Daxue Chubanshe, 2005. 37–57.

Swearingen, C. Jan. "Revisiting Rhetoric's Earliest Borders: Hetairae, Metics, and Other Strangers." *Manifesting a Future for Comparative Rhetoric*, edited by LuMing Mao and Bo Wang, A Symposium of *Rhetoric Review*, vol. 34, no. 3, 2015, pp. 252–56.

Templeton, Joan. "The Doll House Backlash: Criticism, Feminism, and Ibsen." *PMLA*, vol. 104, no. 1, 1989, pp. 28–40.

Tymoczko, Maria. *Translation in a Postcolonial Context: Early Irish Literature in English Translation*. St. Jerome P, 1999.

Wang Ning. *Globalization and Cultural Translation*. Marshall Cavendish Academic, 2004.

Wang, Bo. "Engaging *Nüquanzhuyi:* The Making of a Chinese Feminist Rhetoric." *College English*, vol. 72, no. 4, 2010, pp. 385–405.

———. "Comparative Rhetoric, Postcolonial Studies, and Transnational Feminisms: A Geopolitical Approach." *Rhetoric Society Quarterly*, vol. 43, no. 3, 2013, pp. 226–42.

Wu, Hui, trans. *Once Iron Girls: Essays on Gender by Post-Mao Chinese Literary Women*. Lexington, 2010.

AFTERWORD
AIN'T NO WALLS BEHIND THE SKY, BABY! FUNK, FLIGHT, FREEDOM

ADAM J. BANKS

Funk is dead is what they said, while sitting around cheating at pool.
Their bags were bagging and they weren't bragging; to tell the truth they were looking real cool.
Now they were choked up tight in their white on white, their cocoa brown fronts were down. They wore candy striped ties that hung down to their flies, and they sported gold dust crowns.
It was the 15th frame of a nine-ball game and they all stood digging the play.
With an idle shrug they suddenly dug a strange cat moving their way.
He was a medium built cat with a funny time hat, he looked about 5 years old.
He wore a messed up vine and he needed a shine, and he shivered as if he was cold.
To all the other guys, they surmised this dude was some ordinary flunky,
But to the well trained eyes of how the Mothership flies, you could tell the mutha . . . was funky!

That verse, from George Clinton and Parliament / Funkadelic's 1993 song "Martial Law" links at least three different generations of black oral tradition, as it is a version of the folktale titled either "Hip Bud" or "Billy Bud," but it also provides a poet in one of my favorite movies (*Love Jones*) with the opening lines of his poem as he tries to court photographer Nina Mosely. But as another character in the movie says over his own game of pool, "Let me break this down so it can forever and perpetually be broke." Can I do that? Can we dispense with the pretense of the scholarly essay for a minute so I can do that?

I ask you for permission to do that because my message is not a scholarly one even though it is about our scholarship. It's not even particularly deep, though it is about deep things. And I don't want to use this moment to pretend to speak for our profession in any way, a profession where I learn far more from the gifts and commitments others bring than I can pretend to offer. All I have is my vision of what we do. And that vision, everything I think about who we are, the best of what we do, and who we can be comes down to three words: Funk. Flight. Freedom. Actually, George Clinton's protégé Bootsy Collins says it even better than George did.

"The sky is not the limit! Ain't no walls behind the sky baby, so we just gonna fly on, and reach for the stars if you know what I'm talkin about." That line comes from the lyrics to one of the greatest slow jams I know, Bootsy's "I'd Rather Be with You." Many of you already know that funk and soul music are primary spaces through which I enter this thinking, teaching, and serving work that we do. But beyond the thousands of songs that rotate through my various digital devices and the hundreds of vinyl albums I listen to at least sometimes and the untold numbers of songs I experience because of my friends' Facebook, Twitter, SoundCloud, and Spotify posts, it is this one song from that space bass player from Cincinnati that has stayed with me. Through all our conferences, scholarship, email exchanges, and in-person exchanges, through all of my walking time, coffee-shop time, and library time—even through all of my own internal flights about ways I might escape this moment—I keep coming back to Bootsy, though I'd rather be with you.

Part of that is truly because I would rather be with you—because there is no other academic discipline I would rather be part of than composition. But more than that, I think that this song is the one that wouldn't let me go in all of my thinking about this moment because of its reminder—no, its insistence—that there are no limits, that we need to fly on and reach for the stars, that renews me in a moment when I so needed renewal. Bootsy's song brings together the three themes I believe can guide us as we respond to the call to risk and reward that the program chair for the 2015 Conference on College, Composition, and Communication chose for us: Funk, Flight, and Freedom.

In fact, Bootsy Collins and his Parliament / Funkadelic family, made flight and space travel central themes and images in their music. From the mother ship as the central metaphor for P/Funk's role in the musical universe and the twentieth-century chariot that they invoked to swing down and let us riiiiide, to Bootsy's instruction to his audience that we gonna fly on, past any limits that our day-to-day lives might impose on us, past any constraints that might wear on us, joined in a long line, to a long tradition of tales of flying Africans in which flight—across oceans home to Africa, and across galaxies to as yet unexplored stars and planets—has been an ongoing motif for claiming freedom right here and now.

These ideas—funk, flight, and freedom—speak to the role I believe composition and communication can play in the academy—who we be, to how we go about the work we do, and to what work we see ourselves having come here to do. If our scholarly organization (CCCC) is the "mother ship," I'll extend that metaphor past the Starship *Enterprise* for right now, though. In many ways, I think of composition as the *Deep Space Nine* of the academy. Because we have the opportunity to be part of the academic journey of almost every student who pursues higher education, hub metaphors for our work are not at all new. I use the *Deep Space Nine* metaphor in this sense as well, but with other reasons in mind. I also believe that because of our training—our grounding in rhetoric, composing, and communicating—we have a chance to be a hub for intellectual life on campus for our colleagues in other departments and for administrators as well. Because we are a discipline and at the same time cannot be contained by ideas of disciplinarity, we can be a model and connecting point for the hard work of interdisciplinarity and transdisciplinarity we often hear talked about across campus, but rarely lived out. In fact, I often imagine composition programs and departments operating more like interdisciplinary centers than as programs and departments. And I've always believed we ought to be a hub for connections between the academy and local communities. It is precisely because we do discourse, in all its messiness, that we have the chance to be this kind of hub for intellectual work, and for justice work, on campus and off.

I have funk on my mind not just because it is a genre of music that I love, but because of the ways funk artists imagined the world and our place in it.

One of the things that I love most about composition—one of the reasons I'd rather be with you—is because of ways in which our field has arrived at a disciplinary maturity, and yet remains undisciplined, unable to be disciplined. Funk is on my mind because for me it represents us dropping pretense and embracing boldness, wildness, and irreverence. Poet and scholar Tony Bolden cites writers like Jayne Cortez, Sterling Plummp and Talib Kweli as "funky." Check his description:

> Effusive and amorphous, the funk impulse is a central component of all black music—from antebellum ring shouts and gospels to blues, jazz, funk and hip-hop. Hence, George Clinton's hyperbole: "In the beginning was the funk." Characterized by an aesthetic that foregrounds speed, self-reflexivity, asymmetry, dissonance, and repetition, funkativity bespeaks a kinetic epistemology comprised of dynamic principles stored in a virtual archive of cultural memory, replete with (pre)configuring riffs and rhymes, twists and turns, shakes and breaks that are perpetually (re) sampled and (re)mixed in a manner comparable to electricity.

Bolden also links funk to Latina/o culture by referencing Federico Garcia Lorca's theorizing of the concept of *duende*. He quotes Lorca this way: "The duende climbs up inside you, from the soles of your feet." I yearn for my own writing to one day reflect THAT kind of electric, kinetic, epistemology. Funk is worthy of sustained scholarly attention because it is the sweat and the stank of funk, the sweet and nasty smell of exertion as we break it on down and shake it on down, that signifies not only honest expression, exertion and integrity, but acumen, celebration, commitment to one's work, and yes, intellect. This intellectual, creative, and physical work has helped black folk and audiences across race and culture intervene in the nation's racialized ideologies for Bolden, because those steeped in the funk are free enough to toss those ideologies aside and refuse to play by the rules of the game. Intervention comes from those who are irreverent, from those who are contrary, from those who are wild.

I'm talking about funk as a guiding idea for who we are in our thinking, teaching, making, and doing because for just a minute, I want us to drop our serious, scholarly personae and just talk together. I want us to move forward knowing—as activists in Ferguson and Cleveland and New York and the Bay area teach us—that just as respectability will not save us in the streets or in relationships or in politics, or even in a brilliant presidency, it will not save us in the academy either. So just like Viola Davis took off her wig in *How to Get*

Away with Murder to let the nation know she would not be defined by someone else's oppressive standards, I want us to take off our own respectability politics for now and realize that no matter how much we push our students to dismiss their home languages for some assimilated standardized version, respectability will not save them, or us. I want us to realize that the funkiness of C's the Day and our sparkleponies is one of the best things about us, and that even if we did not have them, the *Chronicle* still wouldn't understand us, much less save us. I'm beyond grateful that sparkleponies roam our halls and listen in on our conference sessions and inspire the connections across people and ideas that open up space for new, imaginative teaching and scholarship and make people feel welcome and at home in the process. I want us to realize the respectability of having fellows like other academic organizations will not save us. I want us to realize that all our citations of high theory will not save us, and neither will trying to show that we are as rigorous and as serious as our literary colleagues save us. And I want us to realize that even the respectability of bigger budgets will not save us. As real as our struggles are, we act like being broke is new. We always been underfunded. We always been figuring it out as we go. We always been dismissed, disregarded, disrespected. But we served anyhow. We took care of our students anyhow. We transformed one discipline and created our own anyhow. And it was women who did that work. It was people of color who did that work. It was queer folk who did that work. It was first-generation students in New York City and across the country demanding open admissions who did that work. It was people of all backgrounds teaching four and five courses a semester, contingent and full-time and sometimes even more time who did that work for us, building and running programs while they taught and theorized.

But sometimes it seems to me that the funk of who we have been throughout our history is dead. Our conferences are sometimes too clean—not so fresh and so clean clean, but serene clean. To paraphrase a poet friend of mine, Thomas Sayers Ellis, all their stanzas and all our conferences and all our conference attendance look alike despite our brochures and our resolutions and our best intentions. As real as the intradepartmental and institutional condescension we face can be, our best work happened in periods of struggle. Our best work happened when we dedicated ourselves to the students the rest of the academy didn't want. Our best work happened when our courses looked more like handcrafted zines and broadsides created on mimeographs than huge productions done and supported by huge corporate publishers. Our universities spend all this time and effort at branding, talking about excellence and distinction and matrices and best practices. But I want us, our courses, our programs and departments to be more than that—I want us to create and work in spaces that look after the students and the teachers and the communities the rest of the academy's pursuit of "distinction" looks at and sneers "ain't nobody got time for that." I want colleagues who will show and tell and teach our students like Elaine Richardson and Rhea Lathan taught us last year, the shame tree truly is dead.

I want funk to be our guide not just because the rest of the academy feels too clean and too serene to me, but because intellectual life is funky. It is messy. Trying to build a society worthy of our aims is messy. It is ratchet. I want funk to be our guide because that is the only way we can close the huge gaps that exist between our professed ideals and our practice, the only way we can own our privilege within oppressive spaces. Funk means we are willing to sweat. Funk means we are willing to deal with messiness and complexity. Funk means we will look unflinchingly at all that pains us, all that is wrong around us and STILL dance and shout and shake and twirl our way out of our constrictions.

My hope for us is that as we worry a little less about being neat and clean, a little less about respectability inside our departments, programs, and universities, that as we embrace boldness, complexity, and even a little irreverence and messiness that we will be able to take flight into intellectual, pedagogical, and programmatic places that we might partially see, but cannot yet fully know. Just like Mos Def and Talib Kweli said, "This ain't no time where the usual is suitable / Tonight alive, let's describe the inscrutable." This is a time for exploration, for experimentation. This is a time when we can create and risk, when we can write graffiti on the walls and color outside the lines. This is a time when we don't have to have it all figured out just yet. I'm also asking us to take flight across both space and time because for me, flight means embracing and investing in innovation. It means creating spaces for innovation not tied to byzantine processes of administrators' or faculty senates' approval. Being willing to really fly on and reach for the stars means that we drop at least some of our worries about what's happening right now and fix our gaze on big challenges and problems and then work backwards.

Because the beloved one and author of *Beloved*, Toni Morrison, tells us, "If you want to fly, you have to let go of the shit that weighs you down," let me say this right now. By the power vested in me for the span of this writing, I hereby promote the essay to dominant genre emeritus. I thank you for your loooonnng and committed service over more than a century. We still love you. We want you to keep an office on campus and in our thinking, teaching, and writing lives. We will continue to throw wonderful parties and give meaningful awards in your name. And yet, we also acknowledge the rise and promotion of many other activities around which writing and communication can be organized. And we realize that if we are going to fly and find new intellectual spaces and futuristic challenges to meet with our students and each other, we have to leave the comfortable ground we have found with you.

For those of you who might be wondering if I've lost my mind at this point, let me state my case this way: the essay is a valuable, even powerful technology that has particular affordances in helping us promote communicative ability, dialogue, and critical thinking. But we have gotten too comfortable relying on those affordances as our writing and communication universe goes through not only intense change, but an ever-increasing tempo of change. I admit that change gets dizzying, and I often find myself relying on the opening words of my favorite artist of the entire funk and soul era, Donny Hathaway, in the painfully, plaintively, beautiful song "Someday We'll All Be Free": "Hang on to the world as it spins around / Just don't let the spin get you down / Never mind your fears." We have been talking about technological changes in communication for more than thirty years thanks to venues like *Computers and Composition* and many of our technical and professional writing scholars. Jackie Royster challenged us years ago to expand our vision of academic discourses in her classic "Small Boats in a Big Sea." And we've been talking about multimodal, multimedia forms of composing for a long time as well.

This is the time for us to take those calls to yet another level. Think with me, about the literacies, about the understandings that the essay has helped us build with students: ethical source use and connection to scholarly community; the ability to value other voices, including those with whom we disagree; the ability to develop compelling support for an idea; experimentation with different rhythms and organizing strategies in our prose. This is obviously only the beginning, but you get the idea. Keep those abilities in mind and consider what the authors of *Confronting the Challenges of Participatory Culture* argue are the literacies we have to develop with our students for right now and for the future:

Play
Performance
Simulation
Appropriation
Multitasking

Distributed Cognition
Collective Intelligence
Judgment
Transmedia Navigation
Networking
Negotiation across diverse communities

But there is more than literacy—more than changing literacies—at stake. As composing becomes more and more enmeshed in digital environments, tools, practices and networks, we need to see this as a crossroads moment for our scholarship too. That crossroads, for me, is one where we see that we have to embrace technology issues not as part of what we do, but central to what we do. Technology is what we do, or what we need to do, not just because literacy is always technologized, not just because of computers AND composition, but because of the big-picture technological issues that are always brought to bear on all facets of our lives and work. Questions about privacy and surveillance, about policy and legal frameworks, about how technologies are marketed, about design, about networks, artificial intelligence, and natural-language processing just to begin the list. So we need to ask different questions about writing with technologies, but also about writing in relationship to big-picture technology issues.

What happens to composing when laptop and desktop computers go the way of the typewriter? How will wearable and implantable technologies change our access to information and our ability to share with each other? Will the constant sharing that sometimes makes us uncomfortable on social media go into warp drive when audio and video recording of everything everywhere becomes as commonplace as clicking and sharing a link are now? How will we respond when the dramatic changes in the pace of change exacerbate racial and gender divides that are already staggering?

What I am trying to suggest is that we need to take the next step in our investigations of technology issues far beyond the boxes and wires, that because writing, communication, composing are always technologized, big-picture technology studies needs to become a crucial, a central part of what we do. It is time for some new journals and book series to take as big a leap forward now as *Kairos* and *Technoculture* and *Computers and Composition* did in their beginnings—journals and book series that are dedicated to exploring the messy big-picture concerns that structure technologies and our relationships to them. In a cultural moment when we are fascinated by the visual because of Instagram and Vine—perhaps blinded by the image, to riff on a classic article by Johndan Johnson-Eilola and Anne Wysocki, we need more work in sound studies and oral composing and audio archives. We need more critical edge when it comes to technology studies so that we don't become hoodwinked every time governments and corporations unite to try to sell us utopian visions about the next new technological hotness that will heal everything that ails us.

And to do all of this, like Malcolm X famously said, we need some new friends. It's time for us to travel across campus, across programs, and into more strategic relationship building by doing more with affiliate faculty and cross-disciplinary courses and certificates. We need deeper connections with the disciplines that get lumped into area studies—long-term and systematic relationships with departments and programs in gender and women's studies, indigenous studies, Latina / Latino studies, Asian and Asian American studies, and Africana studies. We need to build deep and long-term relationships with university libraries and iSchools that go beyond the first-year comp trip to the library to learn about source use. And we need to keep working hard on that fourth *C* in our professional title (Conference on College Composition and Communication): we have to do long-term work, build more on our relationships with communication programs, schools, and departments. Many of our profession's members attend RSA and NCA, but how can we take those individual relationships that exist and use them to deepen our programmatic and organizational connections? What can we do—throughout CCCC and our home departments and programs—to build long-term relationships with Hispanic-serving institutions and tribal colleges and historically black colleges and universities? We need greater connection and collaboration across programs and organizations because even the most brilliant faculty, even the largest writing and rhetoric programs, even the best organizations like CCCC, cannot do this futuristic work alone.

However, to invoke flight—even imagined flight—at a time like this might seem fraudulent, given that none of us on the ground is free. We are not free to fly when one of our own, my sister Dr. Ersula Ore was assaulted and thrown to the street because a police officer didn't like the way she responded to him. And on our own campuses we are not free to take flight when the exploitation of highly skilled teachers and scholars labeled as contingent, labeled as adjunct, minimized with a "part-time" tag is allowed to flourish. It may be that we will never see this society become brave enough to move beyond sexism, homophobia, racism, and economic exploitation. Ta-Nehesi

Coates might have had it right when he stated on Twitter, "Maybe we shall not overcome." But I am still here to ask us to think about freedom as crucial to our work. MeShell Ndegeocello put it best in a song called "Satisfy": I'm asking us to think about how we find "freedom amid this mockery."

I'm asking us to think about freedom in this unfree world because the only freedom we will see, the only freedom we will get is the freedom we take. And the only way we get free is to walk with and learn from those who are out here working to get free. One thing this means is we have to focus less on the rhetorical "exemplars," focus less on "successful" movements. Freedom work is funky rather than refined. It is becoming rather than overcome. It is in process rather than proclaimed. When I was in Syracuse I used to put together community ciphers on different topics; some would have as few as ten or twelve people, some as many as fifty or sixty. And one of the many beautiful things about these groups is that they maintained a focus on what we CAN do, no matter how bad things seemed. And while there were many reasons for that focus, a huge amount of it was due to one woman, someone I sometimes called "mother sister" after the Ruby Dee character in Spike Lee's movies. Any time our conversations seemed to get too world weary or too mired in the obstacles we might see, she would stand up and say "damnit, just ACT like you free!" Ms. Beulah's exclamation was so powerful to us that it became a refrain for almost everyone in the groups because of her insistence that we claim our own agency no matter what the external circumstances.

One major obstacle we have to free ourselves from is the set of handcuffs the same old theory and the same old theorists and the same old scholarship place on us. Movie producer Harvey Weinstein talked to *Vulture Magazine* recently about the lack of diversity in the Oscars, and I think to myself that even the Oscars are less white than our published scholarship and the awards we give for scholarly publications. As my man Thomas Sayers Ellis said, "All their stanzas look alike"—and too much of our theorizing and scholarship do too. As important as people like de Certeau and Jameson and many others can be to our work, there is just as much theoretical richness to be gleaned from Anna Julia Cooper, from Minnie Bruce Pratt, from Vine Deloria, from the Young Lords in New York and Dreamers and Dream Defenders and the Crunk Feminist Collective and from local people and organizations whose names we don't yet know. The moment when we will be free or represent freedom as an organization, as a group of scholars will be not just when the demographics of our conferences and our faculties look like the demographics of our society, but when our citation practices and works-cited lists do too.

I write with my mind stayed on intellectual freedom and racial and social and sexual and economic justice because the only way to gain the freedom we so desperately need as a society and as a discipline is through the very problems that threaten to seem so intractable. Womanist theologian Katie Cannon said it better than I ever could. In a sermon published in the late James Haskin's collection *Keeping the Faith* titled "Living the Life of Jubilee," Cannon transforms the very ideas of jubilee, of liberation. I imagine her words in this sermon as a guide for the work I hope to do and the kind of person I hope to become. She says,

> And in these modern times, what do we do, what do we say, when the powers and principalities, when the spiritual wickedness in high places, say to us go get your sons, go get your daughters, go get your nieces, go get your nephews, go get your grandchildren, go get your great grandchildren, go get your sisters and brothers, and hand them over to us.
>
> Yes, church, what are we saying, what are we doing, when the bureaucrats and the drug dealers, what are we saying, what are we doing, when the global capitalists and the gang bangers, what are we saying when the cold-hearted, mean-spirited power brokers and the misogynistic, bible-thumping homophobes demand the souls of the people in our families, the people in our churches, the people in our communities? When the people who don't mean any good to us demand the souls of our sisters and brothers anywhere in the world?

But it is what she does next in the sermon that is simply transformative. Rather than proclaim jubilee as some moment when those who are enslaved are free or people are relieved of their debts, she challenges her people by flipping the script: instead of a powerful moment of celebration of freedom gained, she challenges them to live the life of jubilee justice. Rather than some mystical majestical moment, jubilee becomes a lifelong commitment to the work of liberation. Being able to reach higher ground, or to fly on, and reach for the stars demands service in the valleys where we live and struggle. And when we see it this way, our service mission, to our students, to our campuses and to our communities becomes the very thing that gives us the freedom to fly.

As real as the obstacles are that we face, on campus, in community, in public, at home, as real as the walls and impediments to movement are here on the ground, let us make this space that we create together be one where we proclaim, "Ain't no walls behind the sky, baby." As we gather to be renewed and to renew each other, let us embrace the funk that keeps us from being completely sanitized by academic silos and conventions. And let us fly on, reaching for stars we cannot yet map, see, or scan. Let us be committed to creating free spaces for ourselves, and to standing with and learning from those who are engaged in freedom struggle, not in the past, but right here, right now. Let us use that freedom we take for those who do not have our protections or our privileges, inside and outside the academy. Let us use it to become a hub for intellectual life and critical dialogue both on campus, and off. And let us use it to *serve* our students, to serve the local communities in which we live, love, work, and play, and to serve our broader society, which needs our attention to discourse and our ability to enter messy public conversations maybe more now than at any point in our recent memory.

CONTRIBUTORS

INDEX

CONTRIBUTORS

Editors

Cheryl Glenn is Distinguished Professor of English at Pennsylvania State University, coeditor of two book series (Studies in Rhetorics and Feminisms, and Rhetoric and Democratic Deliberation), and Director of the Program in Writing and Rhetoric. Her many scholarly publications include *Rhetoric Retold: Regendering the Tradition from Antiquity through the Renaissance*; *Unspoken: A Rhetoric of Silence*; and *Silence and Listening as Rhetorical Arts.*

Roxanne Mountford is Professor of English and Director of Composition, Rhetoric, and Literacy Studies at the University of Oklahoma. Her scholarly publications include the books *The Gendered Pulpit: Preaching in American Protestant Spaces* and *Women's Ways of Making It in Rhetoric and Composition* (with Michelle Ballif and Diane Davis) and numerous articles and chapters.

Other Contributors

A committed teacher, midnight believer, Slow Jam in a Hip Hop World, and a solo soul who peeks out now and then, **Adam J. Banks** is the Faculty Director of the Program in Writing and Rhetoric at Stanford University and Professor in the Graduate School of Education. He is the author of *Digital Griots: African American Rhetoric in a Multimedia Age*; and *Race, Rhetoric, and Technology: Searching for Higher Ground.*

Davida Charney is Professor in the Department of Rhetoric and Writing at the University of Texas at Austin. Her publications include essays in the *Journal of Business and Technical Communication*, *Technical Communication*

Quarterly, Written Communication, Research in the Teaching of English, Journal of Writing Research, College Composition and Communication, and *Rhetoric Society Quarterly,* and the 2015 book *Persuading God: Rhetorical Studies of First-Person Psalms.*

Suellynn Duffey administers the first- and junior-level writing programs and teaches writing and rhetoric courses at the University of Missouri, St. Louis. She has published articles on writing program administration, institutional cultures, basic writing, family stories and race, and silence. She has led national conferences and large-scale writing assessment projects and has received grants to fund research on and development of various writing-related projects.

Lisa Ede is Professor of English, Emerita, at Oregon State University, where for thirty years she directed the Center for Writing and Learning. Ede is the author, coauthor, editor, or coeditor of nine books. Her most recent studies include *Writing Together: Collaboration in Theory and Practice* (2012), coedited with her frequent collaborator Andrea Lunsford; *The Academic Writer: A Brief Guide* (2008, 2011, 2014, 2017); and *Everyone's an Author,* with Andrea Lunsford, Michal Brody, Beverly J. Moss, Carole Clark Papper, and Keith Walters (2013, 2017).

Elizabeth A. Flynn is Professor Emerita of Reading and Composition in the Department of Humanities at Michigan Technological University. She is author of *Feminism beyond Modernism* (2002) and coeditor with Patrocinio P. Schweickart of *Gender and Reading* (1986) and *Reading Sites* (2004) and of *Feminist Rhetorical Resilience* (2012) with Patty Sotirin and Ann Brady.

Melissa A. Goldthwaite is Professor of English at Saint Joseph's University in Philadelphia. Her authored and coauthored books include *Books That Cook: The Making of a Literary Meal; The Little Norton Reader: 50 Essays from the First 50 Years; The St. Martin's Guide to Teaching Writing; The Norton Reader; Surveying the Literary Landscapes of Terry Tempest Williams;* and *The Norton Pocket Book of Writing by Students.*

Gerard A. Hauser is Professor Emeritus of Communication and College Professor Emeritus of Distinction in Rhetoric at the University of Colorado, Boulder. His book publications include *Vernacular Voices: The Rhetoric of Publics and Public Spheres* (recipient of NCA's Nichols Award in Public Address), *Prisoners of Conscience: Moral Vernaculars of Political Agency* (recipient of RSA's Book Award and NCA's Winans-Wichelns Award in Rhetoric and Public Address), and *Introduction to Rhetorical Theory.*

Shirley Brice Heath is Margery Bailey Professor of Dramatic Literature and Professor of Linguistics at Stanford University. A southerner who developed an early curiosity about different voices in life and in literature, she pursues fieldwork and archival research that take her to exotic places at home and in distant countries. Her publications include *Ways with Words: Language, Life, and Work in Communities and Classrooms* (1983) and *Words at Work and Play: Three Decades in Family and Community Life* (2012).

Susan C. Jarratt is Professor Emerita in the Department of Comparative Literature at the University of California, Irvine, where she recently served as Interim Chair of the Department of Classics from 2014 to 2016. She is the author of *Rereading the Sophists: Classical Rhetoric Refigured* (1991) and is at work on a book about the significance of space and the imperial relationship in ancient Greco-Roman rhetoric.

Nan Johnson is Professor of English at the Ohio State University, where she teaches history of rhetoric, theory of rhetoric, and composition theory. She is the author of *Nineteenth-Century Rhetoric in North America* (1991), *Gender and Rhetorical Space in American Life: 1866–1910* (2002), several book chapters, and reviews and articles on the history and theory of rhetoric, composition theory, and the pedagogy of writing.

Shirley Wilson Logan is Professor of English Emerita at the University of Maryland. Her publications include *With Pen and Voice: A Critical Anthology of Nineteenth-Century African American Women*; *"We Are Coming": The Persuasive Discourse of Nineteenth-Century Black Women*; and *Liberating Language: Sites of Rhetorical Education in Nineteenth-Century Black America*. She coedits the book series Studies in Rhetorics and Feminisms.

Alyssa J. O'Brien is a lecturer at the University of Sydney. Her current research focuses on visual rhetoric, affect, and wordplay in intercultural communication. In her previous position, she served as a lecturer in the Program in Writing and Rhetoric at Stanford University, under the leadership of Andrea A. Lunsford. Together with Andrea and Christine Alfano, Alyssa directed the Stanford Cross-Cultural Rhetoric Project from its pilot year in 2005 to its final global videoconference in 2012.

John J. Ruszkiewicz is Professor of Rhetoric and Writing at the University of Texas, Austin, a department he was instrumental in creating. He is the author or a coauthor of numerous books, including *Well-Bound Words*; *The Scott, Foresman Handbook for Writers*; *Bookmarks*; *The Presence of Others*; *Everything's An Argument*; *How To Write Anything*; and *A Reader's Guide to College Writing*.

Bo Wang is Professor of English and Codirector of the Writing Program at California State University, Fresno. Her essays have appeared in the journals *Advances in the History of Rhetoric*, *College Composition and Communication*, *College English*, *JAC*, *Rhetoric Review*, and *Rhetoric Society Quarterly*, and in *Comparative Rhetoric: The Art of Traversing Rhetorical Times, Places, and Spaces*; and *Representations: Doing Asian American Rhetoric*.

INDEX